THE SOCIAL COGNITIVE NEUROSCIENCE OF ORGANIZATIONS

ANNALS OF THE NEW YORK ACADEMY OF SCIENCES
Volume 1118

THE SOCIAL COGNITIVE NEUROSCIENCE OF ORGANIZATIONS

Edited by Carl Senior and Michael J. R. Butler

Published by Blackwell Publishing on behalf of the New York Academy of Sciences
Boston, Massachusetts
2007

Library of Congress Cataloging-in-Publication Data

The social cognitive neuroscience of organizations/editors, Carl Senior and Michael J. R. Butler.
  p. ; cm. – (Annals of the New York Academy of Sciences, ISSN 0077-8923)
  Includes bibliographical references.
  ISBN-13: 978-1-57331-698-9 (alk. paper)
  ISBN-10: 1-57331-698-9 (alk. paper)
  1. Cognitive neuroscience. 2. Social psychology. 3. Psychology, Industrial. 4. Organizational behavior. 5. Interpersonal relations–Physiological aspects. I. Senior, Carl. II. Butler, Michael J. R. (Michael James Richard) III. Series.
  [DNLM: 1. Neuropsychology–methods. 2. Psychology, Industrial. 3. Cognitive Science–methods. 4. Interprofessional Relations. 5. Organizations. W1 AN626YL 2007/WL 103.5 S677 2007]
  QP360.5.S63 2007
  612.8'233–dc22
                                                                2007031927

The *Annals of the New York Academy of Sciences* (ISSN: 0077-8923 [print]; ISSN: 1749-6632 [online]) is published 28 times a year on behalf of the New York Academy of Sciences by Blackwell Publishing with offices at 350 Main St., Malden, MA 02148 USA; 9600 Garsington Road, Oxford, OX4 2ZG UK; and 600 North Bridge Rd, #05-01 Parkview Square, 18878 Singapore.

Information for subscribers: For new orders, renewals, sample copy requests, claims, changes of address and all other subscription correspondence please contact the Journals Department at your nearest Blackwell office (address details listed above). UK office phone: +44 (0)1865 778315, fax +44 (0)1865 471775; US office phone: 1-800-835-6770 (toll free US) or 1-781-388-8599; fax: 1-781-388-8232; Asia office phone: +65 6511 8000, fax; +44 (0)1865 471775, Email: customerservices@blackwellpublishing.com

Subscription rates:
Institutional Premium   The Americas: $4043   Rest of World: £2246
The Premium institutional price also includes online access to full-text articles from 1997 to present, where available. For other pricing options or more information about online access to Blackwell Publishing journals, including access information and terms and conditions, please visit www.blackwellpublishing. com/nyas
*Customers in Canada should add 6% GST or provide evidence of entitlement to exemption.
**Customer in the UK or EU: add the appropriate rate for VAT EC for non-registered customers in countries where this is applicable. If you are registered for VAT please supply your registration number.

Mailing: The *Annals of the New York Academy of Sciences* is mailed Standard Rate. Mailing to rest of world by International Mail Express (IMEX). Canadian mail is sent by Canadian publications mail agreement number 40573520. **Postmaster:** Send all address changes to *Annals of the New York Academy of Sciences*, Blackwell Publishing Inc., Journals Subscription Department, 350 Main St., Malden, MA 02148-5020.

Membership information: Members may order copies of *Annals* volumes directly from the Academy by visiting www.nyas.org/annals, emailing membership@nyas.org, faxing 212-298-3650, or calling 800-843-6927 (US only), or 212-298-8640 (International). For more information on becoming a member of the New York Academy of Sciences, please visit www.nyas.org/membership. Claims and inquiries on member orders should be directed to the Academy at email: membership@nyas.org or Tel: 212-298-8640 (International) or 800-843-6927 (US only).

Copyright and Photocopying:
© 2007 The New York Academy of Sciences. All rights reserved. No part of this publication may be reproduced, stored, or transmitted in any form or by any means without the prior permission in writing from the copyright holder. Authorization to photocopy items for internal and personal use is granted by the copyright holder for libraries and other users registered with their local Reproduction Rights Organization (RRO), e.g. Copyright Clearance Center (CCC), 222 Rosewood Drive, Danvers, MA 01923, USA (www.copyright.com), provided the appropriate fee is paid directly to the RRO. This consent does not extend to other kinds of copying such as copying for general distribution, for advertising or promotional purposes, for creating new collective works, or for resale. Special requests should be addressed to Blackwell Publishing at: journalsrights@oxon.blackwellpublishing.com.

Printed in the USA. Printed on acid-free paper.

Disclaimer: The Publisher, the New York Academy of Sciences and the Editors cannot be held responsible for errors or any consequences arising from the use of information contained in this publication; the views and opinions expressed do not necessarily reflect those of the Publisher, the New York Academy of Sciences, or the Editors.

Annals are available to subscribers online at the New York Academy of Sciences and also at Blackwell Synergy. Visit www.blackwell-synergy.com or www.annalsnyas.org to search the articles and register for table of contents e-mail alerts. Access to full text and PDF downloads of *Annals* articles are available to nonmembers and subscribers on a pay-per-view basis at www.blackwell-synergy.com and www.annalsnyas.org.

The paper used in this publication meets the minimum requirements of the National Standard for Information Sciences Permanence of Paper for Printed Library Materials, ANSI Z39.48_1984.

ISSN: 0077-8923 (print); 1749-6632 (online)
ISBN-10: 1-57331-698-9 (alk. paper); ISBN-13: 978-1-57331-698-9 (alk. paper)

A catalogue record for this title is available from the British Library.

ANNALS OF THE NEW YORK ACADEMY OF SCIENCES

Volume 1118
November 2007

THE SOCIAL COGNITIVE NEUROSCIENCE OF ORGANIZATIONS

Editors
CARL SENIOR AND MICHAEL J. R. BUTLER

CONTENTS

List of Contributors.	ix
Toward an Organizational Cognitive Neuroscience. *By* MICHAEL J.R. BUTLER AND CARL SENIOR	1
Neuroimaging and Psychophysiological Measurement in Organizational Research: An Agenda for Research in Organizational Cognitive Neuroscience. *By* NICK LEE AND LAURA CHAMBERLAIN	18
Hormonal and Genetic Influences on Processing Reward and Social Information. *By* XAVIER CALDÚ AND JEAN-CLAUDE DREHER	43
Neuro-Gov: Neuroscience as Catalyst. *By* DAVID JOHN FARMER	74
Fairness and Cooperation Are Rewarding: Evidence from Social Cognitive Neuroscience. *By* GOLNAZ TABIBNIA AND MATTHEW D. LIEBERMAN	90
Neural Correlates of Corporate Camaraderie and Teamwork. *By* CATHERINE LEVINE	102
Business Change Process, Creativity and the Brain: A Practitioner's Reflective Account with Suggestions for Future Research. *By* ROWENA M. YEATS AND MARTYN F. YEATS	109
Cognitive Accuracy and Intelligent Executive Function in the Brain and in Business. *By* CHARLES E. BAILEY	122

Interviewing Strategies in the Face of Beauty: A Psychophysiological Investigation into the Job Negotiation Process. *By* CARL SENIOR, KARLY THOMSON, JULIA BADGER, AND MICHAEL J.R. BUTLER 142

Neurocognitive Inefficacy of the Strategy Process. *By* HAROLD E. KLEIN AND MARK D'ESPOSITO 163

Being Fed Up: A Social Cognitive Neuroscience Approach to Mental Satiation. *By* ANDREAS MOJZISCH AND STEFAN SCHULZ-HARDT 186

Research Possibilities for Organizational Cognitive Neuroscience. *By* MICHAEL J.R. BUTLER AND CARL SENIOR 206

Index of Contributors 211

The New York Academy of Sciences believes it has a responsibility to provide an open forum for discussion of scientific questions. The positions taken by the participants in the reported conferences are their own and not necessarily those of the Academy. The Academy has no intent to influence legislation by providing such forums.

Contributors

Julia Badger is a research assistant in the School of Life and Health Sciences, Aston University. She has been involved in several projects, including the influence of perceived beauty and the menstrual cycle on decisionmaking, academic sibling rivalry, and the use of modern technologies within education. She has presented her work at several conferences, winning prizes at the British Psychological Society Annual Conference in York, and the Studentské Psychologické Dny in the Czech Republic. She is currently on the MRes degree course in psychological research methods at Aston University.

Charles E. Bailey received his medical degree from the University of Texas at Houston and completed psychiatric residency training at the University of Florida. He practiced as a general psychiatrist in the Orlando, Florida, area for over 20 years. For the past 10 years, he has conducted clinical research in psychopharmacology, participating in more than 150 clinical trials in most diagnostic categories, with children, adolescents, adults, and geriatric populations. He has spent a great deal of time studying human cognitive neuroscience, especially the neuroscience of relationships, organization behavior, and business.

Michael J.R. Butler is a lecturer in management in the Work and Organisational Psychology Group at Aston University. Previously, he was a lecturer in change management in the People and Organisations Group, Cranfield School of Management. He also works as a management consultant across the private and public sectors. His first degree was in history. Michael's teaching reflects his research interests in three core areas: change management, management learning, and social psychology. Along with Professor George Keith, he is co-author of *Language, Power and Identity* (Hodder and Stoughton, 1999) and has contributed to a variety of business and management, public management, and psychology journals. In 2005, he was awarded the Aston Excellence in Teaching Award.

Xavier Caldú studied psychology at the University of Barcelona, where he carried out his doctoral studies. His research focused on the influence of the genetic variants of catechol-o-methyltransferase and the dopamine transporter on brain activation during working memory and emotional processing. Currently, he is a postdoctoral fellow at the Center for Cognitive Neuroscience in Lyon, France, in the reward and decisionmaking team, under supervision of Jean-Claude Dreher.

Laura Chamberlain is an Economic and Social Research Council doctoral candidate at Aston Business School, Aston University. Her research is concerned with the impact of emotional responses on the effectiveness of fear appeal advertisements. She has presented results of this research at international conferences in Italy and Greece, and her work has appeared in the *International Journal of Psychophysiology* and *Qualitative Market Research: An International Journal*.

Mark D'Esposito is professor of neuroscience and psychology and the director of the Henry H. Wheeler, Jr. Brain Imaging Center at the University of California, Berkeley. He has received numerous competitive research grants from the National Institutes of Health (NIH), as well as private sources, such as the Dana Foundation and the American Federation for Aging Research. For his clinical, teaching, and research skills he has earned many awards and honors, such as a citation in "The Best Doctors in America," the Dean's Award for Excellence in Basic Science Teaching, and the Norman Geschwind Prize in Behavioral Neurology from the American Academy of Neurology. He is the editor-in-chief of the *Journal of Cognitive Neuroscience* and has over 200 research publications. He has written and edited four books.

Jean-Claude Dreher studied mathematics, psychology, and cognitive neuroscience in Paris and did his postdoctoral research at the NIH, Bethesda (USA), where he conducted research on the functional organization of the prefrontal cortex and on the reward system. Currently a principal investigator at the Center for Cognitive Neuroscience (Lyon, France), he is leading a research team from the National Research Science Center, focusing on neuroimaging of reward processing and decisionmaking in humans.

David John Farmer is professor of political science and public administration in the L. Douglas Wilder School of Government and Public Affairs, Virginia Commonwealth University. Previously he was employed by the City of New York and by the US federal government. He holds a PhD in economics from the University of London and a PhD in philosophy from the University of Virginia.

Harold E. Klein is associate professor of general and strategic management at the Fox School of Business and Management, Temple University. Concurrently, he is a visiting scholar and affiliate faculty at the Center for Organizational Dynamics, University of Pennsylvania. His general interest and experience has been in strategic planning in dynamically changing environments. He has designed planning systems and directed planning efforts for a number of large corporations and government entities both in the USA and abroad. His particular research focus for much of the last decade has been on the neurocognitive aspects of strategic thinking. He has developed and applied highly effective proprietary technology for scenario planning and knowledge management, based on neurocognitive concepts. His technology has been applied successfully in large corporations. Dr. Klein holds degrees from Columbia University (PhD), Dartmouth (MBA) and City College of New York (BChE).

Nick Lee is a senior lecturer in marketing, and research group convenor at Aston Business School. His research interests include organizational and social psychology and research methodology. Nick's work has appeared or is forthcoming in journals such as the *European Journal of Marketing*, the *International Journal of Psychophysiology*, and the *Journal of the Academy of Marketing Science*. Nick was co-editor of the special issue of the *European Journal of Marketing* on "The State of Research in Marketing," which was recognized with the 2005 Emerald Outstanding Special Issue Award. He was the recipient of the 2002 European Marketing Academy Conference award for best paper based on doctoral work.

Catherine Levine is originally from Bogotá, Colombia and graduated *magna cum laude* with a Bachelor of Science in biological science and minor in English literature. She then went on to train at the Miami Project to Cure Paralysis, Lois Pope Leaders in Furthering Education Center for Neuroscience Research, part of the University of Miami Miller School of Medicine. Her research interests include hypothermia as a treatment option for acute paralysis and computational methods in neuroscience research. Ms. Levine has also presented her work internationally upon invitation at various international conferences, including those held in Stockholm, Sweden and Göttingen, Germany.

Matthew Lieberman is an associate professor in psychology at the University of California, Los Angeles (UCLA). Lieberman's research interests include social cognitive neuroscience topics, such as self-control, self-knowledge, automaticity and control, social rejection, and attitude change. Lieberman has authored more than 50 articles and chapters, including publications in *Science*, *Nature Neuroscience*, *Psychological Science*, *Annual Review of Psychology*, *American Psychologist*, *Psychological Bulletin*, *Journal of Cognitive Neuroscience*, and the *Journal of Personality and Social Psychology*. Lieberman is the founding editor of the journal *Social Cognitive and Affective Neuroscience* and was the 2007 recipient of the American Psychological Association (APA) Distinguished Scientific Award for Early Career Contribution to Psychology.

Andreas Mojzisch is assistant professor at the Economic and Social Psychology Unit, Georg-August University, Göttingen, Germany. He received his PhD from Ludwig-Maximilians-University, Munich. His research interests include group decisionmaking, group performance, social cognition, mental satiation, and stress and work underload in the workplace. He integrates methodology from experimental social psychology, cognitive psychology, psychophysiology, neuroendocrinology, and functional neuroimaging to inform his hypotheses and the designs of his experiments.

Stefan Schulz-Hardt is chair in industrial, economic, and social psychology and head of the Economic and Social Psychology Unit at the Georg-August University, Göttingen, Germany. He received his PhD from the University of Kiel and his habilitation doctorate from Ludwig-Maximilians-University, Munich. Current research interests are group decisionmaking, social information processing, mental satiation, and financial psychology.

Carl Senior is a lecturer in cognitive neuroscience at Aston University. He has published extensively on a range of topics in the cognate disciplines in high-impact journals, such as *Nature, Trends in Cognitive Sciences, Archives of General Psychiatry,* and *Current Biology*. He has edited two books, *Neuroimaging in Psychiatry* (Dunitz Press, 2003) and *Methods in Mind* (The MIT Press, 2006) and was also the guest editor, along with Dr. Gina Rippon, of a special issue of the *International Journal of Psychophysiology* entitled "Cognitive Neuroscience: the New Psychophysiology?"

Golnaz Tabibnia is a postdoctoral scholar in the Department of Psychiatry and Biobehavioral Sciences at UCLA. She received her PhD in the Department of Psychology at UCLA. Her research interests include the neural basis of emotions and emotion regulation. Using functional magnetic resonance imaging, psychophysiology, and behavioral methods, she has studied self-regulation of negative emotions, such as fear, and those associated with unfair treatment, as well as impulse control processes. Her research has been funded in part by a National Science Foundation Graduate Fellowship, the APA Dissertation Award, and a National Research Service Award.

Karly Thomson is a research assistant in the School of Life and Health Sciences at Aston University. Her areas of interest include face perception, beauty, and physiological psychology. She presented her work at the annual British Psychological Society Meeting in Cardiff in 2005. She is due to graduate from the BSc(Hons) in human psychology program at Aston University.

Martyn F. Yeats is the director of Frazier Yeats Associates Ltd, a management consultancy based in the UK. The company specializes in enhancing management capacity in public sector organizations in the health and social care world. Martyn has led a number of major change projects on behalf of organizations and also works closely with company executives and top teams to facilitate and encourage their management creativity and problem-solving abilities. He holds an MBA from the Open University, where he specialized in creativity, innovation, and change. He also holds an MA in Public Sector Management from the University of Sussex and is a master practitioner in neurolinguistic programming.

Rowena M. Yeats is a research assistant at the Cognitive Evolution Laboratory, Harvard University, where she is involved with work examining learning and intelligence in nonhuman primates. Rowena has completed a research internship within the psycholinguistics laboratory, National University of Singapore, where she examined language development in bilingual children. She has previously published work for the British Psychology Society on the benefits of study abroad for undergraduate students and will soon finish her BSc (Hons) in human psychology at Aston University.

Toward an Organizational Cognitive Neuroscience

MICHAEL J.R. BUTLER[a] AND CARL SENIOR[b]

[a]*Aston Business School, Aston University, United Kingdom*
[b]*School of Life & Health Sciences, Aston University, United Kingdom*

ABSTRACT: The research strategy adopted in this article is to connect two different discourses and the ideas, methods, and outputs they contain—these being cognitive neuroscience and organization theory. The main contribution of the article is to present an agenda for the field of organizational cognitive neuroscience. We define what is meant by the term, outline its background, identify why it is important as a new research direction, and then conclude by drawing on Damasio's levels of life regulation as a framework to bind together existing organizational cognitive neuroscience. The article begins by setting the wider debate behind the emergence of organizational cognitive neuroscience by revisiting the nature–nurture debate and uses Pinker to demonstrate that the connection between mind and matter has not been resolved, that new directions are opening up to better understand human nature, and that organizational cognitive neuroscience is one fruitful path forward.

KEYWORDS: organizational cognitive neuroscience; social cognitive neuroscience; organization studies; organizational psychology and social psychology

> The mind, that ocean where each kind
> Does straight its own resemblance find;
> Yet it creates, transcending these,
> Far other worlds, and other seas,
> Annihilating all that's made
> To a green thought in a green shade

—Andrew Marvell (1621–1678): "The Garden"[1]

INTRODUCTION

Emerging research has applied a cognitive neuroscience approach to reveal a deeper understanding of organizational processes. The research findings,

Address for correspondence: Dr. Michael J.R. Butler, Aston Business School, Aston University, Aston Triangle, Birmingham B4 7ET. Voice: +44 (0) 121-204-3053 (Direct/Voicemail), +44 (0) 121-204 3257 (Group Administrator/Voicemail); fax: +44 (0) 121-204-3327.
m.j.r.butler@aston.ac.uk

some of which are highlighted in this volume, together with a growing number of international empirical studies, suggested the development of a new field of inquiry—organizational cognitive neuroscience.

The research strategy adopted connects two different discourses and the ideas, methods, and outputs they contain.[4] The strategy explores how cognitive neuroscience and organizational theory can be connected in symbiosis to create new knowledge. Whereas social psychology has been fully enmeshed in organization studies, cognitive neuroscience has not. The bridge connecting cognitive neuroscience to organizational theory is the more established, yet still young, discipline of social cognitive neuroscience. Some readers may see the connection as more of a juxtaposition of discourses, but the volume, it is hoped, will reveal the benefits and the limitations of pursuing further integration. In the words of Marvell cited at the beginning of the article, the research strategy is to create new knowledge by transcending the separate discourses of cognitive neuroscience and organizational theory.

This article will begin by setting the wider debate behind the emergence of organizational cognitive neuroscience. We revisit the nature–nurture debate and use Pinker to demonstrate that the connection between brain and mind has not been resolved,[3,5] that new directions are opening up to better understand human nature, and that organizational cognitive neuroscience is a fruitful path forward. We discuss the new discipline of social cognitive neuroscience. The main contribution of the article is to focus the debate even further by opening up the new field of organizational cognitive neuroscience. In particular, we define what is meant by the term, outline its background, identify why it is important as a new research direction, and then conclude by drawing on Damasio's levels of life regulation as a framework to bind together existing organizational cognitive neuroscience.[2,6]

NATURE AND NURTURE

The wider debate behind the emergence of organizational cognitive neuroscience is the role of nature and nurture. Pinker makes the following statement in the opening lines of *The Blank Slate*:

> NOT *ANOTHER* BOOK on nature and nurture! ... Haven't we all moved beyond the simplistic dichotomy between heredity and environment and realized that all behavior comes out of an interaction between the two?[7]

He justifies his book by provocatively stating that there is a taboo about the role of nature in human activity:

> To acknowledge human nature many think, is to endorse racism, sexism, war, greed, genocide, nihilism, reactionary politics, and neglect of children and the disadvantaged. Any claim that the mind has an innate organization strikes people not as a hypothesis that might be incorrect but as a thought it is immoral to think.[8]

In response, he states the following:

> An honest discussion of human nature has never been more timely. Throughout the twentieth century, many intellectuals tried to rest principles of decency on fragile factual claims such as that human beings are biologically indistinguishable, harbor no ignoble motives, and are utterly free in their ability to make choices. These claims are now being called into question by discoveries in the sciences of mind, brain, genes, and evolution. If nothing else, the completion of the Human Genome Project, with its promise of an understanding of the genetic roots of the intellect and the emotions, should serve as a wake-up call.[9]

The task, therefore, is to challenge the values we hold which has the positive purpose of improving our lot through self knowledge. In short, there is a philosophical point that "the new sciences of human nature can help lead the way to a realistic, biologically informed humanism."[10]

Lieberman emphasizes Pinker's point by arguing that there is now "an intellectual superhighway" at the intersection of the biomedical sciences and the social sciences and, more specifically, the neurosciences and the social sciences.[11,12] This is only a recent trend that is leading into a new kind of science. The new science recognizes that, ultimately, a full understanding of the social mind depends upon a full understanding of how the brain and body are receptive to socioemotional pressures and produce social behavior. This paradigm will shape future thinking about applied issues such as mental health and the treatment of addiction. The volume focuses on organizations as an applied issue.

Returning to Pinker: He develops and then applies his biologically informed humanism argument to five contemporary social issues or, in his words, hot buttons: politics, violence, gender, children, and the arts.[13] None explicitly deal with organizations, but management is discussed within some of the topics. He does so most noticeably in the chapter on gender, in which he tackles the gender gap in wages and a "glass ceiling" that keeps women from rising to the uppermost levels of power. His biologically informed humanism reveals itself when he concludes his argument with the following:

> Eliminating discrimination against women is important, but believing that women and men are born with indistinguishable minds is not.[14]

His humanism is clear, that discrimination is unjust. The biological aspect pushes Pinker to draw conclusions from a scientific and statistical analysis.[15] This approach starts off from a perspective that human resource scholars and practitioners would recognize and endorse. He argues for a free and unprejudiced labor market, in which people will be hired and paid according to the match between their traits and the demands of the job. His argument, though, takes a more contested turn when he calls for more accurate statistical data that measure jobs and wages when choices and qualifications are equalized. He achieves this goal by phasing the career life cycle. The National Longitudinal

Survey of Youth found that childless women between the ages of 27 and 33 years earn 98 cents to men's dollar.[16] At some point, however, even if both sexes value work and both sexes value children, large surveys of job-related values and career choices reveal that women, more often than men, make choices that allow them to spend more time with their children—shorter or more flexible hours, fewer relocations, skills that do not become obsolete as quickly—in exchange for lower wages or prestige. On the other hand, men's self-esteem is more highly tied to their status, salary, and wealth. Therefore, men say that they are more keen to work longer hours and to sacrifice other parts of their lives—to leave friends and family when they relocate—to climb the corporate ladder. In short, the argument concerns weighing the gender tradeoffs in terms of thinking about human nature, which raises deep new questions that could ultimately improve the lot of working women. The question being considered here is fairness in the workplace. Should we consider people as isolated individuals, or should we consider them members of families who probably will have children at some point in their lives and who probably will care for aging parents at some point in their lives?

During his argument, Pinker links evidence from social science to cognitive neuroscience.[17] To cohere research that links cognitive neuroscience to deciphering the processes behind social behavior, a new discipline has emerged—social cognitive neuroscience. *Monitor on Psychology* proclaims this move as being at the frontier of science, and members of the research agenda belong to one of the fastest-growing research areas in psychology.[18]

SOCIAL COGNITIVE NEUROSCIENCE

We will define social cognitive neuroscience, identify its importance and limitations, and then highlight evidence of the research momentum. Discussing these issues in some detail is important because we will refer to them in the following discussion of organizational cognitive neuroscience. Lieberman defines social cognitive neuroscience in the *Encyclopaedia of Social Psychology*:

> Social cognitive neuroscience is the study of the processes in the human brain that allow people to understand others, understand themselves, and navigate the social world effectively.[19]

Social cognitive neuroscience is embedded in the social sciences because it draws on theories and psychological phenomena from across the social sciences, including social cognition, political cognition, behavior economics, and anthropology.[20] He ends by identifying the methods used to research these subjects.[21] The methods used are also wide ranging, including functional magnetic resonance imaging (fMRI), positron emission tomography (PET), transcranial magnetic stimulation (TMS), event-related potentials (ERP), single-cell recording, and neuropsychological lesion techniques. Indeed, Lieberman is supported by the great Spanish scientist Santiago Ramon Y Cajal, who in his seminal tome *Advice to the Young Investigator* provides a caveat about becoming an "instrument addict":

> This rather unimportant variety of ineffectualist can be recognised immediately by a sort of fetishistic worship of research instruments. They are as fascinated by the gleam of metal as the lark is with its own reflection in the mirror.[22]

The continued evolution of social cognitive neuroscience and its younger cousin, organizational cognitive neuroscience, depends on enthusiastic use of a range of different techniques that converge on the answer to a particular question.

The importance of social cognitive neuroscience is both specific to research about the brain and general in terms of its role within social sciences. Lieberman suggests three benefits to research about the brain.[23] First, two processes that superficially appear similar and are difficult to disentangle with behavioral methods are clearly distinguished when examined with fMRI. An example is encoding social and nonsocial information, which are distinct processes. Encoding nonsocial information in a way that could be later remembered is related to activity in the hippocampus, whereas encoding social information in a way that could be later remembered is related to activity in dorsomedial prefrontal cortex. Of course, the where (in the brain) question is merely a prelude to the when, why, and how questions.

Second, and in contrast, there are sometimes processes that rely on the same mechanisms. An example is social pain resulting from being socially excluded, which produces activity in a similar network of brain regions as the experience of physical pain. The relation between physical and social pain appears to be not just metaphorical. Again, why this should be so is being investigated.

Finally, a future goal is to infer some of the mental processes that individuals are engaged in just from looking at the activity of their brains. The advantage of doing so for organizations would be finding out an individual's mental state, especially when staff may not always want to report the state that they are in.

Azar reports two more benefits.[24] First, social cognitive neuroscience is both theory forming and theory honing because it will help to winnow theories about which cognitive processes facilitate various social behaviors. This concept is important because the topics that social psychologists study tend to be complex and prone to multiple, and equally plausible, explanations. The more that is known about the distinct functional locations of different social processes, the better alternative accounts for a given social cognitive effect or phenomenon can be ruled out.

Second, collaboration is key to form and hone theories. Researchers in the area understand that it is the interdisciplinary nature of social cognitive neuroscience that makes it so powerful. Cognitive neuroscientists realize that they need collaborators to properly examine the social phenomena that they are interested in, and social psychologists know that they cannot do the neuroscience on their own. Azar suggests that neuroscience will help reunify psychology after years of slowly splintering into ever finer subdisciplines by asking more complex research questions that reconnect related disciplines.[25] Linked to asking research questions is the need to train young researchers in both cognitive neuroscience and social psychology.

The limitation of social cognitive neuroscience is again both specific to research about the brain but also more generally in terms of its role within social sciences. Lieberman argues that the key limitation is that fMRI scans are laboratory based, which means that research cannot get directly at actual behavior.[26] This supposition implies further limitations. There can be no face-to-face interactions because when subjects have their brains scanned, they lie on a narrow bed that slides into a long, narrow tube. Subjects must keep their heads absolutely still, and they cannot directly interact with other people. Last, many pictures are taken and then averaged together, which means that experiments are repeated before good information can be extracted from the scans, removing spontaneity from the task.

Azar reports that the key limitation is that some researchers might worry that social cognitive neuroscience will take us down the road of biological reductionism.[27] Pinker is more outspoken about the worry, describing it as "fear and loathing."[28] He identifies four reasons for this fear:

- If people are innately different, oppression and discrimination would be justified.
- If people are innately immoral, hopes to improve the human condition would be futile.
- If people are products of biology, free will would be a myth and we could no longer hold people responsible for their actions.
- If people are products of biology, life would have no higher meaning and purpose.

Tackling the fear of determinism in chapter 10, Pinker succinctly captures why this fear is unfounded by discussing decision making.[29] He sets an experiment that explores whether our actions are determined or open to free will. The experiment involves not deliberating over our actions for the next few days. Pinker concludes by stating the following:

> But a moment's reflection on what would happen if you *did* try to give up decisions should serve as a Valium for the existential anxiety. The experience of choosing is not a fiction, regardless of how the brain works. It is a real neural process, with the obvious function of selecting behavior according to its foreseeable consequences. It responds to information from the senses, including the exhortions of other people. You cannot step outside it or let it go on without you because it *is* you.[30]

Despite these limitations, three pieces of evidence reveal the research momentum that is gathering around social cognitive neuroscience: the publishing of an encyclopedia definition, the growth in research funding, and the emergences of specific routes to disseminate research findings. Lieberman's definition in the *Encyclopaedia of Social Psychology* has already been drawn on.[31] Azar reports that the National Institutes of Health put aside $2.3 million for its last funding cycle to fund pilot research in the area and that the James S. McDonnell Foundation made "Bridging Mind, Brain, and Behavior" one of three primary funding areas.[32] There are currently two specific routes to disseminate research findings. Azar also reports that the field's first conference, hosted by the University of California, Los Angeles, and funded in large part by the National Science Foundation, had to change venues at the last minute because attendance swelled from 70 to 300 participants from around the world.[33] Liebermann indicated that the field has had no journal outlets to publish data.[34] As a consequence, he now edits *Social Cognitive and Affective Neuroscience*, which aims

> ... to be a central home for work that brings together social scientists and neuroscientists to produce top-notch work that has the advantages of both contributing disciplines. In every issue, [*Social Cognitive and Affective Neuroscience*] will publish cutting-edge research from social cognitive neuroscience, social neuroscience, affective neuroscience, neuroeconomics and political neuroscience.[35]

TOWARD AN ORGANIZATIONAL COGNITIVE NEUROSCIENCE

Unlike social cognitive neuroscience, there is currently no notion of organizational cognitive neuroscience. There is, however, cognitive research in organizations and various research streams drawing on neuroscience. This volume, and in particular this article, seeks to fill that gap. This part of the article will define what is meant by organizational cognitive neuroscience, outline the background and history of cognitive research in organizations and the contribution of neuroscience and identify why organizational cognitive neuroscience is important as a new research direction, and then conclude by drawing on Damasio's levels of life regulation as a method to bind together existing organizational cognitive neuroscience.[36]

Definition

The definition proposed is framed in social cognitive neuroscience because organizational cognitive neuroscience may be seen as a more applied form of social cognitive neuroscience. Indeed, where neuroscience has already been allied to organizational theory, in neuroeconomics and neuromarketing, those definitions clearly emerge from the broader area of social cognitive neuroscience.

In the discussion so far, there is an explicit and an implicit link between social cognitive neuroscience and organizations. The explicit link between social cognitive neuroscience and organizations is revealed by returning to part of Lieberman's definition of social cognitive neuroscience.[37] He states that social cognitive neuroscience is embedded in the social sciences and draws on theories and psychological phenomena from social cognition, political cognition, behavior economics, and anthropology. Behavioral economics is not only an independent social science subject but also a field within organizational theory. Most business and management schools have an economics group. Clearly, if behavioral economics is included in social cognitive research, then organizational theory must be too.

The implicit link between social cognitive neuroscience and organizations is revealed by returning to Pinker's notion of biologically informed humanism.[38] Here, we suggest that organizations are a hot button in their own right, and this is for two reasons: one practical and one theoretical. The practical reason concerns the reality that nearly all humans will spend much of their adult daily routine doing work coordinated through a structure of some kind, be it organizational or social. The theoretical reason concerns how academics, and to some extent practitioners (organizational members), have conceptualized the doing of work. That is, there is a body of scholarship that theorizes the doing of work.

Another set of links are those established in the exciting fields of neuroeconomics and neuromarketing. By looking at how the two fields have defined themselves, we will show that those definitions clearly emerge from the broader area of social cognitive neuroscience. Lieberman's definition of social cognitive neuroscience includes the study of the processes in the human brain that allow people to understand others, understand themselves, and navigate the social world effectively.[39]

Similarly, neuroeconomics has been defined as "the application of neuroscientific methods to analyze and understand economically relevant behavior,"[40] whereas neuromarketing has been defined as the uncannily similar sounding, yet distinct, "the application of neuroscientific methods to analyze and understand human behavior in relation to markets and marketing exchanges."[41]

The only difference among the three sets of definitions is the shift from a general focus in social cognitive neuroscience to a specific focus on economics and marketing.

Following the pattern above, organizational cognitive neuroscience is defined as applying neuroscientific methods to analyze and understand human behavior within the applied setting of organizations. This application may be at the individual, group, organizational, and interorganizational levels.

Organizational cognitive neuroscience draws together all the fields of business and management, including their operation in the wider social world. It does this to integrate understanding about human behavior in organizations and, as a consequence, to more fully understand social behavior.

Background and History

The quest to understand our sociality has a long tradition. Lieberman discusses key moments in the exploration of the notion that social behavior and social cognition have biological roots, extending the discussion back to ancient Greece.[42] Many textbooks summarize the results of the exploration.[43] The focus here will be on cognitive research in organizations and the contribution of cognitive neuroscience.

Over the last 20 years, the study of organizational behavior has witnessed a dramatic shift toward a more cognitive and social–cognitive perspective.[44] Organizational behavior has been chastised for lacking a central set of theories, for offering limited theoretical development of the theories it imports from psychology, and for covering topics that lack connection to issues of interest to practitioners.[45] One remedy has been to expand the boundaries of the field to include the study of psychological issues that are relevant to understanding behavior in organizations, for example, social–cognitive psychology and theories of behavioral decision theory. Neale, Tenbrunsel, Galvin, and Bazerman believe that the cognitive revolution and, subsequent, evolution of the social cognitive perspectives has created even more dramatic changes in organizational behavior by specifically incorporating the decision-making process as a primary focus on research—the decisions and the cognitive processing that leads to these decisions by organizational members.[46]

A central question in behavioral decision research is how decision makers actually go about making decisions, using as a comparison the benchmark of optimal (rational) performance. Kahneman and Tversky have provided critical information about specific systematic biases that influence judgment.[47] The importance of this perspective is recognized by the awarding of the 2002 Nobel Prize in Economics to Kahneman. When making decisions, people rely on several simplifying strategies, or rules of thumb called heuristics. The benefit of this strategy is that it provides a simple way of dealing with a complex world producing correct or partially correct judgments. The cost is that individuals often adopt heuristics without being aware of them, and the misapplication to inappropriate situations often leads people astray.

Behavioral decision research is being applied at different levels of analysis. At the micro level, over the last 10 years, there has been increased interest in investigating negotiations—if negotiators do not act rationally, what systematic departures from rationality can be predicted? Still at the micro level, but thinking about group decision making, decision research is used to study the application of individual biases to a group context, the identification of group-specific heuristics, and biases and systematic influences of heuristic thinking at the group level. At the macro level, the most recent focus is on interorganizational relationships highlighting the processes around strategic choice and interactions, as well as the conceptualization of collective cognitive structures to explain organizational and competitive actions and outcomes.[48]

The contribution of cognitive neuroscience is still patchy. Neale *et al.*, for example, do not highlight the contribution of cognitive neuroscience in their comprehensive review of cognitive research in organizations.[49] Their chapter is published in *The Sage Handbook of Organization Studies*, which in turn does not once highlight the contribution of neuroscience.[50]

Nevertheless, research in organizational cognitive neuroscience is gathering pace. Neuroeconomics is already an established field, and neuromarketing is emerging. The literatures in these fields are already burgeoning. As a consequence, this section develops Neale *et al.*'s[51] review by showing that organizational behavior is taking another dramatic turn through the contribution of cognitive neuroscience to decision making.[52]

Morse reviews existing literature to argue that humans are like animals in how we make decisions; more specifically, we have primitive, emotional parts to our brains that have powerful influences on the choices we make.[53] The argument is supported by neuroscience evidence that maps the risk–reward systems in the brain, which drives our best and worst decision making. In more detail, Morse states that we have dog brains with a human cortex stuck on top, a veneer of civilization.[54] This cortex is an evolutionary recent development that plans, deliberates, and decides. Our ancient dog brains confer with our modern cortices to influence choices. Much of the traffic is devoted to the conscious calculation of risks and rewards.

Unlike most animals, we can contemplate what might flow from a decision to chase immediate gratification, and we can get immediate pleasure from the prospect of some future gratification. Hans Breiter and colleagues show that the brain regions that respond to receiving money are the same ones that react to attractive faces, chocolate, cocaine or morphine, music, revenge, sex, and sports cars.[55] This response is beneficial because it motivates high performance at work and other activities. Breiter *et al.*'s work also demonstrates that the amygdala's role in warning us about real and imagined risks appears to extend to the threat of losing money.[56] Again, this action is beneficial because it makes us risk averse. Nevertheless, there can be a cost. One manager may be more risk seeking, whereas another may be more risk avoiding, which will affect how that person manages and makes decisions. Both managers will need different incentive systems to counterbalance their preferred behavior. Being able to do this rests on further research so that it is possible spot these two and other management styles.

Importance of Organizational Cognitive Neuroscience

Expanding the argument from highlighting some of the costs and benefits of the neuroscience of decision making: The debate surrounding the importance of organizational cognitive neuroscience as a new research direction contains similar issues to those extensively discussed in relation to social cognitive neuroscience. In that discussion, the importance and limitations of social cognitive neuroscience were assessed at two levels, those specific to research about the brain and those more general to its role within social sciences. This discussion now targets two caveats currently causing controversy: biological determinism and ethics. Both sides of the controversy are presented, although there is an emphasis on the importance of organizational cognitive neuroscience.

The worry about biological determinism emerged in an exchange of views about evolutionary psychology. The exchange was among Sewell, Markoczy and Goldberg, and Nicholson and took place in *Human Relations*.[57–59] The exchange, in turn, is an impassioned rejection of evolutionary psychology, a robust defense, and a taking stock of its current position. Nicholson first introduced the ideas to the field of business and management.[60–63] He suggests that the most critical point that proponents of evolutionary psychology need to deal with is the following question:

> Does the reflexive capacity of language and self-consciousness make us uniquely masters of our own fate, stretching the gap between distal and proximal influences, such that the former are obviated by the power of social construction?[64]

Is nurture master over nature? Nicholson argues for the development of a coevolutionary research approach:

> If there are any common grounds for reconciliation it will be at two levels: a truly interactionist (bi-directional) account of individual agency and social context, and at the societal/species level an analysis of the co-evolution of human nature and culture.[65]

He uses leadership as an exemplar, which has three interacting elements. First, a wide range of individual differences have a high degree of heritability, for example, social dominance, which will encourage individuals to seek a wide range of leadership positions and to desire to enact leadership behaviors. Second, people will differ in their willingness or ability to enact leadership behaviors; for instance, willingness may be tempered by short-term goals or pressures and ability may be measured by how personal qualities fit any given leadership position. Third, leadership positions are constructions based upon situational demands—environmental contingencies intervene to reinforce the bias for or against any particular model of leadership behavior; for example, will staff follow the leader?

Nicholson's argument suggests that the new discipline of evolutionary psychology raises profound research questions that should be addressed.[66] He is asking us to revisit the essence of leadership. But his argument also addresses the role of women in leadership, that is, their general absence in the private sector and their greater frequency in the public sector. Men's desire for dominance is greater than women's, and men's preferred leadership behaviors are those that require single-mindedness, competitive striving, and political game-playing. Organizational designs reflect such behavior—labor is hierarchically divided, encouraging periodic tournaments for advancement. Status is everything. In this system, women are discriminated against both directly and indirectly and by the self-selection of women away from systems, on the grounds that such systems are unattractive and are a poor fit with women's style.

The worry about ethics emerged in an exchange of views about neuromarketing, albeit in different journals. As neuromarketing emerges, it is facing questions about the ethics of such a practice. The ethical question being asked suggests that the purpose of neuromarketing is to find the "buy button" in the brain so that advertising campaigns will be created that we will be unable to resist.

Lee *et al.* answer by stressing that neuromarketing is more than solely the use of neuroimaging by commercial interests for their benefit.[67] Arguing in a similar vein to Pinker,[68] they emphasize the importance of more scientific analysis to understanding marketing-relevant human behavior.[69] In particular, the self-assessment measures commonly used in marketing research rely totally on the ability and willingness of the respondents to accurately report their attitudes and/or prior behaviors. Physiological responses can be collected when respondents are directly participating in the behavior and are difficult for subjects to control.

They then extend the argument to apply scientific analysis to issues currently facing organizations: trust, pricing, negotiation, and ethics. Focusing on ethics, they move away from the "buy button" criticism to suggest a research agenda that explores exactly what elements of an advertisement are critical to awareness, attitudes, and evaluations of products and whether these differ for different groups. By doing this, organizations should reduce their reliance on the blunt instruments of blanket coverage, shock tactics, or sexual imagery.

Missing Neuroscience Level in Organization Studies

We can express the importance of organizational cognitive neuroscience another way. At the heart of this article is the conviction that there has been a missing cognitive neuroscience level in organization studies. Pinker expressed this clearly, although he did not refer to organizations as a hot button in their own right.[70] He stressed that the task before us is to challenge the values we hold, which has the positive purpose of improving self-knowledge, and the way to achieve this goal is through a biologically informed humanism. In organization studies, to fulfill this ambition, there is the need to consolidate the move to neuroscience in organizations.

Damasio, through his levels of life regulation, captures biologically informed humanism in action.[71] The notion captures such humanism because our inner, private life is being connected to our outer, public interactions:

> Without exception, men and women of all ages, of all cultures, of all levels of education, and of all walks of economic life have emotions, are mindful of the emotions of others, cultivate pastimes that manipulate their emotions, and govern their lives in no small part by the pursuit of one emotion, happiness, and the avoidance of unpleasant emotions ... emotions have become connected to the complex ideas, values, principles, and judgements that only humans can have.[72]

By adapting the notion and transferring it from the neurophysiology of emotions to organizations, scholars from both disciplines have a means of integrating cognitive neuroscience with organizations. This goal can be achieved by relating the notion to the analysis and understanding of organizational behavior at different vertical or hierarchical levels and to different horizontal or functional activities. This, then, is organizational cognitive neuroscience.

In more detail, Damasio identifies four levels of life regulation.[73] The first level is basic life regulation and includes relatively simple, stereotyped patterns of response, such as metabolic regulation, reflexes, the biological machinery behind what will become pain and pleasure, drives, and motivations. The second is emotions or more complex, stereotyped patterns of response, which include secondary emotions and background emotions. The third is feelings, the sensory patterns signaling pain, pleasure, and emotions that become images. The fourth level is high reason when complex, flexible, and customized plans of response are formulated in conscious images and may be executed as behavior. Consciousness is active between levels three and four.

More needs to clarified about the distinction among emotions, feelings, and consciousness. Damasio argues that it is through feelings, which are inwardly directed and private, that emotions, which are outwardly directed and public, begin their effect on the mind.[74] The full and lasting effect of feelings requires consciousness, because only along with the advent of a sense of self do feelings become known to the individual having them. As a consequence, there are three stages of processing: a state of emotion, which can be triggered and executed unconsciously; a state of feeling, which can be triggered and executed unconsciously; and a state of feeling made conscious, which is known to the individual having both emotion and feeling. The processes are separated to facilitate research into the neural underpinnings of this chain of events in humans.

As we have seen, research in organizational behavior has recently turned to understanding cognition, and the most recent turn is to understanding the neuroscience of cognition. Damasio's levels of life regulation helps current and future researchers to conceptualize that turn.[75] To fully apply the notion, it may need to be retitled and extended. Levels of life regulation could be renamed "levels of regulation in organizational behavior." Extra levels could also be added to include the variety of vertical interactions in organizations; high reason can be applied from the individual to the societal level. Also, at each level, extra analysis will be needed to take account of the network of interactions between functions.

ARTICLES IN THE VOLUME

Just as there is a research momentum gathering around social cognitive neuroscience, there is a similar momentum around organizational cognitive neuroscience. The quality and range of articles selected for the volume reflects this momentum. The articles unconsciously draw on the different levels of regulation in organizational behavior and have different perspectives on the emotional aspects of organizing work relationships.

The first set of articles provide a methodological approach to organizational cognitive neuroscience, which nevertheless have affective insights about the workplace. Lee and Chamberlain finish their article with three illuminating hypothetical case studies that exemplify the link between organizational and psychological theory and cognitive neuroscientific approaches. One of their case studies discusses imaging genetics; its association with memory, emotion, and environmental response; and the implications for the nature of leadership. Caldu and Dreher argue for a multilevel array of social neuroscience and focus their article on the hormonal and genetic influences on processing reward and social information. Their findings indicate the neural influence of genes conferring vulnerability to develop neuropathologies, such as drug addiction and pathological gambling. Farmer suggests an innovative approach that uses neuroscience to reunify the fragmented social sciences. Neuroscience does this by revealing and challenging the taken-for-granted concepts of different social science subjects and the language used to express the concepts. Farmer creates the language of "Neuro-gov."

The second set of articles explore the importance of positive emotions in the workplace, with the articles becoming more applied in their discussion as they seek to relate cognitive neuroscience to organizational well-being. Tabibnia and Lieberman review evidence from social cognitive neuroscience to demonstrate that fairness and cooperation motivate staff, arguing that human behavior is not driven solely by material benefits. Levine supports Tabibnia and Lieberman's argument, introducing the notion of corporate camaraderie as an overlooked factor in team effectiveness. She suggests that camaraderie and effective team behaviors can be correlated to neural activity, though future research in needed. Such behaviors are beneficial to offset workplace stress. Yeats and Yeats' article is a reflective account of a management consultant using a business change process to induce creativity in organizational problem solving. Like Levine, they link affective states and social behaviors to specific neural networks during an organizational intervention.

The third set of articles explore how the workplace can be become a toxic environment. Bailey argues that cognitive processes in hierarchical business structures promote the adoption and use of subjective organizational beliefs and, as a consequence, cognitive inaccuracies. In short, we have learned to obey power figures and their heuristics, from parents to leaders, which leads us to accept their interpretations of events. The answer is to improve communication and cooperation to identify a range of possible strategies to in turn offset the limitations of thinking that there is only one best practice. Senior, Thomson, Badger, and Butler focus on one heuristic bias, how humans respond to beauty during the job negotiation process. They found gender differences when female and male interviewers were asked to allocate high-status and low-status job packages to attractive and average-looking interviewees. Women rewarded attractive men, whereas men penalized both attractive women and men. Women and men uniformly penalized average-looking women and men. Klein and D'Esposito take a macro-level business and management function, the strategy process, and challenge the application of two popular tools because they do not facilitate creativity. In contrast, Mojzisch and Schultz-Hardt focus on more routine processes—mental satiation or being fed up with a repeated action. They propose a new model founded on empirical data, which links the cognitive, motivational, and neural processes underlying mental satiation.

This volume consolidates emerging output in the field of organizational cognitive neuroscience with research from distinguished international scholars. Their contributions to this volume are highly valued and received with gratitude. Furthermore, we also thank the various individuals who acted as reviewers for the articles contained within the volume.

REFERENCES

1. MARVELL, A. 1977. The garden. *In* The Penguin Dictionary of Quotations. J.M. Cohen & M.J. Cohen, Eds.: 246–247. Book Club Associates. London.
2. DAMASIO, A. 2000. The Feeling of What Happens – Body, Emotion and the Making of Consciousness. Vintage. London.
3. PINKER, S. 2003. The Blank Slate. Penguin Books. London.
4. NORD, W.R., T.B. LAWRENCE, C. HARDY & S.R. CLEGG. 2006. Introduction. *In* The Sage Handbook of Organization Studies. S.R. Clegg, C. Hardy, T.B. Lawrence & W.R. Nord, Eds.: 1–15. Sage. London.
5. PINKER, S. 2003. op cit.
6. DAMASIO, A. 2000. op cit.

7. PINKER, S. 2003. op cit. vii.
8. PINKER, S. 2003. op cit. viii.
9. PINKER, S. 2003. op cit. xi.
10. PINKER, S. 2003. op cit. xi.
11. LIEBERMAN, M.D. In press. Social cognitive neuroscience. *In* Encyclopaedia of Social Psychology.
12. PINKER, S. 2003. op cit.
13. PINKER, S. 2003. op cit.
14. PINKER, S. 2003. op cit. 371.
15. PINKER, S. 2003. op cit.
16. FURCHTGOTT-ROTH, D. & C. STOLBA. 1999. Women's Figures: An Illustrated Guide to the Economic Progress of Women in America. American Enterprise Institute. Washington, DC.
17. PINKER, S. 2003. op cit.
18. AZAR, B. 2002. At the frontier of science. Monitor on Psychology **33**: 1–8.
19. LIEBERMAN, M.D. In press. op cit.
20. LIEBERMAN, M.D. In press. op cit.
21. LIEBERMAN, M.D. In press. op cit.
22. CAJAL, S.R.Y. 1999. Advice For a Young Investigator. The MIT Press. Cambridge, MA.
23. LIEBERMAN, M.D. In press. op cit.
24. AZAR, B. 2002. op cit.
25. AZAR, B. 2002. op cit.
26. LIEBERMAN, M.D. In press. op cit.
27. AZAR, B. 2002. op cit.
28. PINKER, S. 2003. op cit.
29. PINKER, S. 2003. op cit.
30. PINKER, S. 2003. op cit. 174.
31. LIEBERMAN, M.D. In press. op cit.
32. AZAR, B. 2002. op cit.
33. AZAR, B. 2002. op cit.
34. LIEBERMAN, M.D. 2006. Editorial – Social cognitive and affective neuroscience: When opposites attract. Social Cognitive and Affective Neuroscience **1**: 1–2.
35. LIEBERMAN, M.D. 2006. op cit. 1.
36. DAMASIO, A. 2000. op cit.
37. LIEBERMAN, M.D. In press. op cit.
38. PINKER, S. 2003. op cit.
39. LIEBERMAN, M.D. In press. op cit.
40. KENNING, P. & H. PLASSMANN. 2005. NeuroEconomics: An overview from an economic perspective. Brain Res. Bull. **67**: 343–354. 344.
41. LEE, N., A.J. BRODERICK & L. CHAMBERLAIN. 2007. What is 'neuromarketing'? A discussion and agenda for future research. Int. J. Psychophysiol. **63**: 192–198. 200.
42. LIEBERMAN, M.D. In press. op cit.
43. REED, S.K. 2007. Cognition – Theory and Applications. Seventh Edition. Thomson Higher Education. Belmont, CA.
44. MARKUS, H. & R.B. ZAJONC. 1985. The cognitive perspective in social psychology. *In* The Handbook of Social Psychology. G. Lindzey & E. Aronson, Eds. Random House. New York, NY.

45. O'REILLY, C.A. 1991. Organizational behavior: Where we have been, where we are going. *In* Annu. Rev. of Psychology. Annual Reviews, Inc. Palo Alto, CA.
46. NEALE, M.A., A.E. TENBRUNSEL, T. GALVIN & M.H. BAZERMAN. 2006. A decision perspective on organizations: Social cognition, behavioral decision theory and the psychological links to micro- and macro-organizational behavior. *In* The Sage Handbook of Organization Studies. S.R. Clegg, C. Hardy, T.B. Lawrence & W.R. Nord, Eds.: 485–519. Sage. London.
47. KAHNEMAN, D. & A. TVERSKY. 1979. Prospect theory: An analysis of decision under risk. Econometrica **47**: 263–292.
48. PORAC, J., M. VENTRESCA & Y. MISHINA. 2002. Interorganizational cognition and interpretation. *In* Companion to Organizations. J. Baum, Ed.: 579–598. Blackwell. Oxford.
49. NEALE, M.A. *et al.* 2006. op cit.
50. CLEGG, S.R., C. HARDY, T.B. LAWRENCE & W.R. NORD. 2006. The Sage Handbook of Organization Studies. Sage. London.
51. NEALE, M.A. *et al.* 2006. op cit.
52. MORSE, G. 2006. Decisions and desire. Harvard Bus. Rev. January: 42–51.
53. MORSE, G. 2006. op cit.
54. MORSE, G. 2006. op cit.
55. BREITER, H.C., I. AHARON, D. KAHNEMAN, A. DALE & P. SHIZGAL. 2001. Functional imaging of neural responses to expectancy and experience of monetary gains and losses. Neuron **30**: 619–639.
56. BREITER, H.C. *et al.* 2001. op cit.
57. SEWELL, G. 2004. Yabba-dabba-doo! Evolutionary psychology and the rise of Flintstone psychological thinking in organizational and management studies. Human Relations **57**: 923–955.
58. MARKOCZY, L. & J. GOLDBERG. 2004. Yabba-dabba-doo! A response to unfair accusations. Human Relations **57**: 1037–1046.
59. NICHOLSON, N. 2005. Objections to evolutionary psychology: Reflections, implications and the leadership exemplar. Human Relations **58**: 393–409.
60. NICHOLSON, N. 1997a. Evolutionary psychology and organizational behavior. *In* Creating Tomorrow's Organizations: A Handbook for Future Research in Organizational Behavior. C.L. Cooper & S. Jackson, Eds. Wiley. Chichester.
61. NICHOLSON, N. 1997b. Evolutionary psychology: Toward a new view of human nature and organizational society. Human Relations **50**: 1053–1078.
62. NICHOLSON, N. 1998. How hardwired is human behavior? Harvard Bus. Rev. **76**: 134–147.
63. NICHOLSON, N. 2000. Managing the Human Animal. Thomson/Texere. London.
64. NICHOLSON, N. 2005. op cit.
65. NICHOLSON, N. 2005. op cit. 402.
66. NICHOLSON, N. 2005. op cit.
67. LEE, N. *et al.* 2007. op cit.
68. PINKER, S. 2003. op cit.
69. LEE, N. *et al.* 2007. op cit.
70. PINKER, S. 2003. op cit.
71. DAMASIO, A. 2000. op cit.
72. DAMASIO, A. 2000. op cit. 35.
73. DAMASIO, A. 2000. op cit.
74. DAMASIO, A. 2000. op cit.
75. DAMASIO, A. 2000. op cit.

Neuroimaging and Psychophysiological Measurement in Organizational Research

An Agenda for Research in Organizational Cognitive Neuroscience

NICK LEE AND LAURA CHAMBERLAIN

Organizational Cognitive Neuroscience Centre, Aston Business School, Aston Triangle, Birmingham B4 7ET, United Kingdom

> ABSTRACT: Although organizational research has made tremendous strides in the last century, recent advances in neuroscience and the imaging of functional brain activity remain underused. In fact, even the use of well-established psychophysiological measurement tools is comparatively rare. Following the lead of social cognitive neuroscience, in this review, we conceptualize organizational cognitive neuroscience as a field dedicated to exploring the processes within the brain that underlie or influence human decisions, behaviors, and interactions either (a) within organizations or (b) in response to organizational manifestations or institutions. We discuss organizational cognitive neuroscience, bringing together work that may previously have been characterized rather atomistically, and provide a brief overview of individual methods that may be of use. Subsequently, we discuss the possible convergence and integration of the different neuroimaging and psychophysiological measurement modalities. A brief review of prior work in the field shows a significant need for a more coherent and theory-driven approach to organizational cognitive neuroscience. In response, we discuss a recent example of such work, along with three hypothetical case studies that exemplify the link between organizational and psychological theory and neuroscientific methods.
>
> KEYWORDS: organizational cognitive neuroscience; social cognitive neuroscience; neuroimaging; psychophysiology; neuroeconomics; neuromarketing

INTRODUCTION

The organizational research fields have made tremendous strides in their attempts to understand human behavior and decision making within an organizational context over the last century or so. It is indisputable that we now have far greater insight into how individuals and groups work and interact within organizations, how to effectively manage that process, and how organizational activity can influence various stakeholders (such as employees, consumers, or members of society). Because a significant majority of most individuals' waking lives is spent either working within an organization, or interacting with various organizations and their manifestations, such understanding is of major importance on both a theoretical and a practical level. Although an almost uncountable number of diverse disciplines could be said to fall under the auspices of organizational research—including marketing, strategy, economics, organizational behavior, operations research, and subdisciplines of these fields—they all share a common goal of understanding how humans behave within, or in response to the institutions of, organizations. Further, most of these research areas appear to be based on the development of the behavioral, cognitive, or social psychological fields.

Not surprisingly then, research methods and paradigms within the organizational research fields owe much to psychological research methods. For example, the incorporation by many of the organizational disciplines of latent variable theory and psychometric techniques has, to most minds, advanced understanding considerably, as has the use of experimental methods where appropriate. Conversely, many advances in psychology owe much to organizational and economic contexts as settings for their theoretical and empirical work. Perhaps the most obvious example of this is the 2002 Nobel Prize for Economics awarded to psychologist Daniel Kahneman,[a] for his work with Amos Tversky on "prospect theory," which essentially founded the entire field of behavioral economics,[1] even though Kahneman claims never to have taken an economics course in his life. Other key psychological theories, such as social exchange, social learning, reasoned action, emotions and cognition, and stereotyping, among many others, have also been fruitfully examined in organizational contexts. Such work has provided strong evidence for these theories in a more general context. Thus, a long-held and extremely productive relationship already exists between the psychological and organizational research fields.

However, in more contemporary times, huge advances have been made in the psychological fields that have only begun to filter through in a piecemeal fashion to organizational and economic research. More specifically, in recent years, the ability of researchers to directly observe brain activity has increased exponentially through the use of functional neuroimaging methods such as magnetoencephalography (MEG) and functional magnetic resonance imaging (fMRI). In fact, the 1990s was termed the "Decade of the Brain" by United States President George Bush,[2] and brain imaging research continues

---

[a] While the prize was awarded for his joint work with the late Amos Tversky, the Nobel committee does not make posthumous awards.

to grow in both quantity and sophistication. In 2007, Bandettini reported that, on average, around six to seven papers are published *per day* using fMRI alone.[3] Furthermore, longstanding techniques such as electroencephalography (EEG), eye tracking, and electrodermal response (EDR) remain popular, and have even received renewed interest in conjunction with newer methodologies. Inarguably, advances in neuroscientific methods have allowed us insight into previously poorly understood psychological questions and have also provided new insights into long-held theories and concepts.[4,5] Nevertheless, much of this appears to have passed organizational research by with nary a ripple.

Much as advances in the psychological disciplines have "trickled down" to organizational sciences throughout the 20th century, developments in neuroimaging and other psychophysiological methods seem to have much to offer researchers in more applied research fields. Indeed, social psychological researchers have a long history of applying psychophysiological techniques, such as eye-tracking, EDR, and EEG, to social psychological problems;[6] more recently, the field of social cognitive neuroscience has emerged.[5,7] However, organizational sciences have been slower to incorporate such methods, although their use is not unheard of. Nevertheless, the use of modern neuroimaging techniques—and even long-established psychophysiological methods—remains rare and somewhat ad hoc in the organizational research fields. Certainly, a small number of studies have examined economic decision making and marketing information processing,[8,9] but these efforts appear to have little overall coherence and no overarching research program is obvious. In other words, wherefore *organizational* cognitive neuroscience?

In this article, we provide an integrative overview of the possibilities and caveats of recent developments in neuroimaging and psychophysiological measurement for organizational research. In particular, we discuss and delineate the emergence and scope of an organizational cognitive neuroscience as a distinct branch of cognitive neuroscience. We begin with the latter treatise, and subsequently briefly introduce a number of key neuroimaging and psychophysiological techniques. Following this, we provide an overview of the possible integration of such methods, which may provide the most exciting potential of all. Finally, we provide four illustrative case studies showing how the integration of organizational and cognitive neuroscience could contribute to knowledge in both fields. One of these case studies is a discussion of an exemplary recent study that explored an organizational issue from a cognitive neuroscience perspective; the other three case studies are hypothetical examples showing how advances in cognitive neuroscience theory and technique could be used to help answer pressing organizational research questions.

ORGANIZATIONAL COGNITIVE NEUROSCIENCE

The organizational and economic sciences have a long history of exploring research questions that are essentially concerned with cognitive or social psychology. For example, economic and organizational researchers have long been interested in questions concerning decision making and information processing, as well as many other questions within the cognitive psychological framework. At the same time, topics related to stereotypes, attitudes, group dynamics, persuasion, and social influence have proven to be rich avenues of exploration for organizational researchers. This is unsurprising, as much of one's life is taken up either by interacting with others in a work situation or processing and reacting to information from organizations.

The educated observer can easily see how modern neuroscientific techniques have revolutionized cognitive psychology. Indeed, the cognitive areas of organizational research, such as economic decision making[10,11] and information processing[12,13] have shown the greatest aptitude for incorporating modern brain imaging methodologies. In contrast, neuroimaging and other psychophysiological techniques have yet to make significant inroads into the more social psychologically oriented organizational disciplines—although constructs such as arousal have been of some interest in marketing research, for example.[14]

Nevertheless, techniques such as fMRI have much to offer researchers in both cognitive and social psychological organizational fields. Of particular interest is the recent work in social cognitive neuroscience, which provides a clear framework for the investigation of questions and problems that may fall outside the traditional cognitive neuroscience framework.[5] The roots of social cognitive neuroscience can be found in the work of John Cacioppo and his colleagues throughout the 1980s and 1990s on integrating neuroscience and social psychology to form what was termed *social psychophysiology* and later *social neuroscience*.[15,16] The central thesis of this approach is that social psychological phenomena of interest must be explained by both micro (e.g., neuropsychology, biology, and physiology) and macro (e.g., social context, group dynamics, and economic opportunity) factors.[17] As an example, although all individuals possess the biological factors that support drug abuse, whether an individual actually succumbs to abuse depends on social forces as well.[16]

Although the social neuroscience approach contributed greatly to the integration of social psychology and neuroscience, it has focused primarily on indirect physiological outcomes of cognitive activity,[7] such as autonomic nervous system activity. However, in more recent times, the rise of fMRI has led to the emergence of social cognitive neuroscience as a distinct field of study,[18] as evidenced by ever-increasing research activity and even the creation of two dedicated journals. Although this has apparently not been made explicit in the literature, it seems that the social neuroscience approach has been somewhat absorbed into the social cognitive neuroscience domain (even though social neuroscience work does not necessarily deal solely with cognitive theories or concepts). According to Lieberman,[18] social cognitive neuroscience combines the "tools of cognitive neuroscience with questions and theories from various social sciences" (p. 260), and this is echoed in other work.[5,7,19] Although the development of functional neuroimaging techniques has definitely driven the growth of social cognitive neuroscience,[7] it should not be forgotten that the more indirect psychophysiological techniques used in what was previously termed social neuroscience also have much to offer the social cognitive neuroscientist. Indeed, in part of the present paper we will discuss such techniques, as well as their integration with the newer functional neuroimaging methods.

Nevertheless, cautionary notes have been sounded regarding overenthusiastic application of neuroimaging techniques to social psychological problems. More specifically, scholars such as Lieberman[20] expend considerable effort to explain that simply discovering that certain brain areas show activity, or "light up," when social psychological processes take place is of extremely limited interest. Further, the goals of social cognitive neuroscience are not simply to discover "social modules" in the brain or to map "the brain correlates of social and emotional phenomena," as Ochsner and Lieberman[5] (pp. 729) are at pains to make clear. Certainly, as a first step one must determine which brain areas are associated with which processes but, as Ochsner and Lieberman[5] show, this alone offers little insight into social psychological theories. In fact, the latter approach, which receives implied criticism by Lieberman and others,[5,20] has been termed *blobology* and has been criticized in the more general cognitive neuroscience fields.[21] Instead, research must be strongly grounded in social psychological and other relevant theory to be of more than general interest to the social psychologist.[22] Cacioppo and his colleagues explicitly refer to this idea as exploring "multiple levels" of analysis—social, cognitive, and neural[6,16,17]—and it remains strongly advocated in the social cognitive neuroscience literature.[5] A slightly different way of looking at this issue is to consider a number of different *layers of theory* that one could overlay on the basic neural activity of the brain. The cognitive layer of theory concerns internal mental processes that rely on these neural substrates, such as memory and information processing. The social layer of theory concerns how social interaction can provide an interactive influence in conjunction with cognitive or neurophysiological mechanisms or both. One could overlay social, cognitive, or both theories onto neural activity to develop specific hypotheses regarding human behavior or psychology.

An *organizational cognitive neuroscience* could be defined in relation to social cognitive neuroscience as a distinct field for examination. Much as organizational and economic research has traditionally drawn heavily from social and cognitive psychology, so organizational cognitive neuroscience draws from social cognitive neuroscience. More specifically, organizational cognitive neuroscience is the study of the processes within the brain that underlie or influence human decisions, behaviors, and interactions either (a) within organizations or (b) in response to organizational manifestations or institutions. With the development of organizational cognitive neuroscience, another layer of theory is added to the aforementioned social and cognitive layers, that of the organizational and economic sciences. This layer, in essence, concerns how the specific organizational context has an important interactive influence beyond that of the more general social or cognitive processes. For example, group dynamics within a task-focused work team are considerably different from those in a general social situation. In addition, entire theories—beyond the more general cognitive processing theories—are dedicated to decision making under economic risk.

In recent times, isolated studies have appeared in neuroscientific and psychophysiological outlets dealing with organizationally relevant problems, particularly economic decision making and information processing. Such work has been labeled in various ways, such as *neuroeconomics*,[8] or *neuromarketing*.[23] However, such labeling excludes many areas of organizational research that may benefit from a cognitive neuroscience perspective, and runs the risk of restricting the scope of investigation to a few limited areas. Conversely, there is also a chance that the end result of the present approach is a set of *neurowhatever* ad hoc research studies that are not necessarily theoretically driven. In such cases, we may fall unwittingly prey to exactly the kind of blobological approach that has received criticism in social and general neuroscientific circles.[21]

A further possible benefit of the emergence of a more coherent sense of the overarching organizational cognitive neuroscience research approach is that it may drive an increase in collaboration between scholars in the organizational and neuroscientific fields. At present, certainly from our own experience, such collaboration is rather ad hoc and reliant on serendipitous meetings. Organizational researchers probably see neuroscientific research as something of a mystery,[24] or hold considerable misconceptions about it,[25,26] whereas neuroscientists may find the organizational fields of research as perhaps somewhat "unscientific".[27] Theoretically driven collaborations between the best of both research traditions are perhaps the only way to dispel such myths.[23]

However, some important dangers are inherent in such collaborations. Previously, the necessity for a sound grounding in organizational and cognitive theory was stressed, but there is also a need for a solid grounding for non-neuroscientists in a number of critical aspects of neuroscientific methodology. In their analogous call for a social cognitive neuroscience, Ochsner and Lieberman warn of the risk of theoretical and methodological naivety facing researchers,[5] and it seems pertinent to repeat such counsel here. Yet for many organizational scholars versed in more traditional research methods, the neuroscience methodology literature can seem overwhelming, and it is difficult to know where to begin. Nevertheless, a number of key areas can be defined, inspired by Bandettini's[3] discussion of fMRI. A basic appreciation of all these aspects is important to the organizational cognitive neuroscience researcher. First, one must have an understanding of the actual *physical hardware* to be used; for example, how does an MRI or MEG scanner actually work? Without this knowledge it is hard to truly understand what can and cannot be done or exactly what one *wants* to do. Second, it is important to understand exactly what one is measuring, or the *signal* that is being measured. For example, what do the "lit up" areas on an fMRI scan signify? Third, it is critical to understand how to design appropriate research studies and paradigms. This is especially important for organizational researchers who may have been raised on a diet of large sample, multivariate, cross-sectional work. Most of the paradigms in cognitive neuroscience are fundamentally different from this approach. An understanding of all of these things, coupled with strong theoretical reasoning, is the starting point for fruitful collaboration between organizational and neuroscientific researchers and the development of a true organizational cognitive neuroscience. In this spirit, we provide such a starting point in the balance of this paper.

NEUROIMAGING AND PSYCHOPHYSIOLOGICAL MODALITIES AND THEIR INTEGRATION

Many different modalities could be used by the researcher to investigate brain function, cognition, and, by implication, social and organizational behavior. Perhaps the most well known of these methods is fMRI, and when the same nuclear magnetic resonance technology is used to measure changes in the brain's chemical composition it is termed *magnetic resonance spectroscopy* (MRS[28]). However, MEG and EEG are also used to measure brain activity, in this case by measuring the electromagnetic signals caused by neural activity. Furthermore, EDR and eye-tracking have been used as indirect measures of brain function, although they are not neuroimaging modalities as the term is commonly understood. Whereas it is beyond the scope of this review to introduce in any detail the individual methods, TABLE 1 provides a basic overview of the characteristics, strengths, and weaknesses of these different tools, as well as some introductory references for the interested reader.

Convergence and Integration

As TABLE 1 shows, each modality has distinct features and weaknesses. For example, methods based on electromagnetic signals (e.g., EEG and MEG) have far superior temporal resolution than those based on detecting physiological changes such as blood oxygenation (e.g., fMRI). On the other hand, fMRI does not suffer from the "inverse problem" (see TABLE 1), and thus has superior spatial resolution. One might reasonably assume that increasing temporal or spatial resolution of these techniques would be beneficial and might eventually allow the results from different modalities to converge on single explanations of brain function. However, this is not necessarily the case in all situations,[38] and one must be careful to remain cognizant of the key differences between modalities and their implications for the research questions that can be answered.

Of course, as techniques like MEG and fMRI are ostensibly aiming to measure the same thing—cortical activity—it seems that, by solving the respective spatial and temporal resolution problems, one could expect some form of convergence in activity measurements. However, it remains to be seen what a *lack* of convergence would mean. Would nonconvergence invalidate either the method, the theory, or neither? More specifically, could one interpret nonconvergence as a source of important information about brain function? In particular, both modalities measure different endogenous indicators of activity, one direct (electromagnetic signals) and one essentially indirect (a physiological response to increased activity), and may result in different patterns of activity within the brain. Such nonconvergence could have significant implications for how we think about the interrelationships among cortical areas. In fact, if convergence is a natural consequence of technological development, why use different modalities at all? Surely resources would be better spent investing in the further development of a single method. Thus, it must logically be the case that different modalities give us important, and different, information about cortical activity.

One way to further conceptualize this issue is the idea of the causal connection between a given experimental stimulus and brain activity. More specifically, if one observes differential (e.g., increased) activity at a particular cortical location in response to some task, does this mean that that particular location is *necessary* for the performance of that task? In fact, the answer is no.[38] There are many reasons why cortical activity may be activated in association with a task, such as anticipation or prediction of future behavior, motor functions, or even simply epiphenomenal activity that occurs as a side-effect. For example, the task of a light bulb is to give off light, but as an epiphenomenal consequence it also gives off heat. The following sections will discuss ways to combine different imaging modalities to enhance our understanding of brain activity. However, first we will consider a technique that allows some indication of whether a given brain region is necessary for a given task.

Transcranial Magnetic Stimulation

Transcranial magnetic stimulation (TMS) is not a neuroimaging method *per se*; however, it can be used in conjunction with tools such as fMRI, MEG, and other cognitive study methods, such as behavioral measures. It is most commonly used to create what is called a *virtual lesion* in the brain of an experimental subject. Cognitive psychology has long relied on neuropsychological patients who, as a consequence of various events (e.g., accidents or medical conditions), have some kind of cortical damage, or lesion; more recently, social cognitive neuroscience has explored the possibilities of using such patients.[5] Comparing such patients with "healthy" control subjects has allowed considerable insight into which areas of the brain may be necessary

TABLE 1. Brief overview of neuroimaging and psychophysiological modalities

Modality	Key Features	Strengths	Weaknesses	Key Introductory Reference(s)
EDR	Detects electrical conductance of the skin related to the level of sweat in the eccrine sweat glands as a result of autonomic nervous system activation.	Widely available, commonly used, good temporal resolution, flexible research designs, autonomic responses more valid than behavioral or self-report measures.	Does not measure neural activity directly, link between autonomic response and brain function is theoretical.	Edelberg[29] Naqvi and Bechara[30]
Eye-Tracking	Tracks visual attention and pupil dilation as an indication of attention, arousal, and valence.	Noninvasive, relatively easy to administer, good temporal resolution, flexible in terms of research deigns, sensitive to multiple factors.	Does not measure neural activity directly, link between autonomic response and brain function is theoretical.	Norton and Stark[31] Henderson[32]
EEG	Detects (at scalp surface) electrical potential differences derived from neural activity. Subjects have a number of electrodes attached to their heads.	Widely available, noninvasive, long history of use leading to well-accepted body of theory, excellent temporal resolution.	Does not measure neural activity directly, signal must travel through tissue and skull to surface, relies on the accurate modelling of this path, unable to conclusively determine the actual location of activation in the brain (the 'inverse problem') leading to poor spatial resolution.	Rippon[33]

Continued

TABLE 1. Continued

Modality	Key Features	Strengths	Weaknesses	Key Introductory Reference(s)
MEG	Detects magnetic signals associated with the electrical activity in the brain. Subjects sit in large scanner.	Noninvasive, able to directly measure signals of neural activity, thus more robust than EEG, new techniques can minimize the "inverse problem", excellent temporal resolution.	Expensive to purchase, use, and maintain equipment, suffers from the inverse problem, standardized equipment size can make it unsuitable for some subjects.	Hämäläinen and Hari[34] Singh[35]
MRI	Detects magnetic field distortions that can result from changes in cortical activity, chemical composition of the brain, tissue damage, etc. Imaging of brain function tends to use changes in oxygenated blood (the 'BOLD contrast'), but other contrasts are possible and used for other purposes.	Noninvasive, easy to use, able to locate the source of the signal very accurately (excellent spatial resolution).	Expensive equipment, latest technology not available to all, poor temporal resolution as signal changes occur post-cortical activity, subjects exposed to loud noise due to rapid switching on/off of radiofrequency signal, can be stressful.	Bandettini[36] Russell et al.[37] Hall and Adjamian[28]

for a given task. While this method has several advantages, it does suffer from a number of drawbacks, specifically, the need to wait for a naturally occurring patient, the rarity of a lesion that is located solely in a specific area, and the possibility that the brain may reorganize itself in unique ways to compensate for the lesion[38] which—although undoubtedly good for the patient—leads to a lack of comparability among different cases in research terms.

The use of TMS has considerable advantages. First, the lesion created by TMS is short-term and transient, which means the brain is unable to develop compensation strategies to deal with the reduced functionality. Also, the virtual lesion area can be somewhat more tightly controlled in terms of cortical location, which allows greater control in the behavioral or cognitive effects produced. Finally, TMS subjects are able to be used as their own controls (e.g., in a before–after design), which eliminates between-subject variation and error. That said, one must understand that TMS does not completely "block" cortical activity. Instead, TMS can be considered to "interfere with" the cortical activity, in the same way that electromagnetic signals can create "noise" on a television picture.[38]

The use of TMS alone is not likely to offer significant insight into many of the key organizational research areas. However, when TMS is integrated with other cognitive activity measuring tools—whether behavioral, peripheral, or direct measures—it can provide a new and compelling angle on the causal link between cortical area and behavioral or cognitive functioning. Generally, fMRI, EEG, or MEG is used to determine where to position the TMS coil for stimulation, and behavioral measures (e.g., reaction time, error rate, or another task performance measure) are used as dependent variables in an experimental design. As TMS stimulation is very short (only a few milliseconds), one must be conscious of this when designing experiments. It is possible to either apply TMS during the hypothesized neural processing time (i.e., after presentation of the stimulus and before the behavioral reaction), or prior to the presentation of the stimulus (e.g., repetitive pulses over a few minutes prior to stimulus). However, guidelines specify the duration and strength of TMS pulses that can be applied.[39]

Integration of Different Psychophysiological and Functional Neuroimaging Modalities

Although each of the individual modalities introduced above can offer unique and valuable insight into cortical activity in its own right, it is when they are combined that perhaps the most exciting insights will be developed. The combination of different imaging and psychophysiological measurements is certainly not new; however, as technology and neuroscientific paradigms continue to advance, many new integrations become possible.

In particular, eye-tracking methods have been combined with fMRI. In fact, the importance of gaining an indication of whether subjects are fixating on a stimulus is such that many fMRI scanners actually have eye-tracking facilities inbuilt. However, as Henderson[32] states, such uses "barely scratch the surface" of possibilities for integration (p. 187). As the control of eye fixation is a critical part of cognitive processing,[40] significant insight will likely be gained from linking measurement of how the brain directs attention toward a given stimulus with knowledge of how the brain processes the information generated. However, such integration may be limited by the temporal resolution issues inherent in fMRI. Specifically, if attention occurs prior to processing, the delay in blood oxygen level dependent (BOLD) response to cortical activity may make attempts to link eye tracking with fMRI measurement more difficult. Nevertheless, examples of studies that do link the two can be found. MEG and EEG are also likely to be of considerable utility in conjunction with eye tracking, and do not suffer from the temporal problems outlined previously.

EDR measurement can also fruitfully be combined with other functional neuroimaging modalities. In many cases (especially involving fMRI integration), this involves measurement of the skin response from the plantar (foot) surface, to avoid heating of the electrode that results from the magnetic activity. Furthermore, it is important to select the correct type of conductance measure. If an event-related design is used, one should use phasic measurements, which are of short duration and can be conceptualized as directly related to a stimulus onset.[30] By contrast, tonic measurements are of longer duration, and cannot be causally connected to stimuli. At a most basic level, integrating EDR with functional neuroimaging (and TMS) allows enhanced understanding of which brain areas are implicated in EDR. Although considerable knowledge of these mechanisms has already been gained from lesion studies, direct evidence from normal brain subjects may offer additional insights.[5] EDR can also be used in a manner similar to eye-tracking data, to provide a "check" on the experimental subjects, in this case to determine whether they are exhibiting the expected response to the stimuli.[36] As EDR is a well-validated measure of emotion and arousal, it can also be used to help further understand the neuronal correlates of the fMRI signal.

Although integration between the psychophysiological tools described above and functional neuroimaging tools such as fMRI and MEG can advance our understanding of cortical function considerably, it is the integration of fMRI and MEG or EEG that has been of most interest to neuroscientists in recent years. Given the respective spatial and temporal weaknesses of each method, it is not surprising that some have considered a combination of MEG and fMRI to be the "perfect neuroimaging technique", as Singh[35] puts it (p. 316). The integration of EEG and fMRI is, in fact, relatively common—perhaps driven by its clinical utility for such purposes as locating epileptic foci—and many fMRI scanners have EEG measuring devices already built in. However, the integration of MEG and fMRI is less common, and rather more difficult as it is impossible to simultaneously collect the two sets of data.[36] Simultaneous integration of EEG and fMRI is also not without problems, as the magnetic fields used for fMRI create considerable noise in the EEG signal. However, more recent studies have developed methods of filtering such noise out, or at least reducing its impact.[33]

One of the more intriguing areas in which the integration of EEG or MEG and fMRI data appears to have potential is the aforementioned inverse problem. More specifically, fMRI data can be used to essentially constrain, or bound, the set of possible solutions to the inverse problem.[35] Once fMRI data have been used to infer a source of the EEG or MEG signal, the electromagnetic signals can be used to infer exactly where *and* when neuronal activation occurs.[41] Nevertheless, it is not yet clear that the location of the hemodynamic fMRI signal changes are actually the same as the sources of the electromagnetic activity measured using EEG or MEG, or even whether the fMRI signal change is associated with some types of EEG- or MEG-measurable effects at all.[36] Without this assumption, the use of fMRI to constrain EEG or MEG is questionable.

Because MEG measurements alone contain no information on the location of activity (in contrast to EEG, for which the electrode location is precisely mapped), MRI must be used to create an anatomical scan onto which the MEG signal can be mapped. The accuracy of the coregistration, or transfer between the MRI map and the MEG data, is critical to the use of MRI to constrain the parameters of the inverse solution; even small inaccuracies can result in a solution that is worse than using no MRI information at all.[42] Despite its importance, Singh[35] reports that coregistration is often given a low priority in research efforts. There are many ways to coregister MEG and MRI data, ranging from using corresponding markers on a subject's head to match up the two sets of data to sophisticated digitization of the subject's head. Clearly, it is vital to give the appropriate attention to accurate coregistration. In a similar vein, as MEG and fMRI cannot be collected simultaneously, it is critical that investigators use integrative research designs to remove as much variation as possible among experimental stimuli, treatments, and conditions in the repeated runs necessary. It is difficult to achieve this for obvious practical reasons (e.g., repeating an experiment is prone to many potential problems), but also because the BOLD response is far slower than the MEG signal changes. This problem of experimental repetition will remain something of a quandary with the more complex experimental designs that will probably be necessary to explore social and organizational questions.

Finally, it is also unclear exactly which EEG or MEG activity should be used as a correlate with the fMRI signal. Recent work has shown that many different types of electromagnetic signals measured using MEG are evident in areas that show BOLD signal changes. For example Brookes *et al.*[43] show how evoked response, event-related synchronization, and event-related desynchronization all show signal changes in regions associated with fMRI signal changes, and similar implications can be drawn from findings reported by

Singh.[35] As these results were evident using extremely simple stimuli, such as static checkerboards and moving dots, one can expect that more complex stimuli, such as those usually evident in organizational and social psychological research, will be even more difficult to unravel. Until much more is understood about the types of neuronal activity associated with the BOLD contrast, there will remain many unanswered questions about how to most fruitfully combine MEG with fMRI.

WHAT CAN BRAIN ACTIVITY TELL US ABOUT ORGANIZATIONAL RESEARCH QUESTIONS?

Although an understanding of methodology and technique is very important in designing effective organizational cognitive neuroscience research, it is perhaps more useful to show exactly *how* the organizational and cognitive neurosciences can be linked. In the present section, we (a) provide a brief overview of previous work in the area, (b) pick out and discuss some exemplary current research that has effectively explored organizational questions from a neuroscientific perspective, and (c) provide some hypothetical case studies showing examples of how organizational theory can fruitfully overlay a cognitive neuroscientific base to extend our knowledge of both fields. However, the aim of this section is not to thoroughly review previous research activity, as dedicated and comprehensive reviews are already in existence.[8,9,44] Instead, we aim to explore in more detail how organizational cognitive neuroscience may most effectively be conducted.

Indirect psychophysiological measures of brain function, such as EDR and eye tracking, have received some use in an organizational context. Specifically, research that has explored individual responses to advertising material has probably made the most use of such methods. For example, as early as 1964, Caffyn[45] provided a treatise on how such methods could be productively used in advertising research and reported on the results of work exploring EDR. This was followed by other studies in the area,[46–48] although such work has been surprisingly infrequent, given its potential benefits. That said, eye-tracking work has been somewhat more frequent than the examination of EDR in organizational contexts.[49,50]

EEG has so far probably been the most commonly used of all the direct cortical measuring methodologies within an organizational context. In particular, advertising research has made infrequent use of EEG for nearly 30 years.[14,51–53] Work on economic decisions has also used EEG.[54] Nevertheless, it has never become a particularly popular or well-accepted methodology within organizational research. This may be due to difficulties in collaboration between organizational and psychological researchers, but probably also results from the misconceptions and inaccuracies evident in a few highly critical articles.[25,26] MEG has also been of some recent interest in an organizational context, both in exploring advertising-related information processing and encoding,[12,55] and in research concerned with decision making by consumers [10,56,57] At present, however, such efforts are isolated and appear to depend on the efforts of a small number of cross-disciplinary research teams.

Not surprisingly, given the substantial and growing interest in fMRI research,[2,7] this tool has been something of a method of choice in contemporary research linking neuroscience with organizational issues.[9,44] For example, studies have explored cortical activation in relation to exposure to brands,[58] products of different status,[59] and decision making.[11] Risk, reward, fairness, and trust in decisions have also proved of interest.[60] McLure et al.[61] even recreated the famous Coke–Pepsi taste test using fMRI and blind tastings. That said, despite the wide interest, many studies appear to have taken the "mapping" approach criticized by those such as Lieberman[18] and Kosslyn.[22] Further, the use of fMRI to explore brand- and economic-related decisions has received strident criticism in the neuroscientific literature (e.g., see the July 2004 editorial in *Nature Neuroscience*, p. 683;[27] or the February 2004 edition of *The Lancet*, p. 71[62]). One might wonder whether such criticism is based more on misunderstandings of the more scholarly role of organizational or economic research than on justifiable concerns.[23] Nevertheless, a more theoretically grounded approach to fMRI-based research would surely assist in some way toward assuaging such concerns.

Exemplary Current Research

An excellent example of a research study that used neuroimaging to explore organizational research questions is the study entitled "Salience and choice: neural correlates of shopping decisions" by Ambler et al. in the journal *Psychology and Marketing*.[56] This study demonstrated a number of key features that show how organizational research and cognitive neuroscience can combine theoretical and methodological perspectives to advance our knowledge of human decision-making and behavior in the context of shopping. First, Ambler et al. clearly established the need to determine how consumers make buying decisions. Moreover, Ambler et al. focused not on the commercial applications of such knowledge, but on the need for theoretical research. This was done through a review of prior work that encompassed research done from both a marketing (the relevant organizational discipline) and a cognitive neuroscience perspective. According to this short review, modern cognitive neuroscience research suggests that "the location of brain activation during choice making may indicate the bases for those decisions" (p. 248) and implies that decisions may be made primarily on an emotional, rather than a rational, basis. However, Ambler et al. also showed that marketing theory has tended to emphasize rational choice models, in which individuals trade off product attributes and decision outcomes, even when those outcomes involve emotions. Thus, an investigation based on a cognitive neuroscience perspective can extend our knowledge of organizationally relevant questions. In fact, an organizational cognitive neuroscience perspective may be the only way to resolve the debate over the manner in which consumers make decisions about different brands.

Another key feature of Ambler *et al.*'s work is that it was actually possible to design a neuroimaging paradigm likely to answer the research questions. Given the stimuli and design limitations imposed by many modern neuroscientific techniques (which are evident on reading the literature reported in TABLE 1), this is not always the case for the complex hypotheses suggested by organizational and social theory. First, drawing from existing organizational and neuroscience theory, the authors showed that both the processing time required for, and the neural correlates of, brand-related decisions should differ from basic discrimination of height. MEG was shown to be an appropriate modality for measurement (as opposed to fMRI and positron emission tomography), and was used in conjunction with a "virtual tour" of an English supermarket. Participants were asked to make a series of choices among three brands, ignoring price differentials, and were asked to use a shopping voucher (i.e., not their own money). Subjects later filled in a brand familiarity questionnaire. A control experiment used a repeat of the virtual tour, but subjects were instead asked merely to pick the shortest item.

Ambler *et al.*'s findings are consistent with the cognitive hypotheses advanced, in that reaction times for brand choice were longer than for height discrimination, and differential cortical activation was observed between brand choice and height discrimination. Linking this back to cognitive theory, the investigators suggest that stronger activation of a primary visual response in the occipital cortex for the brand choice condition may be associated with subjects' intended purpose of perception—in other words, complex brand choice rather than simple height discrimination. Similarly, the increased response in areas related to semantic and memory-based processing for the brand choice condition may relate to recognition and recall of previous experiences or associations with the brand. More interestingly, they found increased activation in Broca's area (a brain region associated with speech-related processing) for low-salience brands, which could indicate a "silent vocalization" decision strategy in the absence of easily recalled brand information. This latter finding was unexpected. Further, Ambler *et al.* found little evidence of the frontal lobe activation suggested by prior cognitive work.[63] Thus, the findings reported in Ambler *et al.* are a shining example of how a rigorous organizational cognitive neuroscience approach can both shed light on organizationally relevant research questions and contribute further to our understanding of cognitive psychology in general.

Hypothetical Case Study 1: Decision Making and Leader Development

The manner in which individuals make decisions has occupied the efforts of both cognitive and organizational researchers for some time; the work of Damasio, Bechara, and colleagues[30,63] has suggested that emotions may play the critical role, beyond that of rational choice. The basic theory behind this is termed the *somatic marker hypothesis*, which posits that emotional states are triggered in the brain before and after decision making. Before decision making, a somatic state occurs when contemplating the outcomes of various choices (analogous to a "gut feeling" about a choice). After the choice, the somatic state that results from the outcome—either reward or punishment—works to form learned associations between choice and outcome.[30] Drawing from considerable work with neuropsychological patients,[64–66] Naqvi and Bechara[30] delineate a model of decision making, in which the amygdala—a brain area associated with the emotional evaluation of stimuli—triggers emotional responses to actual decision outcomes that, over time, become learned associations. In turn, the ventromedial prefrontal cortex (VMPFC; an area associated with some types of emotional feelings and the autonomic response to emotional stimuli) expresses these associations prior to future choices, perhaps even before any explicit awareness of the potential outcomes of the decision. These somatic states then bias behavior in a presumably advantageous fashion.

The somatic marker hypothesis seems eminently suitable as a theoretical base from which to explore many questions within the organizational and economic sciences concerning decision making under uncertainty. Such work could enhance our understanding of organizational behavior, as well as cognition and neuropsychology. For example, managers make decisions under risk constantly. This risk can be either conceptualized as economic (e.g., whether to award a contract to one party or another, or whether to introduce a new brand), but also as having social aspects (e.g., which method of punishment to use with a poor performer). Furthermore, employees and managers are frequently placed in positions with some ethical dilemma component. Again, this situation has many different aspects of risk associated with it. From a cognitive perspective, we have little knowledge of whether different types of risk may be associated with different cortical activations. What may be most fruitful at this stage, however, would be to explore further the learning aspects of risky decision making outlined by the theory above. For example, leader development is an area of vast interest to scholars and practitioners. If the ability to make effective decisions depends in some way on prior experience (i.e., leading to an amygdala response, which is later expressed in the VMPFC), how does one most effectively train a future manager to make good decisions without leaving them to learn through trial and error?

One way to begin exploring this issue would be to use fMRI-based research to explore how the location of cortical activation in decision making evolves over long-term leadership decision-making experience. If this work validated the suggestion by Naqvi and Bechara[30] that the amygdala triggers emotional responses to decision outcome experiences, which then become learned associations expressed in the VMPFC, further work could explore how to most effectively bypass the need for experience in leadership decision making. An experiment could be designed to determine which training intervention is most effective, drawing from the bountiful literature on leadership development.[67] Such work would be of major interest to organizational psychologists, but would also contribute to extending our knowledge of the cognitive psychology and neuropsychology of decision making. More specifically, much of the prior work on the somatic marker hypothesis has been conducted using indirect measurement of neural function, such as EDR and other autonomic responses, and has focused on short-term decision-making games using neuropsychological patients.[30] Extending this work to a more ecologically valid and meaningful situation, and incorporating the study of normal subjects in a longitudinal design to explore development, may allow us to understand more clearly how decision making occurs in real life.

Hypothetical Case Study 2: Gender Representations in Advertising

A second hypothetical case study showing how organizational and cognitive neurosciences can work together draws from research on perceptions of beauty and social rewards.[68] Recent neuroimaging work has implicated areas involved in the brain reward system (the amygdala, nucleus accumbens, and orbitofrontal regions[68,69]) in the perception of stimuli involving sexual beauty. Theory suggests that such areas are involved in processing information that served an evolutionary purpose (e.g., important to survival or reproduction).[70] Further, prior neuropsychiatric work has shown that the same areas are implicated in eating disorders in women.[71]

Again, it is not a large leap to see how such theory could inform studies of advertising and other marketing and promotional material. Such work has the potential to extend our understanding of what makes advertising effective, but it also has the potential to inform policymakers about the possible harmful effects of advertising. For example, a link has long been assumed between the representation of women in advertising (and in the media in general) and female body dissatisfaction, which may lead to eating disorders. However, there is little hard evidence for this link, leaving policymakers in something of a quandary regarding the regulation of such representations in the media. It would also be of interest to organizational theorists to explore more fully the ways that males and females are represented in advertising. For example, female-targeted advertising tends to use a wider range of appeals than male-targeted advertising, including sexualized images of women or couples, highly masculine situations, and highly feminized ones. Although behavioral evidence suggests that these various sexual and gender imagery tools appeal to consumers, it is not yet known how they have this effect. For example, does one's gender identity influence the appeal of a particular image? Do such differences correspond to differential brain activity during exposure to the stimuli? Further, theories of beauty and sexual selection have implications for many fields of organizational research as well as advertising.[70]

An fMRI-based study could effectively explore such research questions. For example, subjects could view different sets of advertising appeals and fMRI data could be collected to indicate brain activation for comparison with activation during a control condition. Activation could be compared with subjects' scores on established measuring devices such as the BEM Sex Role Inventory,[72] which would provide evidence as to whether perceived gender roles influence the processing—and effectiveness—of different advertising appeals. Such work would also extend prior cognitive neuroscientific research by using more realistic stimuli, and minimizing cultural restraints, as subjects may have seen the stimuli previously if real advertisements are used. Such work would therefore make a contribution to both organizational science and cognitive neuroscience.

Hypothetical Case Study 3: Natural Leadership, and Leader Development

The final hypothetical case study to be considered here is related to a newer area of neuroimaging research, that of imaging genetics. Imaging genetics is a subfield of the study of the brain's structure, chemistry, or function as it is related to various genetic markers (see Mattay *et al.*[73] for an introduction). Such work is predicated on the assumption that differences in brain morphology or physiology are more accurate representations of genetic differences than are behavioral differences. Although it is beyond the scope of the present review to go into depth regarding the complex chemistry of functional genetic polymorphisms, some of the most compelling findings in this area have concerned the examination of brain chemistry and activation associated with different genetic polymorphisms. For example, recent work[74] has shown that differences in a particular gene are associated with differences in the efficiency of the prefrontal cortex response. However, more recent work has suggested that this efficiency comes at the price of a more adverse response to amphetamines and greater sensitivity to pain.[75] Other work has explored how genes influence serotonin uptake in the amygdala (associated with emotion), which evidence suggests is critical for its functioning.[76] For example, Hariri *et al.*[77] showed that subjects carrying a particular allele showed greater amygdala activation in response to fear-inducing stimuli, which may indicate a hypersensitivity to environmental stimuli. Other work has demonstrated that gene polymorphisms can influence brain structure and function in areas associated with learning and memory (e.g., the hippocampus[78]).

Work on imaging genetics has important implications in general for the debate as to whether it is primarily "nature or nurture" that influences human behavior and cognition.[72] However, in an organizational context, researchers have long been concerned with the question of whether leaders are "born or made". More specifically, are great—or even effective—leaders naturally adept at the necessary skills, or do they develop them in the course of their careers? Of even more relevance to organizational scholars is the question of whether leaders can be trained to be effective. Leadership concerns being able to make good decisions and take effective actions in response to various stimuli, which often have both functional (e.g., the job itself) and social aspects. The discovery of genetic mechanisms that influence the effectiveness of the cortical areas associated with memory, emotion, and environmental response may help to uncover how much of leadership is natural, and how much depends on experience and training. It would be of even greater interest to follow up such discoveries (if they are made) with an exploration of how individuals can become effective leaders even without possessing the genetic advantages outlined above. Are there specific types of leadership development that are more beneficial than others? Conversely, such work could also shed light on *ineffective* leaders, such as those who may be functionally excellent but socially poor.

Research methods to investigate these issues from an imaging genetics perspective are only now emerging. However, they are likely to involve integration of the various modalities discussed herein. For example, MRS can detect chemical differences within the brain, while fMRI and MEG are suited to exploring brain function. Further, EDR is useful in measuring autonomic responses, which are also dependent on specific cortical activations. Behavioral measures, such as memory task performance, will also play a prominent role. Such research will also contribute to more basic psychological research, as well as to the organizationally relevant disciplines. For example, it will be useful to know whether the functional differences associated with gene polymorphisms are in fact associated with "real-world" performance impairments. Further, the links with the somatic marker hypothesis are clear, with findings from imaging genetics research in the area of decision making (e.g., gene polymorphisms affecting the amygdala leading to impaired decision making) providing further corroboration that emotional factors are of primacy in decision making. However, there is much work to be done before any solid conclusions can be drawn.

CONCLUSIONS

By now, the reader should understand that the observation of brain activity in association with organizational processes by itself, and without the benefit of a solid understanding of the concepts presented so far, means very little. The final hypothetical case discussed in the previous section, involving imaging genetics, is an excellent illustration of many of the points raised in this review. First, in the core field there is already a strong theoretical base to draw from, quite apart from newer developments stemming from neuroimaging approaches. That said, ample opportunities exist for the development of this body of knowledge, toward which further research in newer contexts would contribute significantly. Second, the theory has clear implications for how individuals behave in, or in response to, organizations and their manifestations. Third, it appears possible to design neuroimaging research paradigms to test the hypotheses derived from this theory. Finally, a wide variety of modalities could be brought to bear on the problem, providing great flexibility, as well as wide scope to explore the issues from different angles. In so doing, researchers can make a stronger and more robust contribution to both organizational and psychological theory, as well as contribute to methodological advancements in the relevant field(s).

As a final note, it may prove useful to reiterate that the purpose of organizational cognitive neuroscience is to study the brain processes that underlie or influence human decisions, behaviors, and interactions either (a) within organizations or (b) in response to organizational manifestations or institutions. These objectives do not specifically include the benefit of commercial companies. Of course, findings from pure and applied research can often be put to commercial use, but this is not necessarily the remit of the researcher.[23] In fact, findings of some of the research introduced in this review could lead to increased regulation of commercial companies, and a societal benefit rather than a commercial one. Explaining that the goals of organizational cognitive neuroscience are theoretical, not commercial, may help move the field forward in a direction more comfortable to many.[27,62]

The piecemeal, but growing, body of literature exploring organizationally relevant questions from a neuroscientific perspective suggests that we may be on the cusp of a new era in organizational research. When one combines this with recent interest in the mainstream business press, such as the *Harvard Business Review*,[79] it can be seen that organizational cognitive neuroscience has much to offer researchers in the organizational, psychological, and neuroscientific fields. However, to move toward a true organizational cognitive neuroscience, a coherent, theoretically driven research program must emerge, rather than ad hoc commercially driven studies designed to extract money from corporations, in exchange for "[dazzling] them with snazzy imaging technology" (*The Lancet*[62] p. 71). To achieve the vast potential of organizational cognitive neuroscience, scholars from a number of fields must realize that they are inextricably interlinked. Organizational, psychological, neuroscientific, and technical neuroimaging experts all have a role to play in moving the field forward. If this occurs, it is our belief that the emergence of organizational cognitive neuroscience will prove to be of great benefit, not just to organizational scholars, but to the psychological sciences and—perhaps most importantly—to society as a whole.

REFERENCES

1. KAHNEMAN, D. & A. TVERSKY. 1979. Prospect theory: an analysis of decision under risk. Econometrica **47**: 263–292.
2. SENIOR, C. et al. 2007. Mapping the mind for the modern market researcher. Qualitative Market Research: An International Journal **10**: 153–167.
3. BANDETTINI, P. 2007. Functional MRI today. Int. J. Psychophysiol. **63**: 138–145.
4. SENIOR, C & G. RIPPON. 2007. Cognitive neuroscience: contributions from psychophysiology. Int. J. Psychophysiol. **63**: 135–137.
5. OCHSNER, K.N. & M.D. LIEBERMAN. 2001. The emergence of social cognitive neuroscience. Am. Psychol. **56**: 717–734.
6. CACIOPPO, J.T. et al. 2000. Handbook of Psychophysiology. Cambridge University Press. Cambridge, UK.
7. LIEBERMAN, M.D. 2005. Principles, processes, and puzzles of social cognition: an introduction for the special issue on social cognitive neuroscience. NeuroImage **28**: 745–756.
8. BRAEUTIGAM, S. 2005. Neuroeconomics—from neural systems to economic behaviour. Brain Res. Bull. **67**: 355–360.
9. KENNING, P. & H. PLASSMANN. 2005. NeuroEconomics: an overview from an economic perspective. Brain Res. Bull. **67**: 343–354.
10. BRAEUTIGAM, S. et al. 2001. Magnetoencephalographic signals identify stages in real-life decision processes. Neural Plast. **8**: 241–253.
11. SANFEY, A.G. et al. 2003. The neural basis of economic decision-making in the ultimatum game. Science **300**: 1755–1758.
12. IOANNIDES, A.A. et al. 2000. Real time processing of affective and cognitive stimuli in the human brain extracted from MEG signals. Brain Topogr. **13**: 11–19.
13. ROSSITER, J.R. et al. 2001. Brain-imaging detection of visual scene encoding in long-term memory for TV commercials. J. Advert. Res. **41**: 13–21.
14. CACIOPPO, J.T. & R.E. PETTY. 1985. Physiological responses and advertising effects: is the cup half full or half empty? Psychol. Market **2**: 115–127.
15. CACIOPPO, J.T. & R.E. PETTY. 1983. Social Psychophysiology: A Sourcebook. Guildford. New York, NY.
16. CACIOPPO, J.T. et al. 1996. Social neuroscience, principles of psychophysiological arousal and response. In Social Psychology: Handbook of Basic Principles. E.T. Higgins & A.W. Kruglanski, Eds.: 72–101. Guildford. New York, NY.
17. CACIOPPO, J.T. & G.G. BERNTSON. 1992. Social psychological contributions to the decade of the brain: the doctrine of multilevel analysis. Am. Psychol. **47**: 1019–1028.
18. LIEBERMAN, M.D. 2007. Social cognitive neuroscience: a review of core processes. Ann. Rev. Psychol. **58**: 259–289.
19. ADOLPHS, R. 2003. Cognitive neuroscience of human social behavior. Nat. Rev. Neurosci. **4**: 165–178.
20. LIEBERMAN, M.D. 2007. Social cognitive neuroscience. In Encyclopaedia of Social Psychology. R.F. Baumeister & K.T. Vohs, Eds. Sage. Thousand Oaks, CA. In press.
21. SENIOR, C. & T. RUSSELL. 2000. Cognitive neuroscience for the 21st century. Trends Cogn. Sci. **4**: 444–445.
22. KOSSLYN, S.M. 1999. If neuroimaging is the answer, what is the question? Phil. Trans. R. Soc. Lond. B. **354**: 1283–1294.

23. LEE, N. *et al.* 2007. What is 'neuromarketing'? A discussion and agenda for future research. Int. J. Psychophysiol. **63:** 192–198.
24. ROSSITER, J.R. *et al.* 2001. So what? A rejoinder to the reply by Crites and Aikman-Eckenrode to Rossiter et al. (2001). J. Advert. Res. **41:** 59–61.
25. STEWART, D.W. 1984. Physiological measurement of advertising effect: an unfulfilled promise. Psychol. Market. **1:** 43–48.
26. CRITES, S.L., JR. & S.N. AIKMAN-ECKENRODE. 2001. Making inferences concerning physiological responses: a reply to Rossiter, Silberstein, Harris, and Nield (2001). J. Advert. Res. **41:** 23–25.
27. EDITORIAL. 2004. Brain scam? Nat. Neurosci. **7:** 683.
28. HALL, S.D. & P. ADJAMIAN. 2006. The chemistry of cognition. *In* Methods in mind. C. Senior, T. Russell & M.S. Gazzaniga, Eds.: 327–354. MIT Press. Cambridge, MA.
29. EDELBERG, R. 1972. Electrical activity of the skin, its measurement and uses in psychophysiology. *In* Handbook of Psychophysiology. N.S. Greenfield & R.S. Sternback, Eds.: 367–418. Holt, Reinhart and Winston Inc. New York, NY.
30. NAQVI, N.H. & A. BECHARA. 2006. Skin conductance: a psychophysiological approach to the study of decision making. *In* Methods in Mind. C. Senior, T. Russell & M.S. Gazzaniga, Eds.: 103–122. MIT Press. Cambridge, MA.
31. NORTON, D. & L. STARK. 1971. Eye movements and visual perception. Sci. Am. **224:** 34–43.
32. HENDERSON, J.M. 2006. Eye movements. *In* Methods in Mind. C. Senior, T. Russell & M.S. Gazzaniga, Eds.: 171–192. MIT Press. Cambridge, MA.
33. RIPPON, G. 2006. Electroencephalography. *In* Methods in Mind. C. Senior, T. Russell & M.S. Gazzaniga, Eds.: 237–262. MIT Press. Cambridge, MA.
34. HÄMÄLÄINEN, M.S. & R. HARI. 2002. Magnetoencephalographic characterization of dynamic brain activation: basic principles of data collection and source analysis. *In* Brain Mapping: The Methods. A.W. Toga & J.C. Mazziota, Eds.: 227–253. Academic Press. San Diego, CA.
35. SINGH, K. 2006. Magnetoencephalography. *In* Methods in Mind. C. Senior, T. Russell & M.S. Gazzaniga, Eds.: 291–326. MIT Press. Cambridge, MA.
36. BANDETTINI, P. 2006. Functional magnetic resonance imaging. *In* Methods in Mind. C. Senior, T. Russell & M.S. Gazzaniga, Eds.: 193–236. MIT Press. Cambridge, MA.
37. RUSSELL, T.A. *et al.* 2003. Functional neuroimaging: an introduction to the technology, methodology, interpretation, and applucations. *In* Neuroimaging in Psychiatry. C. Senior, C. Fu, T.A. Russell, D. Weinberger & R. Murray, Eds.: 1–50. Dunitz Press, UK.
38. STEWART, L. & V. WALSH. 2006. Transcranial magnetic stimulation in human cognition. *In* Methods in Mind. C. Senior, T. Russell & M.S. Gazzaniga, Eds.: 1–26. MIT Press. Cambridge, MA.
39. WASSERMANN, E.M. 1998. Risk and safety of repetitive transcranial magnetic stimulation: report and suggested guidelines from the International Workshop on the Safety of Repetitive Transcranial Magnetic Stimulation, June 5–7, 1996. Electroen. Clin. Neuro. **108:** 1–16.
40. CHURCHLAND, P.S. *et al.* 1994. A critique of pure vision. *In* Large-Scale Neuronal Theories of the Brain. C. Koch & S. Davis, Eds.: 23–60. MIT Press. Cambridge, MA.
41. AHLFORS, S.P. *et al.* 1999. Spatiotemporal activity of a cortical network for processing visual motion revealed by MEG and fMRI. J. Neurophysiol. **82:** 2545–2555.

42. HILLEBRAND, A. & G.R. BARNES. 2003. The use of anatomical constraints with MEG beamformers. NeuroImage **20:** 2302–2313.
43. BROOKES, M., A. GIBSON, S.D. HALL, *et al.* 2005. GLM-beamformer method demonstrates stationary field: alpha ERD and gamma ERS co-localisation with fMRI BOLD response in visual cortex. NeuroImage **26:** 302–308.
44. KENNING, P. *et al.* 2007. Applications of functional magnetic resonance imaging for market research. Qualitative Market Research: An International Journal **10:** 135–152.
45. CAFFYN, J.M. 1964. Psychological laboratory techniques in cognitive research. J. Advert. Res. **4:** 45–50.
46. GROEPPEL-KLEIN, A. 2005. Arousal and consumer in-store behavior. Brain. Res. Bull. **67:** 428–437.
47. HENSEL, J.S. 1970. Physiological measures of advertising effectiveness: a theoretical and empirical investigation. Ph.D. thesis. Ohio State University, Columbus.
48. KROEBER-REIL, W. 1979. Activation research: psychobiological approaches in consumer research. J. Consum. Res. **5:** 240–250.
49. PIETERS, R. *et al.* 1999. Visual attention to repeated print advertising: a test of scanpath theory. J. Marketing Res. **36:** 424–438.
50. PIETERS, R. & L. WARLOP. 1999. Visual attention during brand choice: the impact of time pressure and task motivation. Int. J. Res. Mark. **16:** 1–16.
51. WEINSTEIN, S. *et al.* 1980. Brain activity responses to magazine and television advertising. J. Advert. Res. **20:** 57–63.
52. WEINSTEIN, S. *et al.* 1984. Brain wave analysis in advertising research: validation from basic research and independent replications. Psychol. Mark. **1:** 83–95.
53. YOUNG, C. 2002. Brain waves, picture sorts®, and branding moments. J. Advert. Res. **42:** 42–53.
54. GEHRING, J.W., & A.R. WILLOUGHBY. 2002. The medial frontal cortex and the rapid processing of monetary gains and losses. Science **295:** 2279–2282.
55. AMBLER, T. *et al.* 2000. Brands on the brain: neuro-images of advertising. Bus. Strategy Rev. **11:** 17–30.
56. AMBLER, T. *et al.* 2004 Salience and choice: neural correlates of shopping decisions. Psychol. Market. **21:** 247–266.
57. BRAEUTIGAM, S. *et al.* 2004. The distributed neuronal systems supporting choice-making in real-life situations: differences between men and women when choosing groceries detected using magnetoencephalography. Eur. J. Neurosci. **20:** 293–302.
58. DEPPE, M. *et al.* 2005. Non-linear responses within the medial prefrontal cortex reveal when specific implicit information influences economic decision making. J. Neuroimaging **15:** 171–182.
59. ERK, S. *et al.* 2002. Cultural objects modulate reward circuitry. Neuroreport **13:** 2499–2503.
60. KING-CASAS, B. *et al.* 2005. Getting to know you: reputation and trust in a two-person economic exchange. Science **308:** 78–83.
61. MCCLURE, S.M. *et al.* 2004. Neural correlates of behavioral preference for culturally familiar drinks. Neuron **44:** 379–387.
62. EDITORIAL. 2004. The Lancet neurology: neuromarketing, beyond branding. Lancet **3:** 71.
63. DAMASIO, A.R. 1994. Descartes' Error: Emotion, Reason, and the Human Brain. Macmillan. London, UK.

64. BECHARA, A. *et al.* 2000. Characterization of the decision-making deficit of patients with ventromedial prefrontal cortex lesions. Brain **123:** 2189–2202.
65. ADOLPHS, R. & D. TRANEL. 2000. Emotion recognition and the human amygdala. *In* The Amygdala: A Functional Analysis. J.P. Aggleton, Ed.: 587–630. Oxford University Press. New York, NY.
66. BECHARA, A. *et al.* 1999. Different contributions of the human amygdala and ventromedial prefrontal cortex to decision-making. J. Neurosci. **19:** 5473–5481.
67. DAY, D.V. 2000. Leadership development: a review in context. Leadership Quart. **11:** 581–613.
68. SENIOR, C. 2003. Beauty in the brain of the beholder. Neuron **38:** 525–528.
69. ISHAI, A. 2007. Sex, beauty and the orbitofrontal cortex. Int. J. Psychophysiol. **63:** 181–185.
70. SENIOR, C. *et al.* 2007. The effects of the menstrual cycle on social decision making. Int. J. Psychophysiol. **63:** 186–191.
71. UHER, R. & J. TREASURE. 2003. Neuroimaging and eating disorders. *In* Neuroimaging in Psychiatry: 171–191. C. Senior, C. Fu, T.A. Russell, D. Weinberger & R. Murray, Eds.: Dunitz Press, UK.
72. WHETTON C. & T. SWINDELLS. 1977. A factor analysis of the BEM Sex-Role Inventory. J. Clin. Psychol. **33:** 150–153.
73. MATTAY, V.S. *et al.* 2006. Imaging genetics. *In* Methods in Mind. C. Senior, T. Russell & M.S. Gazzaniga, Eds.: 263–290. MIT Press. Cambridge, MA.
74. EGAN, M.F. *et al.* 2001. Effect of COMT Val108/158Met genotype on frontal lobe function and risk for schizophrenia. Proc. Natl. Acad. Sci. USA **98:** 6917–6922.
75. MATTAY, V.S. *et al.* 2003. Catechol-O-methyltransferase val158-met genotype and individual variation in the brain response to amphetamine. Proc. Natl. Acad. Sci. USA **100:** 6186–6191.
76. HARIRI, A.R. & D.R. WEINBERGER. 2003. Functional neuroimaging of genetic variation in serotonorgic neurotransmission. Genes and Brain Behavior **2:** 341–349.
77. HARIRI, A.R. *et al.* 2002. Serotonin transporter genetic variation and the response of the human amygdala. Science **297:** 400–403.
78. HARIRI, A.R. *et al.* 2003. Brain-derived neurotropic factor val66met polymorphism affects human memory-related hippocampal activity and predicts memory performance. J. Neurosci. **23:** 6690–6694.
79. KERSTEN, E.L. 2006. The HBR List: breakthroough ideas for 2006. Harv. Bus. Rev. February 2006: 35–67.

Hormonal and Genetic Influences on Processing Reward and Social Information

XAVIER CALDÚ AND JEAN-CLAUDE DREHER

Cognitive Neuroscience Center, Reward and Decision-Making Group, National Center for Scientific Research (CNRS), UMR 5229, Lyon, France

ABSTRACT: Social neuroscience is an emerging interdisciplinary field that combines tools from cognitive, cellular, and molecular neuroscience to understand the neural mechanisms underlying human interactions, emphasizing the complementary nature of different organization levels in the social and biological domains. Previous studies focused on the molecular/neuronal substrates of a variety of complex behaviors, such as parental behavior and pair bonding. Less is known about the various factors influencing interindividual differences in reward processing and decision making in social contexts, both relying upon the dopaminergic system. This review concerns (1) basic electrophysiological findings and recent neuroimaging findings showing that reward processing and social interaction processes share common neural substrates and (2) genetic and hormonal influences on these processes. Recent research combining molecular genetics, endocrinology, and neuroimaging demonstrated that variations in dopamine-related genes and in hormone levels affect the physiological properties of the dopaminergic system in nonhuman primates and modulate the processing of reward and social information in humans. These findings are important because they indicate the neural influence of genes conferring vulnerability to develop neuropathologies such as drug addiction and pathological gambling. Taken together, the reviewed data start to unveil the relationships between genes, hormones, and the functioning of the reward system, as well as decision making in social contexts, and provide a link between molecular, cellular, and social cognitive levels in humans.

KEYWORDS: fMRI; reward system; dopamine; social interaction; genes; COMT; DAT; gonadal steroid hormones; estrogen; progesterone; oxytocin; reward uncertainty; neuroeconomy; cooperation; competition; fairness; trust; social exclusion

Address for correspondence: Dr. Jean-Claude Dreher, CNRS UMR 5229, Reward and Decision-Making Team, Cognitive Neuroscience Center, 67 Bd Pinel, 69675 Bron, France. Voice: 00 33 (0)4 37 91 12 38; fax: 00 33 (0)4 37 91 12 10.
dreher@isc.cnrs.fr

By using classical methods from cognitive neuroscience (e.g., neuropsychology and neuroimaging), as well as molecular and cellular methods, social neuroscience focuses on how the human brain processes social information. Social neuroscience emphasizes the complementary nature of different levels of organization in the social (e.g., relational, collective, societal) and biological (e.g., molecular, cellular, system) domains and investigates how multilevel analyses can foster understanding of the mechanisms underlying human social interactions. Recent studies have tackled problems such as the molecular/neuronal substrates of a variety of complex behaviors, such as parental behavior, pair bonding, monogamy, and the neural changes associated with social experience and social interactions (e.g., evaluation of social status, trust, cooperation, exclusion).[1]

Reward prediction and evaluation are crucial functions for survival in a variable environment and are fundamental for complex behavior such as learning and motivation. The reward system, composed mainly of dopaminergic neurons and their projection sites (structures that include the ventral striatum, the anterior cingulate cortex [ACC], and the orbitofrontal cortex [OFC]), is crucial to represent and detect various types of rewards.[2] Dysfunction of this brain network seriously impairs reward processing, motivation, and decision making, as observed in many neurological and psychiatric disorders (pathological gambling, drug addiction, schizophrenia, Parkinson's disease). Currently, basic electrophysiological properties of the reward system are more fully understood during simple paradigms associating cues and rewards (e.g., classical conditioning) than during complex adaptive behavior requiring choices in social contexts. However, recent functional magnetic resonance imaging (fMRI) studies have started to investigate the neurobiological substrates of more complex reward processing, as well as of social cognition at the system level.[3–5]

Advances in molecular genetics, endocrinology, and neuroimaging start to unravel the relationships between genes, hormonal status, cognition, and functional brain regions and to build new bridges between molecular, cellular, and social cognitive neuroscience systems levels in humans. This approach is fruitful for understanding the genetic/hormonal influences contributing to individual differences in normal and pathological conditions involving dysfunctions of the reward system and of social behavior (e.g., neurodevelopmental disorders, such as autism and schizophrenia, and genetic disorders, such as Williams syndrome).[6–8]

There are important interindividual differences concerning reward processing and decision making.[9] It has been hypothesized that genetic variability in dopaminergic function could be related to these differences. However, exactly how variations of dopamine-related genes influence the reward system remain poorly understood. A major question is therefore to identify genetic polymorphisms influencing dopamine transmission and to investigate how individual differences in dopamine transmission affect the response of the reward system. Elucidating this question should help to clarify biological mechanisms underlying individual differences in reward processing, as well as normal variability and risk for pathological disorders involving the dopaminergic system. To bridge the gap between genetics and behavior, recent studies combined genetics and personality assessment with brain imaging as an intermediate endophenotype, an approach based on the assumption that brain activation is causally more directly linked to genotype than is behavior.[10]

Similarly, there is a within-subject variability in mood and cognitive functions according to variations in hormone levels. How gonadal steroid hormones and neuropeptides regulate brain physiology is helpful not only to understand sex-specific behaviors in health and disease but also to clarify how brain activity changes with these factors during social interactions and processing of reward information. For example, during the menstrual cycle, plasma concentrations of gonadal steroid hormones such as estradiol and progesterone vary systematically, which is associated with cyclic modulations of mood and cognitive abilities,[11,12] and have been shown to modulate the activity of the reward system.[13]

In this article, we will first focus on basic processing of reward information in nonhuman primates and in humans. Second, we will review recent fMRI evidence in humans showing that processes involved in social interaction share common neural substrates with basic reward processing. Finally, we will review the recent literature on hormonal and genetic influences on reward and social interaction functions, illustrating the current integration between molecular, cellular, and brain imaging levels.

BASIC PROCESSING OF REWARD INFORMATION

Seeking rewards and avoiding punishments is a common behavior of animals, including humans. This behavior is based on the capacity to represent the value of rewarding and punishing stimuli, which is essential to predict when they might occur, and to use these predictions to make decisions prospectively.[14] Rewards are those stimuli that increase the frequency of behavior leading to their acquisition.[2] Three functions of reward have been proposed[15]: they induce learning (positive reinforcement), they induce approach and consummatory behavior for acquiring the reward object, and they induce positive emotions.[15] Rewards can serve as goals of behavior if the reward and the contingency between action and reward are represented in the brain during the action. By contrast, punishments induce avoidance and withdrawal behaviors, as well as negative emotions. Although animal studies commonly use juice as the (primary) reward, most human neuroimaging studies have used monetary (secondary) reward. Several factors may explain why money has been widely used for the study of the reward system in humans. First, it is motivationally salient and valued for most people. Second, it is scalable, allowing comparison across different amounts. Third, it is reversible, allowing comparison between rewarding (i.e., gain) and aversive (i.e., loss) circumstances.[16]

Electrophysiological Studies on Dopaminergic Neurons in Monkeys

Neurons that respond to rewards and reward-predicting stimuli have been identified in a number of brain structures receiving projections from midbrain dopaminergic neurons, such as the ventral striatum, the dorsolateral prefrontal cortex (DLPFC) and orbital prefrontal cortex, the ACC, and the amygdala.[2] The integrity of midbrain dopaminergic neurons is particularly important for the efficient functioning of this system. Electrophysiological studies in monkeys indicate that midbrain dopaminergic neurons exhibit two modes of firing: a phasic signal that varies linearly with reward probability and a sustained signal that varies highly nonlinearly with reward probability and that is highest with maximal reward uncertainty (reward probability = 0.5).[17]

It has been proposed that the phasic mode of dopamine neuronal activity codes a reward prediction error, that is, a discrepancy between the reward obtained and the reward that was predicted to occur.[2,18] Indeed, after learning, if a reward is not present at the expected time of delivery, or if it is lower than expected, the firing of dopamine neurons is depressed below their basal rates. In contrast, unexpected rewards or rewards higher than expected produce a phasic increase in the firing rate of the dopamine neurons at the time of their delivery. Moreover, after repeated pairings of a cue followed by a reward, the phasic activity of dopaminergic neurons shifts from the time of the reward delivery to the cue onset. This phasic dopamine signal may be used as a teaching signal by other structures to learn reward-directed behavior, through the repeated comparison between the expected and the actual outcomes. Moreover, at the time of the conditioned stimulus, this phasic activity increases with the expected value (product of reward probability and magnitude).[17,19]

In addition to their phasic activity, dopamine neurons also exhibit a sustained mode of activity after learning that is maximal with highest reward uncertainty (i. e., $P = 0.5$). This activity grows from the onset of the conditioned stimulus to the time of the reward delivery.[17] This sustained mode of activity occurring with maximal reward uncertainty may be related to a specific form of attention,[20] to motivational processes in the context of reward uncertainty, or to the expectation of reward information following rules from information theory.[21] According to this theory, the more uncertain the outcome (reward or no reward), the more information it conveys. Thus, monkey electrophysiological studies have shown that two different modes of dopaminergic activity may code apparently distinct statistical parameters of reward information: a phasic mode of activity coding a reward prediction error and a sustained mode of activity reflecting reward uncertainty.

fMRI Studies on Reward Prediction Error and Reward Uncertainty

A number of fMRI studies have investigated the neural correlates of the reward prediction error signal. The administration of juice and water in an unpredicted manner was found to elicit greater blood oxygen level-dependent (BOLD) changes in the ventral striatum than administration in a predicted fashion.[22] Also consistent with this reward prediction error theory, the BOLD signal in the ventral striatum has been found to change through the course of conditioning experiments.[23–25] Before training, the delivery of a reward generates a positive prediction error response. With training, this prediction error shifts to the time of the conditioned stimulus, and this prediction error signal is reflected in striatal activity.[24,25] Furthermore, the omission of a reward at its predicted time of delivery generates a negative prediction error. The ventral striatum has also been found to be activated when distinguishing the anticipatory period before the potential reward[26] from the outcome phase at the time of reward delivery.[27] In addition to the ventral striatum, some fMRI studies also reported that the DLPFC, inferior frontal gyrus and OFC correlate with the prediction error signal, either related to abstract stimulus-response associations or to taste reward.[22,24,28–30]

A recent functional neuroimaging study extends the notions of learning signals by assessing the neural substrates of a fictive error signal.[3] This signal encodes ongoing differences between experienced returns and returns that could have been experienced if decisions had been different, that is, a learning signal associated with the actions not taken. The authors used a sequential investment task in which after each decision, information was revealed regarding whether higher or lower investments would have been a better choice. The natural learning signal for criticizing each choice was the difference between the best return that could have been obtained and the actual gain or loss, that is, the fictive error. Behaviorally, the fictive error was found to be an important determinant of the next investment. The analysis of the fMRI data revealed that the fictive error signal produced a response in the ventral caudate that was not explained by the temporal difference error signal. Taking into account the fictive error signals into learning models may provide additional insight into both normal and altered decision making.

Until recently, although a number of studies have investigated the neural correlates of the prediction error, it was still unclear whether distinct brain networks code separately the prediction error and reward uncertainty signals. To answer this question, we have used fMRI to distinguish the phasic and sustained modes of reward activity in humans.[31] Using an event-related fMRI paradigm that systematically varied monetary reward probability, magnitude and expected reward value, we found that the dopaminergic midbrain responded transiently both to higher reward probability at the cue and to lower reward probability at the rewarded outcome, and in a sustained manner to reward uncertainty during the delay period (FIG. 1). These results support the view that midbrain dopaminergic neurons follow the same basic principles of neuronal computation in humans and monkeys.

Furthermore, we observed distinct activity dynamics in target regions of the dopaminergic neurons, the prefrontal cortex responding to the transient

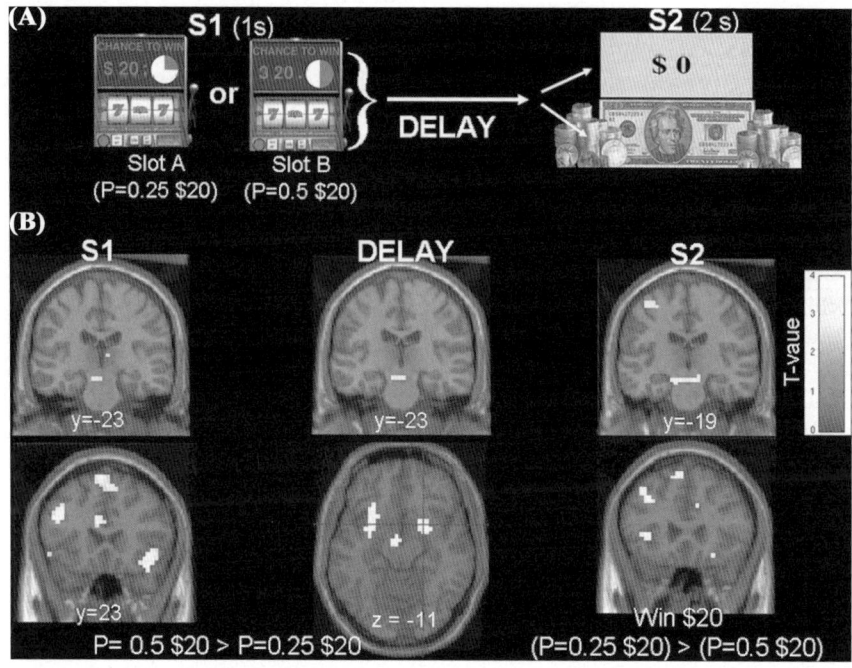

FIGURE 1. (**A**). Task design. Four types of "slot machines" were presented pseudo-randomly on a screen. The probabilities of winning different amounts of money or nothing were indicated, respectively, by the red and white portions of a pie chart above the slot machines. Each trial consisted of a brief (1 s) presentation of the cue (stimulus S1, one of the four slot machines), followed after a fixed delay (14 s) by the outcome S2 (either $0 or a picture of a $10 or $20 bill, lasting 2 s). (**B**). Location of transient (S1 and S2) and sustained (during delay) brain responses in humans. *Left and right*. The midbrain and a prefrontal network covaried with the prediction error signal at the cue S1 and at the time of the rewarded outcome S2. *Middle*. Location of sustained midbrain and ventral striatum activities covarying with the reward uncertainty signal ($P = 0.5$) during the delay period. Consistent with electrophysiological recordings, the human midbrain region was transiently activated with higher reward probability at the cue S1, with lower reward probability at the rewarded outcome S2 and showed higher sustained activity with reward uncertainty during the delay period. Reprinted and modified with permission from REF.[31] © (2006) Oxford University Press.

prediction error signal, and the ventral striatum covarying with the sustained reward uncertainty signal. Our findings may indicate that dopaminergic projection sites can distinguish the two signals.[31] These targets may also show independent transient (prefrontal cortex) and sustained (ventral striatum) activities and/or may help to shape differentially the phasic and sustained modes of midbrain firing. Because the development of the mesolimbic/nigrostriatal dopaminergic pathways occurred earlier than the mesocortical pathway during evolution, our findings suggest that specific functional brain networks developed to code distinct aspects of the statistical properties of reward information.[31] The absence of activation in the ventral striatum/putamen covarying with the prediction error signal could be explained by the fact that nothing had to be learned in our task.[31]

Importantly, our monetary reward task was purposely designed to use a long delay interval (=14 s) between the cue (slot machine) and the outcome, which allowed us to disentangle the phasic signal from the sustained activity. This critical temporal dimension of our task is important to remember when considering different paradigms and also varying reward magnitude, probability, and/or uncertainty, which could not fully distinguish phasic and sustained aspects. For example, in one fMRI study, the ventral striatum was found more activated during anticipation (=2 s) of rewards of increasing magnitude but not of increasing probability,[32] while other studies reported increased ventral striatal activation with both higher reward magnitude and probability.[33–35]

Concerning reward uncertainty, stimuli associated with higher uncertainty (variance) have been reported to elicit increased activity in the lateral OFC.[35] Moreover, in a guessing card task in which subjects were presented with a cue card and had to decide whether the next card would be higher or lower, activity in anterior cingulate and orbitofrontal cortices was modulated by outcome uncertainty during the anticipatory period.[36] In a similar paradigm varying expected reward and risk simultaneously, in which subjects had to place a bet before actually seeing the first card, the ventral striatum showed both an immediate response with increasing reward probability and a delayed response related to risk (reward variance).[37] Finally, tasks using nonmonetary stimuli also reported modulation by categorization uncertainty[38] and decision uncertainty[39] in a network that included prefrontal, parietal, and insular cortices. The exact reasons for the discrepancies between these findings are certainly multiple, probably involving timing and task designs, and future studies will need to address these issues.

Predictive Value Coding in the Orbitofrontal Cortex and the Amygdala

In addition to the ventral striatum and the ventral tegmental area, involved in coding prediction error and reward uncertainty, distinct functions have been attributed to other components of the reward system. The two structures most consistently activated are the OFC and the amygdala, both responding to primary[40–42] and secondary[43–45] rewards.

For example, the OFC is involved in coding stimulus reward value and in concert with the amygdala and the ventral striatum is implicated in representing predicted future reward.[14] In monkeys, OFC neurons code the relative value, rather than the absolute value, of reward.[46] These neurons can discriminate between different rewards, reflecting animals' relative preferences among the available rewards rather than physical reward properties, suggesting that they process the motivational value of rewarding outcomes. Also, neurons in the OFC respond to a particular taste or odor when the animal is hungry but decrease their firing rate after satiation.[47-49] Similarly, in humans, the OFC and the amygdala are less activated for devaluated than for nondevaluated cues for food after consumption of one food to satiation.[50] Similarly, the amygdala may play a complementary role in coding reward intensity. Although the amygdala has been traditionally linked to aversive stimuli, new evidence has emerged concerning the amygdala responding to both pleasant and unpleasant stimuli.[51,52] Two recent studies in the olfactory and gustatory domains dissociated responses to valence and intensity of the stimuli and reported that the amygdala responds to intensity but not to valence of the stimuli, whereas the OFC showed the opposite pattern.[53,54]

Neuroeconomic Approach: From Basic Reward Processing to Real-Life Purchasing Behavior

There has been a recent explosion in applying game theory and economic methods to understand how the brain responds to the various influences of cognitive and emotional bias on the decisions of purchasers, salesmen, savers, etc. One example is human loss aversion, which reflects that when deciding between risky options, humans are about twice as sensitive to the possibility of losing goods or money than to the possibility of winning them. Some studies suggest that the representation of losses entails emotional processes and consequently engages structures such as the amygdala or the anterior insula.[34,55-58] Consistent with this notion, Kuhnen and Knutson investigated why investors systematically deviate from rationality when making financial decisions.[56] Using event-related fMRI, they investigated whether anticipatory neural activity would predict optimal and suboptimal choices in a financial decision-making task and showed that distinct neural systems were engaged during financial decision making. Using a task that elicited a range of investment behaviors, including risk-seeking and risk-averse financial choices, they observed that activation in the nucleus accumbens preceded risky choices and risk-seeking mistakes, whereas activation of the anterior insula preceded riskless choices and risk-aversion mistakes. The authors indicate that the relative activation of each one of these systems may lead to different risk preferences underlying risk-seeking choices (e.g., gambling) and risk-averse choices (e.g., buying insurance). Moreover, during a purchase paradigm using neuroeconomic methods to separate distinct components of the purchase decision process in individual consumers, product preference activated the nucleus accumbens, whereas excessive prices activated the insula and deactivated the medial prefrontal cortex.[59] Response in these three brain regions predicted subsequent decisions to purchase. These results suggest that the brain frames preference as a potential gain and price as a potential loss, and that activation of brain structures such as the nucleus accumbens, related to anticipation of potential gains precedes purchasing decisions. From a neuromarketing perspective, these findings have implications for the design of more effective sales strategies, on the basis that anticipatory activation of the nucleus accumbens by certain reward cues may increase the likelihood that individuals engage in risk-seeking behaviors. Moreover, diminishing the salience of payments (e.g., credit cards) or creating the illusion that products have no cost (e.g., rewarding frequent clients) may also decrease the effect of excessive prices.[56,59]

A recent fMRI study challenged the view that loss aversion engages a distinct emotion-related brain network (e.g., amygdala/insula) and identified a common brain network whose activity increases with potential gains and decreases with potential losses.[58,60] The authors assessed the brain activation related to the decision of whether to accept a gamble. They isolated a gain-responsive network consisting of brain regions previously associated with anticipation and receipt of monetary rewards, which included the dorsal and ventral striatum, the ventromedial prefrontal cortex, the anterior cingulate gyrus, the orbitofrontal gyrus, and the dopaminergic midbrain regions. Most of these areas also showed decreasing activity as the size of potential loss increased. Interestingly, in the striatum and the ventromedial prefrontal cortex, the slope of the decrease in activity for increasing losses was greater than the slope of the increase of activity for increasing gains, indicating that loss aversion behavior may be linked to the brain's greater sensitivity for losses than gains. These results agree with those of studies showing increased and decreased activity in the striatum for experienced monetary gains and losses,[27,45] and they support the notion that the same neural structures code losses and gains.

In the context of an organization, money is not the only reward possible. The intrinsic enjoyment derived by the task, social recognition, the opportunity to grow, autonomy, and even positive feedback from managers or peers are examples of rewarding aspects of a job and, as such, affect motivation, satisfaction, and behavior of the members of the organization. To design suitable reward plans that can motivate a heterogeneous group of workers, one must account for differences in the valuation of available rewards. For example, generational differences are reflected in the rewarding value of different job features, so different rewards might be necessary to attract a technology-savvy and innovative young worker or to retain an experienced veteran.[61]

Taken together, these studies provide important new insights into the functional properties of the reward system and of economic decision making in humans. They are particularly relevant for several neuropsychiatric and behavioral disorders, such as substance abuse and pathological gambling, that are associated with increased risk taking and impulsive behavior.

NEURAL BASES OF SOCIAL INTERACTION

The strong interdependence showed between humans, even with nonkin, might have been a key element of our evolutionary success. An example might be the high levels of cooperation that humans express with each other, which are unmatched in the animal world. The study of social interaction has received much attention by social sciences and has recently been spotlighted by cognitive and neural sciences. Using neuroimaging techniques and adaptations of games used by economists to model social interactions, several studies have assessed the neural basis of different forms of social interaction such as cooperation, competition, punishment, and rejection.

Neuroimaging Studies on Cooperation and Competition

Inferring others' mental states is essential to cooperate and to compete. Mentalizing is the ability to explain and predict others' behavior by means of attributing them independent mental states, such as thoughts, beliefs, wishes, and intentions, which might be different from ours. One way of assessing the neural substrates of mentalizing involves comparing subjects while playing with a human (or believing they do so) versus playing with a computer. These studies have often reported that the medial prefrontal cortex and the ACC are crucial in the formation of others' mental states.[4,62,63]

Cooperation is pervasive in human societies. In consequence, effective social interactions must differentiate between those who do and do not reciprocate to decide whom to approach and whom to avoid. Mathematical models and computer simulations combining biological and economical methods demonstrate the evolutionary advantage of mutual cooperation.[64] Recent neuroimaging studies have explored the neural substrates of cooperation.[65–68] In one experiment,[65] subjects competed, cooperated, or played alone in a tokens game while they were scanned. Competition and cooperation toward a common goal, compared with playing alone, were found to activate a common frontoparietal network subserving executive functions, as well as the anterior insula, involved in the sense of agency and autonomic arousal. Cooperation activated the OFC, whereas competition activated inferior parietal and medial prefrontal cortices. According to the authors, activation in the OFC might be indicative of the socially rewarding properties of cooperation.

Data from other studies suggest that cooperative behavior engages several brain areas from the reward circuitry. In one study, subjects were scanned while playing the Prisoner's Dilemma game, in which two players independently choose to either cooperate with each other or not. The amount of money each one wins depends on his or her choices, so that the highest outcome is obtained if one defects and the partner collaborates, and the lowest outcome results the other way around. Mutual cooperation has been found to activate brain areas involved in reward processing, such as the nucleus accumbens, the caudate nucleus, and the ventromedial frontal/OFC.[66] Furthermore, reciprocated and unreciprocated cooperation have, respectively, been associated with positive and negative BOLD responses in the ventromedial prefrontal cortex and ventral striatum.[67] These results might reflect the rewarding effects of arranging and/or experiencing a mutually cooperative social interaction. They also parallel single-neuron recordings showing that unexpected rewards activate midbrain dopaminergic neurons, whereas omission of an expected reward reduces the firing rates of these neurons.[18] In the Prisoner's Dilemma game, defection by the partner after having decided to cooperate might be seen as the omission of an anticipated reward, which may lead to the reduced activity or deactivation of the midbrain dopaminergic region and possibly of the targets to which they project. These effects might reflect the positive and negative prediction errors related to a reciprocated and unreciprocated cooperation, respectively, that would be used to learn whom we can trust to reciprocate favors and whom we cannot.

Singer *et al.* subtly used the Prisoner's Dilemma game to investigate the processing of relevant cues that acquired significance through learning in an interactive context.[68] Unlike in other studies, subjects were not scanned during the game proper but while making judgments based on the sex of people with whom they had previously interacted during the game. The insula, the OFC, the left amygdala, and the left putamen showed greater responses to cooperator faces relative to neutral faces. Defector faces induced increased activity in the ventromedial prefrontal cortex. Response in several brain regions related to reward processing, including OFC and ventral striatum, was higher for unconstrained cooperators than for cooperators that were forced to follow a predetermined pattern of response. The activation of several reward areas led the authors to propose that mutual cooperation inherently possesses a rewarding value.

Neuroimaging Studies on Fairness and Trust

Humans do not always behave rationally about money. Clear evidence comes from a study using the Ultimatum Game.[69] In this game, a proposer makes an offer to the responder on how a certain amount of money should be split between them, and the responder can either accept or reject the offer. If the offer is accepted, each participant gets the amount of money proposed, whereas if it is rejected, none of the players gets anything. The reasonable way to play the game is for the proposer to offer the smallest possible amount of money and for the responder to accept any proposal, no matter how small it may be, because a small amount is better than none. Behaviorally, participants accepted all offers considered fair (those splitting the amount around 50%), but the rate of rejection increased as the offers were considered less fair. Unfair offers elicited activation in the anterior insula, DLPFC, and ACC. Moreover, activation in the anterior insula was correlated with the degree of unfairness of an offer, and activity therein predicted acceptance of unfair offers. Interestingly, the insula has been related to the experience of several negative events, such as pain,[70] and to the evaluation of negative emotions like anger or disgust.[71,72] Activation of the DLPFC was attributed to the fact that unfair offers require more cognitive demands to overcome the emotional impulse of rejecting the offer. Finally, ACC activation was interpreted as detecting the conflict arising between accepting an unfair (but economically reasonable) offer and emotionally rejecting it. Authors indicate that activation in the DLPFC and the anterior insula could be responsible for two opposite demands in the ultimatum game, namely, the cognitive goal of accumulating money and the emotional goal of resisting unfairness. This study stresses the importance of emotional states on decision making.

Many social interactions strongly depend on fairness and trust. Trust is essential for friendship, trade, and leadership, and plays an important role in economic exchange and politics.[73,74] Many employees believe that the outcomes they receive from an organization should be linked to the contributions they make to the organization. The reciprocation of trust in an organizational context could be exemplified by the fact that members will work harder and exhibit higher commitment if they consider that they are fairly treated. The perception of members and employees of being treated fairly has been related to many important outcomes, including employee satisfaction, commitment to the organization, trust in one's leader, and task performance, and it has been considered an important mediator of the positive effects of reward on motivations, perceptions, attitudes, and behavior of the members.[75] Unfair behaviors by leaders and managers (e.g., to show who the boss is and assert their authority) may lead to nonreciprocation by the members of the organization, culminating in demonstrations and strikes when conflicts cannot be solved more easily.

Not only do we punish unfair treatment, even when doing so is costly, but we may also obtain satisfaction from it. Altruistic punishment—the predisposition to punish social norms violators even when this imposes a cost on the punisher—is basic for the evolution and maintenance of social cooperation.[76–78] The dorsal striatum activates when subjects administer monetary punishments to defectors.[5] Moreover, activation of this region during costless punishment predicted the cost that punishers were willing to assume to punish defectors. The more the activation, the more the cost assumed. The authors conclude that caudate activation reflects the expected satisfaction from punishing. A later study reported increased activation in reward-related areas when observing unfair partners receiving pain induced by a third person.[81] The brain areas reported to be activated in these studies coincide with those activated by rewarding cooperators,[66] linking two diametrically opposite behaviors by means of a common psychological experience: the anticipation of a satisfying (or rewarding) outcome.[80]

Interestingly, in an organizational context, an early study revealed that subjects reported positive affect when deserved sanctions were administered to a group member.[81] Moreover, subjects were more willing to work hard, felt more satisfied, expected higher levels of group performance, and perceived fairer treatment from their supervisors when the supervisors punished a team member who performed poorly than when a poor-performing team member received no punishment.[81]

In most of the studies concerning social interaction, only one of the two interacting subjects was scanned. The term *hyperscanning* refers to the ability that allows the link between magnetic resonance scanners through the Internet, so that the activity of two actually interacting agents can be recorded at the same time.[82] Using hyperscanning and a multiround format of the trust game, King-Casas *et al.* assessed the neural correlates of trust. Pairs of subjects were scanned simultaneously, one of them being the investor and the other one, the trustee.[83] The investor is endowed with a certain amount of money, which he or she can invest in any portion with the trustee. The amount of money invested appreciates, so that the trustee actually receives, say, three times the amount invested. Finally, the trustee decides how much of the amount received he will repay to the investor. At the behavioral level, reciprocity by one player was the strongest predictor of subsequent increases or decreases in trust in the other player, as measured by an increased or decreased repayment in the next round. The analysis of the fMRI data revealed that activation of the trustees' caudate nuclei was higher in response to benevolent reciprocity, that is, an increase in the investment as a response to a previous defection of the trustee, compared with malevolent reciprocity, a reduction in the investment after a generous repayment by the trustee. Moreover, the activation in the caudate nucleus dynamically varied with the increases and decreases in the amount of money returned in the subsequent trial, being higher when trustees increased the repayment in the next round. The authors conclude that the activity of the trustee's caudate nucleus computes information about the fairness of a decision and the intention to repay that decision with trust. Interestingly, there was a shift in the peak of the response for the intended increases in trust. In the initial rounds this peak was observed after the investor's decision was revealed and progressively became anticipatory and occurred before the revelation of the investor's decision. These results parallel those obtained in monkey neurophysiological studies showing a shift in the phasic response of dopamine neurons through conditioning from the time of the presentation of the reward to the time of the presentation of the reward-predicting stimulus.[18] In a social interaction context, this shift might be interpreted as the development of a reputation for the partner.

Neuroimaging Studies on Social Exclusion

Given the adaptive importance of social bonds for human beings, it has been suggested that the social attachment system and the physical pain system share a common neural basis. Confirming this hypothesis, the ACC and the right ventral prefrontal cortex, both related to the affective aspects of physical pain, also respond to social pain.[84] The ACC, anterior insula, and right ventral prefrontal cortex were activated when subjects were excluded from a ball-tossing game by the other players. Moreover, activation of the ACC and the right ventral prefrontal cortices correlated positively and negatively, respectively, with self-reported distress. Activation of these two brain areas was negatively correlated, which supports the notion that the ventral prefrontal cortex may implement a self-regulatory mechanism for mitigating the distressing effects of social exclusion. A later study found a dissociation between dorsal and ventral aspects of the ACC.[85] Subjects were scanned while viewing faces and either forming a first impression (saying whether they liked the person) or predicting whether the other person liked them. After their judgments, subjects were given feedback indicating whether the other person liked them. The fMRI data revealed that the dorsal ACC responded to expectancy violation, that is, when feedback matched versus did not match the subjects' first impressions or predictions. On the other hand, the ventral ACC responded to feedback type (positive or negative). For the authors, these data agree with a classical dissociation within the ACC, its rostral and dorsal aspects being responsible for emotional and cognitive functions, respectively.[86]

Taken together, these studies indicate a strong link between certain aspects of social interaction (e.g., cooperation) and the processing of rewards. Similarly, social exclusion could be related to aspects such as punishment or loss aversion. In fact, the ACC has been reported to be activated during experiencing both social rejection[84,85] and financial losses.[59,87] However, further studies including several aversive outcomes of different natures in the same experiment are necessary to clarify to what extent these processes share common neural substrates.

Most economic analyses are based on two major assumptions of human nature: Individuals are rational decision makers and they have purely self-regarding preferences. Altogether, behavioral and neuroimaging studies show that people often violate these assumptions,[88] especially in social settings.[89] In fact, emotions play an important role in decision making.[90,91] However, how the violation of these assumptions might affect aggregate entities, like markets and organizations, is not clear, given that there is still a share of subjects who do not violate these assumptions. This latter type of subject shapes aggregate outcomes, making them closer to those predicted by a model assuming rationality and self-regard by all the agents.[88] Furthermore, some brain regions, such as the medial prefrontal cortex and the anterior insula, may be characteristic of the interactions between human partners compared with computer partners, suggesting that decisions made during social interactions depend on something else than merely economic outcomes.[89]

HORMONAL INFLUENCES

Given the fundamental role of the dopaminergic system in reward processing and social interactions, some researchers have begun to test the hypothesis that naturally occurring differences in dopaminergic transmission between and within subjects may affect these functions. Hormones are a source of both intraindividual and interindividual differences, some of them directly affecting the dopaminergic system.

Estrogen and Progesterone Effects on Reward Processing and Social Decision Making

Behavioral, biochemical, and physiological data in animals show that gonadal steroid hormones affect behavior and modulate neuronal activity.[92–95] Estrogen and progesterone receptors are densely expressed in structures of the dopaminergic reward system, such as the midbrain dopaminergic neurons, the ventral striatum, and the amygdala.[92] Many preclinical data, including behavioral and neurochemical differences between sexes, across the estrous cycle, and in postovariectomy hormone replacement,[96,97] demonstrate the neuroregulatory effects of estrogen and progesterone on the dopaminergic system.[98,99] These effects are not restricted to the tuberoinfundibular dopaminergic system involved in control of the anterior pituitary and important for ovulation and reproductive behavior but also to the mesocortical and mesolimbic dopaminergic systems relevant for cognition, affect, and reward processing. For instance, estrogen has a neuroprotective effect on the nigrostriatal dopaminergic system during methamphetamine-induced neurotoxicity in female rats, but not in male rats.[100] Furthermore, female rats show the highest rates of cocaine self-administration briefly after estradiol peaks, and administering estradiol to ovariectomized rats enhances cocaine self-administration.[99,101]

In women, the normal 28-day menstrual cycle is divided into two main phases. The follicular phase extends from the first day of menses until the 14th day and is characterized by low levels of progesterone and increasing levels of estradiol, which reaches a peak at ovulation. The remaining days constitute the luteal phase, characterized by high levels of progesterone and a second peak of estradiol in the midluteal phase.[102]

Hormonal changes during the menstrual cycle phases influence spatial and verbal cognitive abilities,[12,103,104] attention,[105] mood,[106] and vulnerability to drugs of abuse.[107] In a recent study, we used fMRI and an event-related monetary reward paradigm to investigate the neurophysiological effects of gonadal steroid hormones on the human reward system.[13] Women were scanned during the midfollicular and luteal phases of the menstrual cycle while performing a monetary reward task that distinguished neural concomitants of anticipating uncertain rewards from those of reward outcome. We observed that during the midfollicular phase, women showed higher activation, relative to the luteal phase, of the OFC and the amygdala during anticipation of uncertain rewards (FIG. 2). During reward delivery, we found higher activation in the midbrain, striatum, and frontopolar cortex during the follicular phase than during the luteal phase. These data support an increased reactivity of the reward system

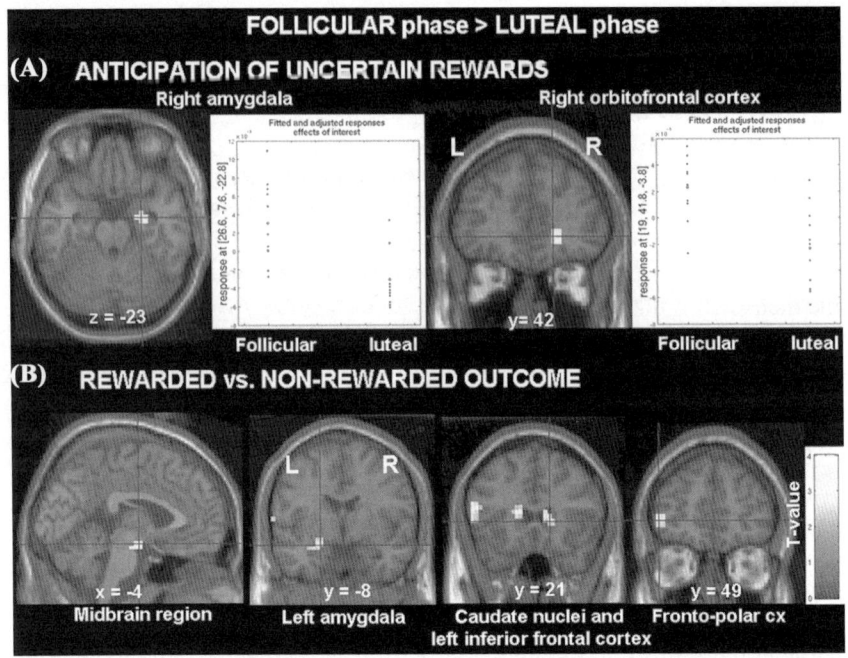

FIGURE 2. Cross–menstrual cycle phase differences in BOLD response during anticipation of uncertain rewards and at the time of the rewarded outcome. (**A**) *Left*. Statistical maps overlaid onto structural MRI showing BOLD fMRI responses greater in follicular than luteal phase during reward anticipation in the right amygdala and OFC. *Right*. Distributions of BOLD signal response for each woman. (**B**) Greater BOLD response during follicular than luteal phase at the time of the outcome in midbrain, left amygdala, heads of the caudate nuclei, left inferior frontal gyrus, and left frontopolar cortex. Reprinted and modified with permission from REF.[13] © (2007) The National Academy of Sciences.

in women during the midfollicular phase, during which estrogen is unopposed by progesterone.

Moreover, between-sex differences comparing the group of women with a group of men matched for age and level of education revealed that men activated the ventral putamen more than women during anticipation of uncertain rewards, whereas women showed stronger activation of the anterior medial prefrontal cortex during reward delivery. Finally, correlational analysis between the brain activity and the gonadal steroid levels revealed a positive correlation between activation in the amygdalo–hippocampal complex and the estradiol level, regardless of menstrual cycle phase. From an evolutionary point of view, the increased activity observed during the follicular phase may underlie the increased availability, receptivity, and desire during the ovulatory period, which has been thought to facilitate procreation.[13]

Recent neuroimaging studies have also been able to detect changes in brain activation related to menstrual cycle phase during negative emotional processing. Activity of the anterior-medial OFC for negative verbal stimuli was increased premenstrually and decreased postmenstrually, whereas the inverse pattern was observed in the lateral OFC.[108] Another study reported greater activity during the early follicular phase in response to negative, high-arousing stimuli in a set of areas involved in the response to stress, including the amygdala, the OFC, and the anterior cingulate gyrus.[109] These studies demonstrate that generally arousing stimuli may modulate similar brain networks across the menstrual cycle phases.

At the behavioral level, the effect of the menstrual cycle on social decision making was recently studied in a group of young women participating in a mock job scenario.[110] There is evidence that women's preferences for male faces shift across the menstrual cycle, with higher preference for relatively masculine traits in the follicular phase.[111–113] Participants had to assign minimum, low, high, or maximum status resources to a series of men previously rated to look either dominant (e.g., squarer jaws, smaller pupil-to-brow distance) or nondominant. A first analysis revealed that female observers assign resources of high status to dominant-looking men and resources of low status to nondominant-looking men. Further analyses showed that during the follicular phase more high-status resources were allocated to the dominant-looking men than to nondominant-looking men. Thus, women actively manipulate male status cues in a manner that is specific to the different phases of the menstrual cycle. Awareness of these and other biases, such as the influence of past and future expected interactions in reward allocation,[114] may be useful for trainings in management and human resources.

Testosterone Effects on Reward Processing and Social Behavior

In men, testosterone levels vary during the day[115,116] and with age, starting to decrease at around 40 years old.[117] Animal studies have demonstrated a relationship between testosterone and aggression.[118] In humans, a role of androgens in aggression has been inferred from studies in which samples were selected on the basis of violent behavior.[119] Although there is some evidence in favor of a positive relationship between testosterone and aggression in humans, results are not conclusive.[118–120] Dominance, that is, the enhancing of one's status over that of other people, which is often expressed nonaggressively, has also been related to higher levels of testosterone in both men and women.[121,122] Testosterone may partly explain the sex differences observed in some cognitive functions. In women, testosterone administration was found to improve spatial abilities,[123,124] putatively considered male-advantage abilities. Less is known about testosterone influences on the reward system. Testosterone levels correlated with brain activation in the OFC and the insula during processing of visual sexual stimuli in men,[125] demonstrating that these brain areas respond to sexual arousal and not merely to a state of general motivational arousal. Activation of the OFC was interpreted as the neural correlate of an appraisal process through which visual stimuli are categorized as sexual incentives. In women, testosterone has also been reported to influence economic decision making.[126] Administering testosterone produced a more disadvantageous pattern of decision-making response in the Iowa Gambling Task, indicating reductions in punishment sensitivity and heightened reward dependency. In this task, subjects must draw a card from one of four available decks with the objective of gaining as much money as possible. Two of the decks are disadvantageous; they produce immediate large rewards, but these are accompanied by substantial money losses due to more extreme punishments. The other two decks are advantageous, because reward is modest but consistent and punishment is low. A similar study showed that low cortisol levels were related to impaired performance on this task in both men and women.[127]

Another study assessed the influence of cortisol on interpersonal trust.[128] Subjects' cortisol levels were measured before and after psychosocial stress exposure. Cortisol elevation induced by social stress was negatively correlated with the scores of General Trust Scale, suggesting that subjects with higher interpersonal trust have lower activation of the hypothalamic–pituitary–adrenal axis when exposed to social stress.

Oxytocin Effects on Social Interactions

Evidence from animal studies indicates that another class of hormone, neuropeptides oxytocin and vasopressin, play an important role in complex social behaviors, including parental care, affiliation, and pair bonding.[129,130] The study of two species of voles showing distinct reproductive strategies has provided most of the evidence. Comparative studies of prairie and montane voles, which are monogamous and polygamous, respectively,[131] have shown a different pattern of expression of oxytocin and vasopressin receptors in the brain that appears to be associated with these reproductive strategies.[129,132] Regions exhibiting such differences are the nucleus accumbens, where prairie monogamous voles have higher density of oxytocin receptors than montane voles do, and the ventral pallidal area, a major output of the nucleus accumbens, which shows higher density of vasopressin receptors in prairie voles.[130] The functional importance of these receptors is demonstrated by the fact that oxytocin agonists and antagonists specifically facilitate and block social behaviors such as pair bonding in female voles. In male voles, it is vasopressin that appears necessary for bond formation.[133,134] It has been suggested that these receptors link social information to reward circuits in the brain, providing a neurobiological mechanism for partner preference formation and social attachment.[1,130]

In humans, oxytocin has been associated with trustworthiness[137,138] and with improved ability to infer others' mental states,[137] both essential for human social interactions. In a double-blind study,[74] participants received either an intranasal dose of oxytocin or placebo before taking part in a trust game. The data showed that oxytocin increased investors' trust, as demonstrated by the larger amounts of money transferred by the investors in the oxytocin group than those in the placebo group. Moreover, this effect of oxytocin was specific to trusting behavior in social interactions, as suggested by there being no differences in the amount of money transfers between the oxytocin and the placebo groups when investors faced the same choices as in the trust game but this time with a random mechanism determining the investor's risk. Thus, the effect of oxytocin on trust is not due to a general increase in the readiness to bear risks; on the contrary, oxytocin specifically affects an individual's willingness to accept social risks arising through interpersonal interactions. The influence of oxytocin on social behavior may be mediated, at least in part, by its effects on the amygdala, which is a central component of the circuitry of fear and social cognition and shows a high expression of oxytocin receptors. Confirming this hypothesis, a recent neuroimaging study reported reduced fear-induced activation in the amygdala after administration of oxytocin.[138]

GENETIC INFLUENCES

The study of the genetic basis of human differences in complex behaviors appears as one of the most promising fields in neuroscience, favored by the advances in molecular genetics and in noninvasive functional neuroimaging techniques.[139] From the point of view of the generalist genes hypothesis, it is assumed that one gene might affect many traits and that many genes affect a trait.[140] In social organization, it has become increasingly accepted that traits, attitudes, and behaviors relevant to the workplace have a genetic component.[141] Several studies have assessed the genetic influence on some job-related variables such as leadership role occupancy,[142,143] job and occupational switching,[144] and job satisfaction.[145] These studies have been conducted on twins and have reported that around 30% of the variance observed in these variables may be explained by genetic influences.

Both reward processing and social interaction engage brain structures that lie on the ascending dopaminergic pathways. Thus, an important axis of current research is to study the brain influence of genes that affect dopaminergic transmission, to clarify the biological mechanisms underlying interindividual differences and vulnerability to pathology related to the dopaminergic system.[139,146] Behavioral and neuroimaging studies have explored the relationship between dopamine-related genes and some personality traits and behaviors related to reward, and more recently, with reward-related brain activation. These studies have focused on the genetic variations of dopamine receptors

(DRs), especially DRD2 and DRD4, and other genes coding for enzymes and transporters involved in the dopaminergic transmission, such as the catechol-O-methyltransferase (COMT) and the dopamine transporter (DAT).

At the behavioral level, genetic variations in DRD4 have been related to novelty seeking[147–149] and pathological gambling.[150] DRD2 has been related to drug addiction[151,152] and reward deficiency syndrome.[153,154] Neuroimaging studies have recently begun to assess the effects of dopamine-related genes on reward processing. Cohen et al. studied the effect of the DRD2 gene in reward processing by using an fMRI gambling task that allowed them to separate anticipation and reception of rewards.[155] Although they found no differences during reward anticipation between carriers and noncarriers of the A1 allele of the DRD2 gene, the presence of the A1 allele of the gene significantly affected neural responses at the time of the outcome. Subjects with the A1 allele showed lower response in the medial OFC, amygdala, hippocampus, and nucleus accumbens during reward outcome. This lower differentiation between receiving and not receiving rewards agrees with the idea that a reduced concentration of DRD2 receptors in the reward system reduces sensitivity to rewards. This finding may explain why individuals with the A1 allele are more likely to develop addictive or reward deficiency disorders.

Another gene implicated in the dopaminergic transmission is the COMT gene. This gene codes for the COMT enzyme, which is involved in dopamine degradation.[156–158] In humans, a functional polymorphism leads to the substitution of the amino acid valine (Val) by methionine (Met) at codon 158.[159] The enzyme containing Met is unstable at body temperatures and shows significantly lower activity than the enzyme containing Val,[160] presumably leading to higher levels of synaptic dopamine.[159,161] Although somewhat inconsistently, behavioral studies have linked the Val allele of the COMT with personality traits such as novelty-seeking[162] and risk-seeking[163] scores. Cognitively, the COMT genotype has been studied mainly on prefrontal function, the Val allele often being associated with worse performance in executive functioning.[146,164,165] This finding has received further support from our own[166] and other fMRI studies relating the number of Val alleles to lower prefrontal efficiency (higher activation for a similar level of performance) during performance of working memory tasks.[146,167] However, the effect of COMT on brain activity depends on the task at hand.[168] For instance, during the performance of emotional tasks, BOLD response in the amygdala and prefrontal connected areas correlated with the number of Met alleles during unpleasant stimuli.[169] Similarly, viewing faces expressing negative emotions elicits brain activation in the hippocampus and ventrolateral prefrontal cortex that is related in a dose-dependent fashion to the number of Met alleles.[170]

Another gene involved in dopamine transmission is the gene coding for the DAT, which terminates dopamine transmission by reuptaking released dopamine back into the presynaptic neuron. The DAT gene displays a 40-base-pair variable number of tandem repeats, with 9 and 10 repeats being the

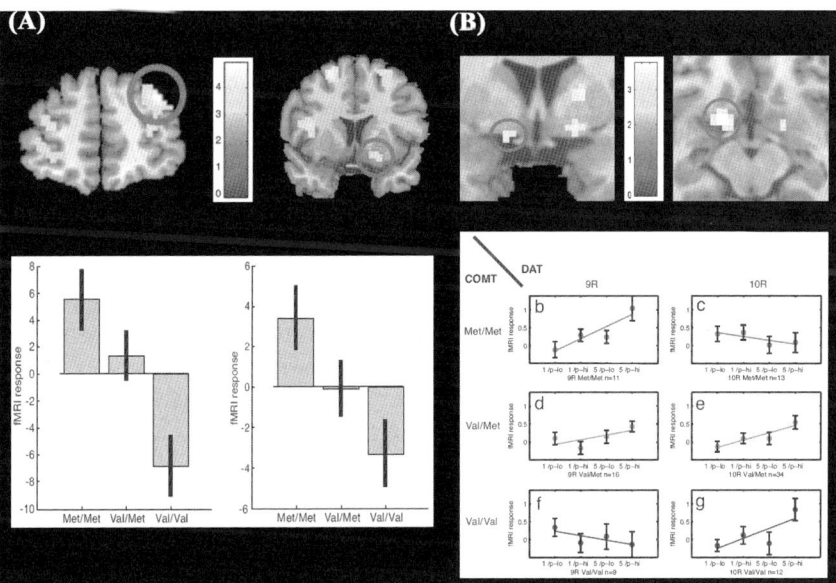

FIGURE 3. Genetic effects on brain response during reward anticipation. (**A**) Statistical maps overlaid onto structural MRI showing the effect of COMT genotype on reward anticipation–related activation in the prefrontal cortex (*left*) and the ventral putamen (*right*). Met/Met subjects (less enzyme activity) show highest activation levels, whereas Val/Val subjects show the lowest. (**B**) (*Up*) Functional interaction between COMT and DAT genotypes in the left ventral striatum. (*Down*) fMRI responses from the left ventral striatum as a function of reward probability (*p*-low vs. *p*-high), magnitude (1€ vs. 5€), and genotype. In all groups except DAT 10R COMT Met/Met and DAT 9R COMT Val/Val, activation increases according to probability and magnitude of rewards. The blunted response in DAT 10R COMT Met/Met and DAT 9R COMT Val/Val subjects may reflect suboptimal neural encoding of rewards. Reprinted and modified with permission from REF.[10] © (2007) The National Academy of Sciences.

most common.[171] Although this configuration does not affect the corresponding protein's structure, it does influence gene expression[172–174] and protein availability.[175–177] Despite the somewhat controversial results, there seems to be stronger evidence for higher DAT availability and gene expression related to the 10-repeat allele, which would lead to lower dopamine levels. Moreover, disruption of the DAT gene in DAT-knockout mice has been shown to alter their "social" behavior.[178]

A recent study assessed the effect of COMT and DAT genotypes on anticipation of monetary rewards that varied in probability and magnitude.[10] Neuronal activity in the prefrontal cortex and in the striatum was modulated by the COMT genotype. Subjects homozygous for the Met allele, and thus with presumably greater dopamine availability, showed larger responses to anticipated rewards than those who were homozygous for the Val allele. Activation in the ventral striatum was also scaled as a function of both reward probability and magnitude, but this activation was affected by neither the COMT nor DAT genotype independently. However, the results found an interaction effect between the two genotypes. This effect came from the fact that subjects homozygous for the Met allele and for the 10-repeat allele and subjects homozygous for the Val allele and carriers of the 9-repeat allele showed a weakened striatal response to increasing expected values, suggesting a nonoptimal reward encoding (FIG. 3). This observation is consistent with the notion that both very low and very high dopamine levels are detrimental for some cognitive functions as, for example, working memory.[179]

In a recent study, we have also observed synergistic effects of COMT and DAT genotypes.[180] These effects are found in the ventral striatum and the DLPFC during anticipation of uncertain rewards and in the lateral OFC at reward delivery. Subjects homozygous for the Met allele and carriers of the 9-repeat allele exhibited the highest activation, presumably reflecting a functional change consecutive to higher synaptic dopamine availability.

In conclusion, there is now compelling evidence that genetic variations in dopamine-related genes modulate the physiological response of the dopaminergic system, which may help explain the interindividual differences commonly observed in compulsive behavior, such as pathological gambling and drug addiction, and vulnerability to neuropathologies (e.g., schizophrenia).

CONCLUSIONS

In recent years, the combination of molecular genetics, endocrinology, and neuroimaging with economic and social theories has provided many data that help in understanding the biological mechanisms influencing reward processing and social interaction. These studies have demonstrated that genetic and hormonal variations affecting dopaminergic transmission affect the physiological response of the dopaminergic system and its associated cognitive functions, and that these variations may account for some of the interindividual and intraindividual behavioral differences observed in reward processing and social cognition. Although this review emphasizes biological influences on reward-related behavior and social interactions, complex behaviors such as social interactions result from the interplay between genetic and environmental influences. Genes provide the foundation of behavior, but environmental traits and early experience play an important role in modulating the expression of these behaviors through their effect on the underlying physiological mechanisms.[181]

In conclusion, the multilevel analysis used in social neuroscience has now proved to be a useful approach for assessing the neurobiological mechanisms underlying variations in social behavior. Identifying the molecular and cellular markers of reward processing and social interaction provides new insights into the basic mechanisms underlying interindividual differences in susceptibility to disorders such as pathological gambling and drug addiction.

REFERENCES

1. INSEL, T.R. & R.D. FERNALD. 2004. How the brain processes social information: searching for the social brain. Annual Review of Neuroscience **27**: 697–722.
2. SCHULTZ, W. 2000. Multiple reward signals in the brain. Nature reviews. Neuroscience **1**: 199–207.
3. LOHRENZ, T. et al. 2007. Neural signature of fictive learning signals in a sequential investment task. Proc. Natl. Acad. Sci. USA **104**: 9493–9498.
4. MCCABE, K. et al. 2001. A functional imaging study of cooperation in two-person reciprocal exchange. Proceedings of the National Academy of Sciences of the United States of America **98**: 11832–11835.
5. DE QUERVAIN, D.J. et al. 2004. The neural basis of altruistic punishment. Science (New York, N.Y.) **305**: 1254–1258.
6. HAFNER, H. 2003. Gender differences in schizophrenia. Psychoneuroendocrinology **28**(Suppl 2): 17–54.
7. MEYER-LINDENBERG, A., C.B. MERVIS & K.F. BERMAN. 2006. Neural mechanisms in Williams syndrome: a unique window to genetic influences on cognition and behaviour. Nat. Rev. Neurosci. **7**: 380–393.
8. MEYER-LINDENBERG, A. & D.R. WEINBERGER. 2006. Intermediate phenotypes and genetic mechanisms of psychiatric disorders. Nat. Rev. Neurosci. **7**: 818–827.
9. TREPEL, C., C.R. FOX & R.A. POLDRACK. 2005. Prospect theory on the brain? Toward a cognitive neuroscience of decision under risk. Brain Res. Cogn. Brain Res. **23**: 34–50.
10. YACUBIAN, J. et al. 2007. Gene-gene interaction associated with neural reward sensitivity. Proc. Natl. Acad. Sci. USA **104**: 8125–8130.
11. DENNERSTEIN, L., C. SPENCER-GARDNER & G.D. BURROWS. 1984. Mood and the menstrual cycle. J. Psychiatr. Res. **18**: 1–12.
12. ROSENBERG, L. & S. PARK. 2002. Verbal and spatial functions across the menstrual cycle in healthy young women. Psychoneuroendocrinology **27**: 835–841.
13. DREHER, J.C. et al. 2007. Menstrual cycle phase modulates reward-related neural function in women. Proceedings of the National Academy of Sciences of the United States of America **104**: 2465–2470.
14. O'DOHERTY, J.P. 2004. Reward representations and reward-related learning in the human brain: insights from neuroimaging. Current Opinion in Neurobiology **14**: 769–776.
15. SCHULTZ, W. 2004. Neural coding of basic reward terms of animal learning theory, game theory, microeconomics and behavioural ecology. Current Opinion in Neurobiology **14**: 139–147.
16. KNUTSON, B. et al. 2003. A region of mesial prefrontal cortex tracks monetarily rewarding outcomes: characterization with rapid event-related fMRI. NeuroImage **18**: 263–272.
17. FIORILLO, C.D., P.N. TOBLER & W. SCHULTZ. 2003. Discrete coding of reward probability and uncertainty by dopamine neurons. Science. **299**: 1898–1902.
18. SCHULTZ, W., P. DAYAN & P.R. MONTAGUE. 1997. A neural substrate of prediction and reward. Science. **275**: 1593–1599.

19. TOBLER, P.N., C.D. FIORILLO & W. SCHULTZ. 2005. Adaptive coding of reward value by dopamine neurons. Science. **307:** 1642–1645.
20. PEARCE, J.M. & G. HALL. 1980. A model for Pavlovian learning: variations in the effectiveness of conditioned but not of unconditioned stimuli. Psychol Rev. **87:** 532–552.
21. SHANNON, C.E. 1948. A mathematical theory of communication. Bell Syst. Tech. J. **27:** 379–423.
22. BERNS, G.S. et al. 2001. Predictability modulates human brain response to reward. J Neurosci. **21:** 2793–2798.
23. MCCLURE, S.M., G.S. BERNS & P.R. MONTAGUE. 2003. Temporal prediction errors in a passive learning task activate human striatum. Neuron. **38:** 339–346.
24. O'DOHERTY, J.P. et al. 2003. Temporal difference models and reward-related learning in the human brain. Neuron. **38:** 329–337.
25. MCCLURE, S.M., M.K. YORK & P.R. MONTAGUE. 2004. The neural substrates of reward processing in humans: the modern role of FMRI. Neuroscientist. **10:** 260–268.
26. KNUTSON, B. et al. 2001. Dissociation of reward anticipation and outcome with event-related fMRI. Neuroreport. **12:** 3683–3687.
27. DELGADO, M.R. et al. 2000. Tracking the hemodynamic responses to reward and punishment in the striatum. J Neurophysiol. **84:** 3072–3077.
28. FLETCHER, P.C. et al. 2001. Responses of human frontal cortex to surprising events are predicted by formal associative learning theory. Nat Neurosci. **4:** 1043–1048.
29. PAULUS, M.P. et al. 2004. Trend detection via temporal difference model predicts inferior prefrontal cortex activation during acquisition of advantageous action selection. Neuroimage. **21:** 733–743.
30. CORLETT, P.R. et al. 2004. Prediction error during retrospective revaluation of causal associations in humans: fMRI evidence in favor of an associative model of learning. Neuron. **44:** 877–888.
31. DREHER, J.C., P. KOHN & K.F. BERMAN. 2006. Neural coding of distinct statistical properties of reward information in humans. Cereb Cortex. **16:** 561–573.
32. KNUTSON, B. et al. 2005. Distributed neural representation of expected value. J Neurosci. **25:** 4806–4812.
33. ABLER, B. et al. 2006. Prediction error as a linear function of reward probability is coded in human nucleus accumbens. Neuroimage. **31:** 790–795.
34. YACUBIAN, J. et al. 2006. Dissociable systems for gain- and loss-related value predictions and errors of prediction in the human brain. J Neurosci. **26:** 9530–9537.
35. TOBLER, P.N. et al. 2007. Reward value coding distinct from risk attitude-related uncertainty coding in human reward systems. J Neurophysiol. **97:** 1621–1632.
36. CRITCHLEY, H.D., C.J. MATHIAS & R.J. DOLAN. 2001. Neural activity in the human brain relating to uncertainty and arousal during anticipation. Neuron. **29:** 537–545.
37. PREUSCHOFF, K., P. BOSSAERTS & S.R. QUARTZ. 2006. Neural differentiation of expected reward and risk in human subcortical structures. Neuron. **51:** 381–390.
38. GRINBAND, J., J. HIRSCH & V.P. FERRERA. 2006. A neural representation of categorization uncertainty in the human brain. Neuron. **49:** 757–763.
39. HUETTEL, S.A., A.W. SONG & G. MCCARTHY. 2005. Decisions under uncertainty: probabilistic context influences activation of prefrontal and parietal cortices. J Neurosci. **25:** 3304–3311.

40. O'DOHERTY, J.P. et al. 2002. Neural responses during anticipation of a primary taste reward. Neuron. **33:** 815–826.
41. KRINGELBACH, M.L. et al. 2003. Activation of the human orbitofrontal cortex to a liquid food stimulus is correlated with its subjective pleasantness. Cereb Cortex. **13:** 1064–1071.
42. GOTTFRIED, J.A., J. O'DOHERTY & R.J. DOLAN. 2002. Appetitive and aversive olfactory learning in humans studied using event-related functional magnetic resonance imaging. J Neurosci. **22:** 10829–10837.
43. THUT, G. et al. 1997. Activation of the human brain by monetary reward. Neuroreport. **8:** 1225–1228.
44. KNUTSON, B. et al. 2000. FMRI visualization of brain activity during a monetary incentive delay task. Neuroimage. **12:** 20–27.
45. BREITER, H.C. et al. 2001. Functional imaging of neural responses to expectancy and experience of monetary gains and losses. Neuron. **30:** 619–639.
46. TREMBLAY, L. & W. SCHULTZ. 1999. Relative reward preference in primate orbitofrontal cortex. Nature. **398:** 704–708.
47. ROLLS, E.T., Z.J. SIENKIEWICZ & S. YAXLEY. 1989. Hunger Modulates the Responses to Gustatory Stimuli of Single Neurons in the Caudolateral Orbitofrontal Cortex of the Macaque Monkey. Eur J Neurosci. **1:** 53–60.
48. CRITCHLEY, H.D. & E.T. ROLLS. 1996. Hunger and satiety modify the responses of olfactory and visual neurons in the primate orbitofrontal cortex. J Neurophysiol. **75:** 1673–1686.
49. ROLLS, E.T. 2000. The orbitofrontal cortex and reward. Cereb Cortex. **10:** 284–294.
50. GOTTFRIED, J.A., J. O'DOHERTY & R.J. DOLAN. 2003. Encoding predictive reward value in human amygdala and orbitofrontal cortex. Science. **301:** 1104–1107.
51. HAMANN, S. & H. MAO. 2002. Positive and negative emotional verbal stimuli elicit activity in the left amygdala. Neuroreport. **13:** 15–19.
52. HOMMER, D.W. et al. 2003. Amygdalar recruitment during anticipation of monetary rewards: an event-related fMRI study. Ann N Y Acad Sci. **985:** 476–478.
53. ANDERSON, A.K. et al. 2003. Dissociated neural representations of intensity and valence in human olfaction. Nat Neurosci. **6:** 196–202.
54. SMALL, D.M. et al. 2003. Dissociation of neural representation of intensity and affective valuation in human gustation. Neuron. **39:** 701–711.
55. DE MARTINO, B. et al. 2006. Frames, biases, and rational decision-making in the human brain. Science. **313:** 684–687.
56. KUHNEN, C.M. & B. KNUTSON. 2005. The neural basis of financial risk taking. Neuron. **47:** 763–770.
57. KAHN, I. et al. 2002. The role of the amygdala in signaling prospective outcome of choice. Neuron. **33:** 983–994.
58. DREHER, J.C. 2007. Sensitivity of the brain to loss aversion during risky gambles. Trends Cogn Sci. **11:** 270–272.
59. KNUTSON, B. et al. 2007. Neural predictors of purchases. Neuron. **53:** 147–156.
60. TOM, S.M. et al. 2007. The neural basis of loss aversion in decision-making under risk. Science. **315:** 515–518.
61. REYNOLDS, L.A. 2005. Communicating total rewards to the generations. Benefits Q. **21:** 13–17.
62. GALLAGHER, H.L. et al. 2002. Imaging the intentional stance in a competitive game. Neuroimage. **16:** 814–821.

63. AMODIO, D.M. & C.D. FRITH. 2006. Meeting of minds: the medial frontal cortex and social cognition. Nat Rev Neurosci. **7:** 268–277.
64. AXELROD, R. & W.D. HAMILTON. 1981. The evolution of cooperation. Science. **211:** 1390–1396.
65. DECETY, J. *et al.* 2004. The neural bases of cooperation and competition: an fMRI investigation. Neuroimage. **23:** 744–751.
66. RILLING, J. *et al.* 2002. A neural basis for social cooperation. Neuron. **35:** 395–405.
67. RILLING, J.K. *et al.* 2004. Opposing BOLD responses to reciprocated and unreciprocated altruism in putative reward pathways. Neuroreport. **15:** 2539–2543.
68. SINGER, T. *et al.* 2004. Brain responses to the acquired moral status of faces. Neuron. **41:** 653–662.
69. SANFEY, A.G. *et al.* 2003. The neural basis of economic decision-making in the Ultimatum Game. Science. **300:** 1755–1758.
70. SINGER, T. *et al.* 2004. Empathy for pain involves the affective but not sensory components of pain. Science. **303:** 1157–1162.
71. DAMASIO, A.R. *et al.* 2000. Subcortical and cortical brain activity during the feeling of self-generated emotions. Nat Neurosci. **3:** 1049–1056.
72. PHILLIPS, M.L. *et al.* 1997. A specific neural substrate for perceiving facial expressions of disgust. Nature. **389:** 495–498.
73. DAMASIO, A. 2005. Human behaviour: brain trust. Nature. **435:** 571–572.
74. KOSFELD, M. *et al.* 2005. Oxytocin increases trust in humans. Nature. **435:** 673–676.
75. PODSAKOFF, P.M. *et al.* 2006. Relationships between leader reward and punishment behavior and subordinate attitudes, perceptions, and behaviors: a meta-analytic review of existing and new research. Organ. Behav. Hum. Decis. Process. **99:** 113–142.
76. BOWLES, S. & H. GINTIS. 2004. The evolution of strong reciprocity: cooperation in heterogeneous populations. Theor Popul Biol. **65:** 17–28.
77. BOYD, R. *et al.* 2003. The evolution of altruistic punishment. Proc Natl Acad Sci USA. **100:** 3531–3535.
78. FEHR, E. & S. GACHTER. 2002. Altruistic punishment in humans. Nature. **415:** 137–140.
79. SINGER, T. *et al.* 2006. Empathic neural responses are modulated by the perceived fairness of others. Nature. **439:** 466–469.
80. KNUTSON, B. 2004. Behavior. Sweet revenge? Science. **305:** 1246–1247.
81. O'REILLY, C.A. & S.M. PUFFER. 1989. The impact of rewards and punishments in a social context: A laboratory and field experiment. J. Occup. Psychol. **62:** 41–53.
82. MONTAGUE, P.R. *et al.* 2002. Hyperscanning: simultaneous fMRI during linked social interactions. Neuroimage. **16:** 1159–1164.
83. KING-CASAS, B. *et al.* 2005. Getting to know you: reputation and trust in a two-person economic exchange. Science. **308:** 78–83.
84. EISENBERGER, N.I., M.D. LIEBERMAN & K.D. WILLIAMS. 2003. Does rejection hurt? An FMRI study of social exclusion. Science. **302:** 290–292.
85. SOMERVILLE, L.H., T.F. HEATHERTON & W.M. KELLEY. 2006. Anterior cingulate cortex responds differentially to expectancy violation and social rejection. Nat Neurosci. **9:** 1007–1008.
86. BUSH, G., P. LUU & M.I. POSNER. 2000. Cognitive and emotional influences in anterior cingulate cortex. Trends Cogn Sci. **4:** 215–222.

87. AKITSUKI, Y. et al. 2003. Context-dependent cortical activation in response to financial reward and penalty: an event-related fMRI study. Neuroimage **19:** 1674–1685.
88. CAMERER, C.F. & E. FEHR. 2006. When does "economic man" dominate social behavior? Science. **311:** 47–52.
89. LEE, D. 2006. Neural basis of quasi-rational decision making. Curr Opin Neurobiol. **16:** 191–198.
90. HASELHUHN, M.P. & B.A. MELLERS. 2005. Emotions and cooperation in economic games. Brain Res Cogn Brain Res. **23:** 24–33.
91. MELLERS, B., I. RITOV & A. SCHWARTZ. 1999. Emotion-based choice. J. Exp. Psychol. **128:** 332–345.
92. MCEWEN, B. 2002. Estrogen actions throughout the brain. Recent Prog. Horm. Res. **57:** 357–384.
93. MCEWEN, B.S. & S.E. ALVES. 1999. Estrogen actions in the central nervous system. Endocr Rev. **20:** 279–307.
94. PFAFF, D.W. et al. 2000. Estrogens, brain and behavior: studies in fundamental neurobiology and observations related to women's health. J Steroid Biochem Mol Biol. **74:** 365–373.
95. PFAFF, D. 2005. Hormone-driven mechanisms in the central nervous system facilitate the analysis of mammalian behaviours. J Endocrinol. **184:** 447–453.
96. BECKER, J.B. & J.H. CHA. 1989. Estrous cycle-dependent variation in amphetamine-induced behaviors and striatal dopamine release assessed with microdialysis. Behav Brain Res. **35:** 117–125.
97. BECKER, J.B., T.E. ROBINSON & K.A. LORENZ. 1982. Sex differences and estrous cycle variations in amphetamine-elicited rotational behavior. Eur J Pharmacol. **80:** 65–72.
98. CREUTZ, L.M. & M.F. KRITZER. 2004. Mesostriatal and mesolimbic projections of midbrain neurons immunoreactive for estrogen receptor beta or androgen receptors in rats. J Comp Neurol. **476:** 348–362.
99. LYNCH, W.J. et al. 2001. Role of estrogen in the acquisition of intravenously self-administered cocaine in female rats. Pharmacol Biochem Behav. **68:** 641–646.
100. DLUZEN, D. & M. HORSTINK. 2003. Estrogen as neuroprotectant of nigrostriatal dopaminergic system: laboratory and clinical studies. Endocrine. **21:** 67–75.
101. JACKSON, L.R., T.E. ROBINSON & J.B. BECKER. 2006. Sex differences and hormonal influences on acquisition of cocaine self-administration in rats. Neuropsychopharmacology. **31:** 129–138.
102. LACREUSE, A. 2006. Effects of ovarian hormones on cognitive function in nonhuman primates. Neuroscience. **138:** 859–867.
103. HALPERN, D.F. & U. TAN. 2001. Stereotypes and steroids: using a psychobiosocial model to understand cognitive sex differences. Brain Cogn. **45:** 392–414.
104. HAUSMANN, M. et al. 2000. Sex hormones affect spatial abilities during the menstrual cycle. Behav Neurosci. **114:** 1245–1250.
105. BEAUDOIN, J. & R. MARROCCO. 2005. Attentional validity effect across the human menstrual cycle varies with basal temperature changes. Behav Brain Res. **158:** 23–29.
106. RUBINOW, D.R. & P.J. SCHMIDT. 2006. Gonadal steroid regulation of mood: the lessons of premenstrual syndrome. Front Neuroendocrinol. **27:** 210–216.
107. JUSTICE, A.J. & H. DE WIT. 1999. Acute effects of d-amphetamine during the follicular and luteal phases of the menstrual cycle in women. Psychopharmacology (Berl). **145:** 67–75.

108. PROTOPOPESCU, X. *et al.* 2005. Orbitofrontal cortex activity related to emotional processing changes across the menstrual cycle. Proc Natl Acad Sci USA. **102:** 16060–16065.
109. GOLDSTEIN, J.M. *et al.* 2005. Hormonal cycle modulates arousal circuitry in women using functional magnetic resonance imaging. J Neurosci. **25:** 9309–9316.
110. SENIOR, C., A. LAU & M.J. BUTLER. 2007. The effects of the menstrual cycle on social decision making. Int J Psychophysiol. **63:** 186–191.
111. PENTON-VOAK, I.S. *et al.* 1999. Menstrual cycle alters face preference. Nature. **399:** 741–742.
112. PENTON-VOAK, I.S. & D.I. PERRETT. 2000. Female preference for male faces changes cyclically: Further evidence. Evol. Hum. Behav. **21:** 39–48.
113. JOHNSTON, V.S. *et al.* 2001. Male facial attractiveness. Evidence for hormone-mediated adaptive design. Evol. Hum. Behav. **22:** 251–267.
114. ZHANG, Z.X. 2001. The effects of frequency of social interaction and relationship closeness on reward allocation. J Psychol. **135:** 154–164.
115. GRANGER, D.A. *et al.* 2003. Salivary testosterone diurnal variation and psychopathology in adolescent males and females: individual differences and developmental effects. Dev Psychopathol. **15:** 431–449.
116. SWAAB, D.F. *et al.* 1996. Biological rhythms in the human life cycle and their relationship to functional changes in the suprachiasmatic nucleus. Prog. Brain Res. **111:** 349–368.
117. FELDMAN, H.A. *et al.* 2002. Age trends in the level of serum testosterone and other hormones in middle-aged men: longitudinal results from the Massachusetts male aging study. J Clin Endocrinol Metab. **87:** 589–598.
118. ARCHER, J. 1991. The influence of testosterone on human aggression. Br J Psychol. **82**(Pt 1): 1–28.
119. RUBINOW, D.R. & P.J. SCHMIDT. 1996. Androgens, brain, and behavior. Am J Psychiatry. **153:** 974–984.
120. VAN BOKHOVEN, I. *et al.* 2006. Salivary testosterone and aggression, delinquency, and social dominance in a population-based longitudinal study of adolescent males. Horm Behav. **50:** 118–125.
121. MAZUR, A. & A. BOOTH. 1998. Testosterone and dominance in men. Behav Brain Sci. **21:** 353–363; discussion 363–97.
122. GRANT, V.J. & J.T. FRANCE. 2001. Dominance and testosterone in women. Biol Psychol. **58:** 41–47.
123. POSTMA, A. *et al.* 2000. Effects of testosterone administration on selective aspects of object-location memory in healthy young women. Psychoneuroendocrinology. **25:** 563–575.
124. ALEMAN, A. *et al.* 2004. A single administration of testosterone improves visuospatial ability in young women. Psychoneuroendocrinology. **29:** 612–617.
125. REDOUTE, J. *et al.* 2005. Brain processing of visual sexual stimuli in treated and untreated hypogonadal patients. Psychoneuroendocrinology. **30:** 461–482.
126. VAN HONK, J. *et al.* 2004. Testosterone shifts the balance between sensitivity for punishment and reward in healthy young women. Psychoneuroendocrinology. **29:** 937–943.
127. VAN HONK, J. *et al.* 2003. Low cortisol levels and the balance between punishment sensitivity and reward dependency. Neuroreport. **14:** 1993–1996.
128. TAKAHASHI, T. *et al.* 2005. Interpersonal trust and social stress-induced cortisol elevation. Neuroreport. **16:** 197–199.

129. YOUNG, L.J., Z. WANG & T.R INSEL. 1998. Neuroendocrine bases of monogamy. Trends Neurosci. **21:** 71–75.
130. YOUNG, L.J. *et al.* 2001. Cellular mechanisms of social attachment. Horm Behav. **40:** 133–138.
131. WINSLOW, J.T. *et al.* 1993. Oxytocin and complex social behavior: species comparisons. Psychopharmacol Bull. **29:** 409–414.
132. INSEL, T.R. & L.E. SHAPIRO. 1992. Oxytocin receptor distribution reflects social organization in monogamous and polygamous voles. Proc Natl Acad Sci USA. **89:** 5981–5985.
133. INSEL, T.R. & T.J. HULIHAN. 1995. A gender-specific mechanism for pair bonding: oxytocin and partner preference formation in monogamous voles. Behav Neurosci. **109:** 782–789.
134. INSEL, T.R. *et al.* 1995. Oxytocin and the molecular basis of monogamy. Adv Exp Med Biol. **395:** 227–234.
135. ZAK, P.J., R. KURZBAN & W.T. MATZNER. 2004. The neurobiology of trust. Ann N Y Acad Sci. **1032:** 224–227.
136. ZAK, P.J., R. KURZBAN & W.T. MATZNER. 2005. Oxytocin is associated with human trustworthiness. Horm Behav. **48:** 522–527.
137. DOMES, G. *et al.* 2007. Oxytocin improves 'mind-reading' in humans. Biol Psychiatry. **61:** 731–733.
138. KIRSCH, P. *et al.* 2005. Oxytocin modulates neural circuitry for social cognition and fear in humans. J Neurosci. **25:** 11489–11493.
139. HARIRI, A.R. & D.R. WEINBERGER. 2003. Imaging genomics. Br Med Bull. **65:** 259–270.
140. KOVAS, Y. & R. PLOMIN. 2006. Generalist genes: implications for the cognitive sciences. Trends Cogn Sci. **10:** 198–203.
141. ILIES, R., R.D. ARVEY & T.J. BOUCHARD. 2006. Darwinism, behavioral genetics, and organizational behavior: a review and agenda for future research. J. Organ. Behav. **27:** 121–141.
142. ARVEY, R.D. *et al.* 2006. The determinants of leadership role occupancy: Genetic and personality factors. Leadersh. Q. **17:** 1–20.
143. ARVEY, R.D. *et al.* 2007. Developmental and genetic determinants of leadership role occupancy among women. J Appl Psychol. **92:** 693–706.
144. MCCALL, B.P., M.A. CAVANAUGH & R.D. ARVEY. 1997. Genetic influences on job and occupational switching. J. Vocat. Behav. **50:** 60–77.
145. ARVEY, R.D. *et al.* 1989. Job satisfaction: Environmental and genetic components. J. Appl. Psychol. **74:** 187–192.
146. EGAN, M.F. *et al.* 2001. Effect of COMT Val108/158 Met genotype on frontal lobe function and risk for schizophrenia. Proc Natl Acad Sci USA. **98:** 6917–6922.
147. BENJAMIN, J. *et al.* 1996. Population and familial association between the D4 dopamine receptor gene and measures of Novelty Seeking. Nat Genet. **12:** 81–84.
148. EBSTEIN, R.P. *et al.* 1996. Dopamine D4 receptor (D4DR) exon III polymorphism associated with the human personality trait of Novelty Seeking. Nat Genet. **12:** 78–80.
149. ROGERS, G. *et al.* 2004. Association of a duplicated repeat polymorphism in the 5'-untranslated region of the DRD4 gene with novelty seeking. Am J Med Genet B Neuropsychiatr Genet. **126:** 95–98.
150. PEREZ DE CASTRO, I. *et al.* 1997. Genetic association study between pathological gambling and a functional DNA polymorphism at the D4 receptor gene. Pharmacogenetics. **7:** 345–348.

151. COMINGS, D.E. *et al.* 1994. The dopamine D2 receptor gene: a genetic risk factor in substance abuse. Drug Alcohol Depend. **34:** 175–180.
152. NOBLE, E.P. 2000. Addiction and its reward process through polymorphisms of the D2 dopamine receptor gene: a review. Eur Psychiatry. **15:** 79–89.
153. BOWIRRAT, A. & M. OSCAR-BERMAN. 2005. Relationship between dopaminergic neurotransmission, alcoholism, and Reward Deficiency syndrome. Am J Med Genet B Neuropsychiatr Genet. **132:** 29–37.
154. BLUM, K. *et al.* 1996. The D2 dopamine receptor gene as a determinant of reward deficiency syndrome. J R Soc Med. **89:** 396–400.
155. COHEN, M.X. *et al.* 2005. Individual differences in extraversion and dopamine genetics predict neural reward responses. Brain Res Cogn Brain Res. **25:** 851–861.
156. AXELROD, J. & R. TOMCHICK. 1958. Enzymatic O-methylation of epinephrine and other catechols. J Biol Chem. **233:** 702–705.
157. MANNISTO, P.T. & S. KAAKKOLA. 1999. Catechol-O-methyltransferase (COMT): biochemistry, molecular biology, pharmacology, and clinical efficacy of the new selective COMT inhibitors. Pharmacol Rev. **51:** 593–628.
158. NAPOLITANO, A., A.M. CESURA & M. DA PRADA. 1995. The role of monoamine oxidase and catechol O-methyltransferase in dopaminergic neurotransmission. J Neural Transm Suppl. **45:** 35–45.
159. LACHMAN, H.M. *et al.* 1996. Human catechol-O-methyltransferase pharmacogenetics: description of a functional polymorphism and its potential application to neuropsychiatric disorders. Pharmacogenetics. **6:** 243–250.
160. LOTTA, T. *et al.* 1995. Kinetics of human soluble and membrane-bound catechol O-methyltransferase: a revised mechanism and description of the thermolabile variant of the enzyme. Biochemistry. **34:** 4202–4210.
161. CHEN, J. *et al.* 2004. Functional analysis of genetic variation in catechol-O-methyltransferase (COMT): effects on mRNA, protein, and enzyme activity in postmortem human brain. Am J Hum Genet. **75:** 807–821.
162. TSAI, S.J. *et al.* 2004. Association study of catechol-O-methyltransferase gene and dopamine D4 receptor gene polymorphisms and personality traits in healthy young chinese females. Neuropsychobiology. **50:** 153–156.
163. ENOCH, M.A. *et al.* 2003. Genetic origins of anxiety in women: a role for a functional catechol-O-methyltransferase polymorphism. Psychiatr Genet. **13:** 33–41.
164. DE FRIAS, C.M. *et al.* 2005. Catechol O-methyltransferase Val158Met polymorphism is associated with cognitive performance in nondemented adults. J Cogn Neurosci. **17:** 1018–1025.
165. BRUDER, G.E. *et al.* 2005. Catechol-O-methyltransferase (COMT) genotypes and working memory: associations with differing cognitive operations. Biol Psychiatry. **58:** 901–907.
166. CALDÚ, X. *et al.* 2007. Impact of the COMT Val108/158 Met and DAT1 genotypes on prefrontal function in healthy subjects. Neuroimage. **37:** 1437–1444.
167. BERTOLINO, A. *et al.* 2006. Additive effects of genetic variation in dopamine regulating genes on working memory cortical activity in human brain. J Neurosci. **26:** 3918–3922.
168. HEINZ, A. & M.N. SMOLKA. 2006. The effects of catechol O-methyltransferase genotype on brain activation elicited by affective stimuli and cognitive tasks. Rev Neurosci. **17:** 359–367.

169. SMOLKA, M.N. *et al.* 2005. Catechol-O-methyltransferase val158met genotype affects processing of emotional stimuli in the amygdala and prefrontal cortex. J Neurosci. **25:** 836–842.
170. DRABANT, E.M. *et al.* 2006. Catechol O-methyltransferase val158met genotype and neural mechanisms related to affective arousal and regulation. Arch Gen Psychiatry. **63:** 1396–1406.
171. GELERNTER, J., H. KRANZLER & J. LACOBELLE. 1998. Population studies of polymorphisms at loci of neuropsychiatric interest (tryptophan hydroxylase (TPH), dopamine transporter protein (SLC6A3), D3 dopamine receptor (DRD3), apolipoprotein E (APOE), mu opioid receptor (OPRM1), and ciliary neurotrophic factor (CNTF)). Genomics. **52:** 289–297.
172. FUKE, S. *et al.* 2001. The VNTR polymorphism of the human dopamine transporter (DAT1) gene affects gene expression. Pharmacogenomics J. **1:** 152–156.
173. MILL, J. *et al.* 2002. Expression of the dopamine transporter gene is regulated by the 3' UTR VNTR: Evidence from brain and lymphocytes using quantitative RT-PCR. Am J Med Genet. **114:** 975–979.
174. VANNESS, S.H., M.J. OWENS & C.D. KILTS. 2005. The variable number of tandem repeats element in DAT1 regulates in vitro dopamine transporter density. BMC Genet. **6:** 55.
175. HEINZ, A. *et al.* 2000. Genotype influences in vivo dopamine transporter availability in human striatum. Neuropsychopharmacology. **22:** 133–139.
176. JACOBSEN, L.K. *et al.* 2000. Prediction of dopamine transporter binding availability by genotype: a preliminary report. Am J Psychiatry. **157:** 1700–1703.
177. VAN DYCK, C.H. *et al.* 2005. Increased dopamine transporter availability associated with the 9-repeat allele of the SLC6A3 gene. J Nucl Med. **46:** 745–751.
178. RODRIGUIZ, R.M. *et al.* 2004. Aberrant responses in social interaction of dopamine transporter knockout mice. Behav Brain Res. **148:** 185–198.
179. TUNBRIDGE, E.M., P.J. HARRISON & D.R. WEINBERGER. 2006. Catechol-o-methyltransferase, cognition, and psychosis: Val158Met and beyond. Biol Psychiatry. **60:** 141–151.
180. DREHER, J.C. *et al.* Heritable variation in dopamine genes influences hyperresponsivity of the human reward system. (Unpublished data)
181. CUSHING, B.S. & K.M. KRAMER. 2005. Mechanisms underlying epigenetic effects of early social experience: the role of neuropeptides and steroids. Neurosci Biobehav Rev. **29:** 1089–1105.

Neuro-Gov

Neuroscience as Catalyst

DAVID JOHN FARMER

Virginia Commonwealth University

ABSTRACT: Neuroscience promises to act as a catalyst, in the longer run, in seeking re-unification of the fragmented social sciences (e.g., political science and economics) and social action subjects (e.g., public administration and business administration) that concern governance. Neuroscience can achieve this because it reveals that taken-for-granted concepts, and the language used to express them, should be challenged. What should be sought is a language called in this paper Neuro-Gov.

KEYWORDS: governance; neuroscience; interdisciplinarity; neuropolitical; neuro-economic; neurophilosophical; neuropsychological

To show the fly the way out of the fly-bottle.
Wittgenstein, 1953[1]

Should social science and social action thinkers embrace neuroscience? Yes, more should, from the social science disciplines, such as economics (ECON) and political science (POLI), and from social action fields, such as public administration (PA) and business administration (BA). Embracing neuroscience could help to generate and promote a needed new language of governance. It could serve as a catalyst, giving needed life to attempts to reverse the increasing fragmentation of disciplines.

"Catch up, and go beyond!" could be a slogan for individual disciplines. Catch up with neuroscientific advances in social sciences (e.g., in fringes in political science and in economics, as well as in social psychology) and in social action subjects (e.g., in even smaller fringes in public administration and business administration). Catch up in philosophy! Yet in embracing neuroscience, go beyond the scope and methods of such traditional disciplines. In this paper, transcending scope, for instance, means coverage of the full range of governance. The term *governance* is used here in the sense of governmentality, referring to the gamut of dynamically interrelated governing activities, including not only public but also private, non-profit, and even self-governing

Address for correspondence: D.J. Farmer, Virginia Commonwealth University, L. Douglas Wilder School of Government and Public Affairs, 923 W. Franklin Street, Box 842028, Richmond, Virginia 23284-2028.
dfarmer@vcu.edu

enterprises. This marriage between neuroscience and governance is termed *Neuro-Gov*.

Yet there are pitfalls. There may be failure to recognize that embracing neuroscience does not mean biological determinism—nor even that biology is trumps. Turning to neuroscience implies neither abandoning insights available from the particular social sciences, nor from Shakespeare, nor from the multi-perspectival play. On the contrary, such embrace requires multidisciplinarity of its own.

Neuroscience is itself a language, which has different dialects. There are direct contributions that this language can make to the various social science and social action subjects. As an example of the social sciences (psychology), consider the neuroscientific claim that the brain is plastic, and—within limits— shaped by its environment.[2] As an example of a social action discipline (such as policy analysis), consider the neuroscientific claim that 1 out of 500 babies is born with afflictions such as anencephaly if mothers do not ingest folic acid within the first three weeks of pregnancy.[3] Of course, there are softer dialects, e.g., under the social neuroscience heading.

Before discussing Neuro-Gov, attention should be directed to: (1) the movement to repair increasing fragmentation of the social sciences, and (2) the neuro-benefits sought by some of the social sciences and other disciplines.

REPAIRING THE FRAGMENTATION

Fragmentation of knowledge has occurred during the modern period, especially (but not exclusively) in the social sciences and in social action fields. Or, to put it another way, increasing specialization and proliferation are characteristic of modernity, especially in these disciplines. Klein has described the "modern connotation of disciplinarity" as a nineteenth century product, for example, and links it with the "evolution of the modern natural sciences, the general 'scientification' of knowledge, the industrial revolution, technological advancements, and agrarian agitation."[4] He adds that, as modern universities developed, disciplinarity was encouraged by industries demanding specialists, by disciplines recruiting students, and by more expensive instrumentation in some fields.

Social science and social action subjects are now atomized, hindering examination of cross-disciplinary issues and confining insights to limited perspectives.[5] Flexner gives as an example from the United States, the "history of the curriculum in American higher education has been one of increasing diversification and specialization."[6]

The social sciences are more liable to fragmentation than the physical sciences because they tend to be low paradigm fields. This reflects a distinction that has been drawn between high paradigm (such as physics) and low paradigm (such as sociology) subjects.[7] This distinction can be understood as equivalent to that between highly codified (e.g., mathematics) and less codified (e.g., social sciences) subjects. There are differences in this respect between social sciences. For instance, economic theory is more high-paradigm or codified than political theory.

Throughout the modern period, concerns have been expressed regarding the fragmentation of knowledge and there have been calls to restore the lost unity by a long list of philosophers, e.g., including Bacon and Comte.[8] More recently, the biologist E.O. Wilson wrote about consilience and the unity of knowledge, uniting the sciences and, ultimately, union with the humanities. Wilson defined consilience as "literally a lumping together of knowledge by the linking of facts and fact-based theory across disciplines to create a common groundwork for explanation."[9]

During the past century, there has been a rich variety of attempts at interdisciplinarity. For historical surveys of these attempts, see Klein[10] and Flexner.[11] Interdisciplinarity has been applied to the functional aspects of disciplines such as general education, professional education, the training of researchers, basic research, and applied research. An account of developments in the United States and elsewhere would include descriptions of national and other organizations (such as the Social Science Research Council in the 1920s, the 1948 Foundation for Integrative Education, and the National Science Foundation's programs); as well as descriptions of externally driven developments (e.g., those resulting from World War II, such as the Manhattan Project), and internally driven ones (e.g., those resulting from synthetic theories, such as structuralism and general systems theory).

It is fair to complain of the continuing proliferation. While there have been some successes at transdisciplinarity, it is fair to say that the attempts to achieve interdisciplinarity have mainly resulted in what has been called an "interdisciplinary archipelago" of new disciplines.[12]

Recall that there are various strategies for reversing the trend toward fragmentation. Elsewhere, the author[13] has discussed a tailored and ad hoc approach, in which the better model for knowing (as Deleuze & Guattari explain[14]) is not the "orderly" tree but the "disorderly" rhizome. Rather than seeking a massive top-down structural reorganization of disciplines, the latter strategy is modeled on the tailored activities of eclectic thinkers like Herbert Marcuse. Marcuse, for instance, offers analyses—for particular purposes—that include materials from philosophy, psychoanalysis, politics, economics and other disciplines.[15]

The strategy of aiming to restore the lost unity can be expected to evolve only on a gradual or evolutionary basis. The long-term aim may well be to create a gathering together of all the subjects connected with what is called here governance—all knowledge concerned with governing or being governed. But it is reasonable to anticipate that this development will start with a few disciplines, and then evolve to others. That is one reason why this paper has chosen to focus on a few of the social science and social action disciplines;

others may have opted to include different ones.[16] It is reasonable to suppose that a catalyst is required for such an aim to combat the balkanized character of the social science and social action terrain.

It is proposed that this catalyst is now available, in the nature of the accelerating research results of neuroscience. Neuroscience promises to act as a catalyst in seeking reunification in the longer run, because it challenges the taken-for-granted concepts of disciplinary orthodoxy in the social science and social action disciplines.

PAY-OFFS SOUGHT BY INDIVIDUAL SOCIAL SCIENCES

The following should be read in the context of the neuroscientific revolution symbolized during the Decade of the Brain (1990–1999) and the development of the Human Genome Project (1990–2003). The momentum of the revolution was brought home also when attending the 2006 annual conference of the Society for Neuroscience. There were more than 30,000 attendees, representing fields as diverse as molecular neuroscience, cellular neuroscience, systems neuroscience, behavioral neuroscience, cognitive and affective neuroscience, social neuroscience, neuro-ethics—and even "neuroscience and architecture." Neuro-afficianados were also present from the neuropolitical, the neuro-economic, the neurophilosophical, and the neuropsychological—subtopics considered, in turn, here.

The existing fragmentation between the social science disciplines (and between these subjects) is clear. Each discipline has its own distinctive subculture, e. g., including governing structure and recognized practices. There is some interdisciplinarity, as indicated earlier; and in fact a social scientist (e.g., a political scientist) interested in neuroscience is in itself a form of interdisciplinarity. Yet these disciplines are fundamentally separate; each has, as will be explained in this paper, its own language game.

Consider disciplines dipping their toes into neuroscience, taking the examples of economics and political science. Within each of them, there is limited interest in neuroscience—"limited" meaning that the interest is confined to a minority of the practicing political scientists and economists.

A critical question is whether the interest aims to preserve the disciplinary status quo or to achieve fresh and possibly counter-disciplinary conclusions. On the one hand, the interest of neuro-economists may be in gaining support for the dominant neoclassical paradigm. This is not in terms of cooking the books, but rather of setting the research questions and agenda in a way that is friendlier or more open to the status quo. On the other hand, the interest of neuro-economists may be in following wherever the research leads, even if it clashes with the dominant paradigm.

This will be explained in terms of a central assumption in economic modeling, which, as discussed later in more detail, is that the allocation of scarce resources among competing needs may be studied exclusively in terms of rational decision making. On the one hand, the neuro-economist may set the research agenda merely to find out more about the nature of rational decision making, e.g., studying risk taking or other unchallenging topics. On the other hand, the neuro-economist may be open to the neuroscientific claim that people are basically emotional,[17] rather than merely rational. The latter undermines the dominant language game (or set of language games) in economics.

It is reasonable to expect that initial interest in neuroscience would support existing disciplinary concerns, if only because rewards accrue to disciplinary members primarily from within their disciplines.

Note in the following comments how the neuro-economists are interested in neuroscientific topics clearly supportive of the rational man assumption, just mentioned. Note in the following comments the neuropolitical interest in setting a research agenda, e.g., perhaps even to prevent the neuro-economists from setting it.

It is also reasonable to expect that, in the shorter run, there would be even more fragmentation. Indeed, recall that this has been the experience to date with programs to reverse such fragmentation. It is difficult to specify how short, or long, such a shorter run would be, which would depend partly on historical accidents. But the argument here is that, in the longer run, the catalytic power of neuroscience is so great that it would repair the fragmentation. The suggestion is that, in the longer run, there can only be delay in the evolutionary progress toward Neuro-Gov. Such delay would be shorter to the extent that the various social sciences come to understand that the open or consilience approach should be attempted.

Neuropolitical

Decision making, motivation, emotion and stereotyping are among topics that can be profitably investigated from a neuroscientific perspective. Such a claim was made by political scientists leading a training session on, "What neuroscience has to offer political science," a short course preceding the 2006 annual conference of the American Political Science Association (APSA).[18] Attention should be paid to this claim to the extent that it is true. The impression that *much show-me-what-you've-got neuropolitical benefit is for the future* should not decrease, and should even increase, enthusiasm.

The APSA short course underscored three other points. First, some neuro-political-scientists want to shape the choice of research questions, e.g., focusing on the political aspects, rather than leaving the neuro-field to economists. Second, some work directly with fMRI functional magnetic resonance imaging (imaging the workings of the living brain), and are not limited to passive using. This is mentioned only because it is suggestive of the range of interest. In my view, such positivist activity is incidental to the hermeneutic major league action; white coat-ism is not suggested. Neuropolitics is a fringe area of political science activity in terms of quantity, even though it is important at this margin. The 2006 APSA Conference's main program contained a single panel on "neuroscientific advances in the study of political science,"[19] including significant topics, such as the neurological basis of representative democracy,[20] neuroscience and analytical narratives,[21] and considerations on the neuroscience of power.[22]

Neuro-economics

Neuro-economics is further along than neuropolitics. The *fourth* informal annual meeting of the Neuroeconomics Society was held in September 2006. The aims of neuro-economics are bi-directional: on the supply side, to provide what economics can offer neuroscience, via mathematical economics; and, on the demand side, to use what neuroscience can give to economics.

Paul Glimcher describes the supply-side neuro-economic contribution as repairing the failure adequately to incorporate probability theory for understanding the relationship between behavior and brain. In his book sub-titled "The Science of Neuroeconomics," Glimcher explains that "mathematical theories of decision making that include probability theory must form the core of future approaches to understanding the relationship between behavior and brain, because understanding the relationship between behavior and brain is fundamentally about understanding decision making."[23] Neuroscience is a massive interdisciplinary set of inquiries, including both heavy-duty physical science and social science. Experimental neuroscience includes developmental neurobiology, molecular neurobiology, neuro-anatomy, neurochemistry, neuro-ethology, neuropharmacology, neuropsychology, and computational neuroscience. In the latter area, economists, including game theorists, can readily contribute.

On the demand side, the fourth Annual Conference of the Neuro-economics Society included papers on significant topics friendly to the economics paradigm, such as the neural basis of discounting future gains, loss aversion, risk, marketing, learning, choice, sociality and even time, as well as studies on trust and addiction. The Conference included papers with titles such as neural substrates of risky decision making,[24] the neurobiology of intertemporal choice,[25] brain mechanisms of persuasion,[26] subsecond dopamine release during economic decision making in rodents,[27] rats under uncertainty,[28] the neural basis of charitable giving,[29] and so on.

Neurophilosophy

Neurophilosophy applies neuroscienctific concepts to traditional philosophical questions. An example of an exciting neurophilosophical issue is the nature of a unified self; other examples include the nature of psychological states (e.g., emotions, beliefs and desires) and perceptual knowledge. Neurophilosophy is usually distinguished from philosophy of neuroscience. The latter is concerned with foundational issues in neuroscience, e.g., descriptive, normative and constructive questions about the nature of neuroscientific explanations. The exchange between neuroscience and philosophy, in an ideal world, thus would be bi-directional—the same ideal as in neuropolitics and neuroeconomics.

Being concerned with such issues as the nature of consciousness, cognition, action and knowledge, it is not surprising that philosophy has long been involved with neuroscience. It is difficult to know when neuroscience started; but one view is that the philosopher Rene Descartes was the founder of neuroscience, but the pace has obviously increased in recent decades. Thus, Patricia Churchland[30,31] attempts to "introduce" neuroscience to philosophers and philosophy-of-science to neuroscientists. Earlier, there was excitement about a couple of corner topics—sociobiology[32] and the selfish gene.[33]

Neuropsychology

There is also the cluster of emerging and important study areas that relate to neuropsychology—an even larger area. Social neuroscience is generally concerned with the neurological features associated with the processes that have traditionally been studied in social psychology. This description appeared in the first issue of the journal *Social Neuroscience*, in March 2006.[34] The lead article discussed the anatomic correlates of stigma[35]; another one was concerned with the visual analysis of emotional actions.[36] Social neuroscience is closely related to cognitive neuroscience and affective neuroscience, these two fields leading to another new journal, *Social Cognitive and Affective Neuroscience,* in 2006.

Surely this would suggest that James Watson and Edward O. Wilson were right in claiming that the 21st century is the century of neurobiology? Does this not imply that, in the longer run, the catalytic power of the neurosciences will lead to Neuro-Gov? It is time to develop this argument in this paper by turning to look at this catalytic power to challenge existing language games.

THE LANGUAGE GAME

Does Neuro-Gov, among others, have the substance and the momentum to release the coming generation from the traditional, common-sensical languages speaking about governance? Substance is taken to mean catalytic power to generate, and momentum means "muscle" power to induce, to seduce—such compelling power as is exerted by hard science on the upswing. Reading neuroscience seems to highlight the undesirability of the social mis-construction of common sense—and to emphasize the desirability of deconstructing such misleading constructions.

Recall the previous discussion about the existing fragmentation, the aims in current research, and the nature of future research. It is argued here that the catalytic power, the unifying power, of neuroscience is in attacking the taken-for-granted orthodox concepts, which are constituents of disciplinary language games. Wittgenstein explained language games in terms of the manner of the discourses of a community, such as the discourse of economists or physicists. Wittgenstein explained that, for him, language is an activity or a form of life, and that people participate in a variety of language games. Wittgenstein gives the example of a builder and an assistant to illustrate a primitive language,[37] consisting of the words *block*, *pillar*, *slab* and *beam*. The builder calls out the words and the assistant brings him things. Clearly, economics has a language game (e.g., speaking of marginality, optimization of returns) that political science does not, and vice-versa. Public administration has a language game that differs from business administration.[38]

Neuro-Gov, to repeat the earlier explanation, is the study of governance that relies importantly on insights and research results from neuroscience. Governance refers to the full range of activities that are implicated in governing. As a starting point, the evolution of Neuro-Gov would include disciplines such as those mentioned here; eventually the evolution is expected to extend to all disciplines concerned with all kinds of governing and being governed.

Neuroscience v. Common-Sensical Language

The first journal issue of *Social Neuroscience* claims that social neuroscience forces the recognition that common-sense language does not match what is going on at various neuroscientific levels.[39] Common-sense ways of conceptualizing X are not reflected in X's neural signature. For instance, if a single concept such as empathy (if it is viewed as such) has two neuro scientific manifestations (two neural signatures), that might be a double reminder that the concept is socially constructed and should be deconstructed. This is also true of other areas of neuroscience.

Neuroscience can be another perspective that tips the balance against the constraints of common sense. This parallels the way that most paradigm shifts in hard science show the hollowness of the common-sense language game, e.g., space-time understandings show the hollowness of talking about "ascending" into Heaven, understandings about sub-atomic particles are at variance with... (fill in the blank).

Consider heart and mind, as another example. Before William Harvey's 17th-century discovery of circulation of the blood, it seems that it was not widely recognized that the heart is a mere pumping station. It is claimed that Aristotle, the first biologist as he is often called, concluded—unlike others, including Hippocrates—that the brain is a cooling system, while the heart is the seat and source of sensation. Looking at the fluid-filled ventricles in human brain coloring books[40] suggests that such a conclusion is reasonable, even if it is false. It is more reasonable than the Egyptian idea that the brain is mere stuffing, so that Egyptian morticians used hooks to tear it out. From the point of view of language, there is much mis-speak about the heart. "I love you with all my heart;" no, "I love you with all my stuffing." Our commonsense language, in this and other respects, is misleading.

Neuro-Gov v. Political Science Language

This paper now focuses more directly on three points about opportunities for recognizing the social construction, and the need for the deconstruction, of traditional discourse.

Consider as a preface traditional public administration (PA), often thought of as a component and subordinate element of political science. We might want to deconstruct the idea of *public* that supports the artificial construction of the *commonsense* understanding of the boundaries of PA. Deconstruction is taken in the sense coined by Jacques Derrida and recognized in political science and PA.[41] Jurgen Habermas' work includes what amounts to a "deconstruction" of the meaning of the concept of *public*, for example, with unintended implications for "public" administration.[42] He points to shifts in movements in the meaning of public and private, e.g., how the concept *public* meant open conversation in the 18th century, whereas now it includes government activities (e.g., military, national security), which are not public in the same sense. The point is that the distinction between public and private, which is important for PA (no less than for the language of economics), is problematic. This gives weight to questions such as, "How can we get PA (public administration) away from confinement to the P (public)?"

Turn now to common-sensical political science talk. First, George Marcus (President of the International Association of Political Psychology, speaking at the APSA training session) described neuroscientific results as showing that it is false to suppose that perceptions yield understandings that are "veridical, comprehensive, capable of instantaneous representation, and able to provide mindful control."[43] (As he explained it, perceptions are preceded by values and are necessary for motivations like survival.) Assume that this claim is itself veridical, etc. If this is so, would this claim be consistent with Michel Foucault's "deconstructive" observations on normalization and the connection between truth and power—fundamentally significant for thinkers about PA and BA bureaucracy? Does it not suggest the desirability of deconstructing the traditional urge for definite easy-to-understand answers? Does it not encourage recognition of the value of "hesitation" in making pronouncements? Does it not suggest the value of appreciating that, in governance and all other areas, there is value in skepticism, and rarely is there ready access to the truth, the whole truth and nothing but the truth?

Second, with regard to the neurophilosophical, the issue of the neural nature of the unified self should be noted. Does that not offer hope of further "filling in" the concept of a person-in-herself in-her-differences, a concept much discussed in the literature on feminism?[44] Surely, this can be filled out better with insights from literatures on pathology of the brain and identity?[45] So, Restak, for instance, claims that knowlege of the human brain is changing our understanding of ourselves and our inter-relationships so dramatically that by mid-century, what he calls "a neurosociety" will emerge.[46]

Third, consider the example of understanding and encouraging extraordinary creativity in governance. Andrew Modell,[47] writing about metaphors and neuroscience, claims that metaphors—which are at the center of the imagination—are not merely figures of speech. They are neural features, the way the brain yields meaning. He emphasizes that "the construction of meaning is very different from the processing of information."[48] For him, the metaphor is the brain's primary mode of understanding and remembering the world.

Fourth, even perception of space is socially constructed. With damage to both sides of the posterior portions of the cortex, some people are still able to see objects, but they cannot see space. As Lynn Robertson puts it, for them there is no "there" there. People with the rare condition of "Balint's syndrome lose explicit spatial awareness but retain spatial information at an implicit level."[49] Others see only part of a space, such as the right side of a picture—parallel to the partial blindness often described for the traditional PA and POLI games. Surely this suggests the value of deconstructing the traditional over-emphasis on things out there, rather than the person?

Neuro-Gov v. Econ Language

To go on to the neuro-economic part of governance, the neural basis of discounting future gains has already been mentioned. While this might encourage deconstructing the over-emphasis on the short term and the micro in the traditional language of PA and BA, it is more symbolic of the concern, expressed by neuro-enthusiasts outside that discipline, over whether construction by neuro-economists confirms, or undermines, economic theory. Yet, the contention in this paper is that neuroscience will eventually prompt insights that will result in significant adjustments even in the language of mainstream economics.

Beyond traditional ideas of time in economics and in such studies as discounting future gains, Chevalier points out that both St. Augustine and Gilles Deleuze view "time as a product of 'narrative contemplation,' a meditative process whereby the past and the future become integral dimensions and contradictions."[50] In a way that is very foreign to economics, he goes on to say that "traces of the past are like scars that mark the passage of time. They are signs not of past wounds but of the present fact of having been wounded."[51] This is the same thinker who writes of the neurological features of explicit-declarative and implicit-emotive memories and remembering. "Different memory functions and interchanges proceed along cortical pathways involving the posterior and anterior lobes and the two hemispheres, but memories are also modulated by sub-cortical and subattentional processing mechanisms."[52] Thus, while philosophy has raised fundamental issues about time,[53] hard science, such as neuroscience, perhaps has the momentum to induce adjustments that philosophy has hitherto failed to generate—even in traditional economics.

Some neuroscientific insights are supportive, while others are disruptive, and the latter should stimulate disciplinary reassessment. To return to a central assumption of economic theory—the idea of rational economic man totally absorbed in optimizing his own utility—on the supportive side, note views about the brain's sensory systems being "narcissistic."[54] On the disruptive side, the idea of rationality is brought into a different perspective by the neuroscientific view that humans are emotional beings who think, rather than thinking beings who have emotions.[55]

Disruptive seems an understatement, because the concept of rational *economic man*—the rational utility optimizer—is so central in mainstream economics, as noted earlier. Economic man is super-rational in the sense that perfect competition can speak of him as having (among other things) full information about the performance and quality of, and the costs of the alternative ways of producing goods and services. In other words, as a buyer, he is not content to purchase the first available product that is satisfactory to him; he wants to optimize, without recognizing bounded rationality.[56] To repeat the claim, neuroscience has the power, in the long run, to act as a catalyst in undermining such disciplinary assumptions.

Neuro-Gov v. Other Languages

Other aspects of neuro-governance, such as governance of the self or even the governance that is represented in religion, should be included. The point is that neuro-governance requires treatment as a whole, and should be open to re-reading and re-writing of common-sensical languages throughout the range.

Return to the self, for instance, and consider neuro-psychology and neuro-psychotherapy. Antonio Damasio re-constructs the word "feelings," correcting the common-sensical. He argues, as James-Lange did before him, that an emotional feeling is identical to the bodily sensation that expresses it; that emotions do not cause bodily symptoms, but vice-versa; and that his theory of emotions can be generalized to all mental states. Damasio claims that of "all the mental phenomena we can describe, feelings and their essential ingredients—pain and pleasure—are the least understood in biological and specifically neurobiological terms."[57] As another and possibly better instance, literature in the neuroscience of psychotherapy suggests that there are attempts to re-write the language of psychotherapy. The sub-title of Cozolino's book, reflecting his re-writing neuroscience project, is "Building and Rebuilding the Human Brain."[58]

Consider, for example, how insights about the self can be gained, for instance, from evolutionary psychology—a combination of evolutionary biology and cognitive psychology. Pinker[59] emphasizes the leading view in evolutionary biology that brain processes consist of many specific-purpose modules that have evolved, rather than a general-purpose problem-solving program. These modules are for specific purposes, such as avoiding dangers and selecting mates. The unconscious role of the amygdala in registering fear has relevance to stereotyping, a topic much discussed in social neuroscience.[60] Unconscious brain preference in selecting mates may have relevance to the insistence on balance in PA and BA organization charts—a lesser example, among many others. Evolutionary biologists describe a preference for body symmetry as an indicator of good genes.

On the neuropsychological features in religious activity, for instance, Persinger tells us that "God experiences are... correlated with transient electrical instabilities within the temporal lobe of the human brain. These temporal lobe transients (TLTs) are normal changes that are precipitated by maturation, personal dilemma, grief, fatigue, and a variety of physiological conditions."[61] Showing the relevance for changing not only the language of religion (if such change is desirable) but also the languages of traditional PA and BA, Persinger goes on to say that "Production of TLTs create an intense sense of meaningfulness, profundity, and conviction."[62] How many TLTs are there among attendees at mainstream meetings of traditional thinkers (e.g., at the American Society for Public Administration), compared with "deviants" at fringe meetings?

EPILOGUE

Neuroscience can be a catalyst in seeking re-unification of the fragmented social sciences (e.g., political science and economics) and social action subjects that concern governance (e.g., public administration and business administration). The study of neuroscience can be used to undermine taken-for-granted concepts that constitute the current fragmented state of the social sciences and social action subjects. This paper recommends *Neuro-Gov*.

Yet the process is evolutionary and longer term. The shorter run can be expected to result in the temporary effect of increasing proliferation. But surely, there is good reason to expect that the catalytic effect of neuroscience will be successful in the longer term. The longer term effect can be hastened (and the shorter term effect lessened) with further research on the catalytic effects of alternative research agendas. Such further research is needed (e.g., in neuro-economics and neuropolitical science) on which agendas would best undermine the language games of existing orthodoxies, e.g. in how best to achieve appropriate research agendas.

Faced by "the bewitchment of our intelligence by misleading common sense,"[63] Ludwig Wittgenstein observes that the aim of philosophy is to "show the fly the way out of the fly-bottle."[64] To release governance flies from their language games, would it not be desirable for more people to turn to such research agendas for *Neuro-Gov*?

REFERENCES

1. WITTGENSTEIN, L.J. 1953. Philosophical Investigations: 105. Macmillan. New York.
2. BEAR, M.F., B.W. CONNERS & M.A. PARADISO. 2007. Neuroscience: Exploring the brain. 3rd edition, 687–723. Lippincott Williams & Wilkins. New York.
3. BEAR, M.F., B.W. CONNERS & M.A. PARADISO. 2007. Neuroscience: Exploring the brain. 3rd edition, 182–183. Lippincott Williams & Wilkins. New York.
4. KLEIN, J.K. 1990. Interdisciplinarity: History, theory, and practice: 21. Wayne State University. Detroit, Michigan.
5. See FARMER, D.J. 2005. To kill the king: Post-traditional governance and bureaucracy. M.E. Sharpe. Armonk, New York.
6. FLEXNER, H. 1979. The curriculum, the disciplines, and interdisciplinarity in higher education. *In* Interdisciplinarity and higher education. J.J. Knockelmans, Ed.: Pp. 84137. University Press: Pennsylvania State University Press. p. 93.
7. KLEIN, J.K. 1990. Interdisciplinarity: History, theory, and practice: 104–105. Wayne State University. Detroit, Michigan.
8. See FARMER, D.J. 1995. The language of public administration: Bureaucracy, modernity, and postmodernity: 218–226. University of Alabama Press. Tuscaloosa, Alabama.
9. WILSON, E.O. 1998. Consilience: The unity of knowledge: 8. Alfred Knopf. New York.
10. KLEIN, J.T. 1990. Interdisciplinarity: History, theory and practice. Wayne State University Press. Detroit, Michigan.
11. FLEXNER, H. 1979. The curriculum, the disciplines, and interdisciplinarity in higher education. *In* Interdisciplinarity and higher education. J.J. Knockelmans, Ed.: 84–101. University Press: Pennsylvania State University Press.
12. CENTER FOR EDUCATION RESEARCH AND INNOVATION (CREI). 1972. Interdisciplinarity: Problems of teaching and research in universities: 35. Organization for Economic Co-operation and Development. Paris, France.
13. FARMER, D.J. 2005. To kill the king: Post-traditional governance and bureaucracy: 26–28. M.E. Sharpe. Armonk, New York.
14. DELEUZE, G. & F. GUATTERI. 1987. A thousand plateaus. University of Minnesota Press. Minneapolis, Minnesota.

15. See MARCUSE, H. 1955. Eros and civilization. Beacon Press. Boston, Massachusetts.
16. See FARMER, R.L., K.J. BENTLEY & J. WALSH. 2006. Advancing social work curriculum in psychopharmacology and medication management. Social Work Educ. **42**: 211–229.
17. See LEDOUX, J. 1996. The emotional brain: The mysterious underpinnings of emotional life. Simon and Schuster. New York.
18. MCDERMOTT, R.J. et al. 2006. What neuroscience has to offer political science. Short course #4. Annual meeting. American Political Science Association. Philadelphia, Pennsylvania.
19. ALFORD, J.R. 2006. Neuroscientific advances in the study of political science. Conference panel. American Political Science Association. Philadelphia, Pennsylvania. September 1.
20. HIBBING, J.R. & J.R. ALFORD. 2006. The neurological basis of representative democracy. Conference paper. American Political Science Association. Philadelphia, Pennsylvania. September 1.
21. SCHIEMANN, J.W. 2006. Neuroscience and analytical narratives. Conference paper. American Political Science Association. Philadelphia, Pennsylvania. September 1.
22. VALK, F.V. & D. PARISI. 2006. Considerations on the neuroscience of power. Conference paper. American Political Science Association. Philadelphia, Pennsylvania. September 1.
23. GLIMCHER, P.W. 2003. Decisions, uncertainty, and the brain: The science of neuroeconomics: 177–178. MIT. Cambridge, Massachusetts.
24. WEBER, E. 2006. Neural substrates of risky decision-making. Conference paper. The Society for Neuroeconomics. Park City, Utah. September 8.
25. CAMPBELL, T. 2006. The neurobiology of intertemporal choice. Conference paper. The Society for Neuroeconomics. Park City, Utah. September 8.
26. KLUCHAREV, V. 2006. Brain mechanisms of persuasion: fMRI study of persuasive nature of advertising. Conference paper. The Society for Neuroeconomics. Park City, Utah. September 9.
27. PHILLIPS, P.E. 2006. Subsecond dopamine release during economic decision making in rodents. Conference paper. The Society for Neuroeconomics. Park City, Utah. September 9.
28. KEPECS, A. 2006. Rats under uncertainty: Orbital frontal neurons support updating of decision strategy. Conference paper. The Society for Neuroeconomics. Park City, Utah. September 10.
29. HARBAUGH, W. 2006. The neural basis of charitable giving. Conference paper. The Society for Neuroeconomics. Park City, Utah. September 10.
30. CHURCHLAND, P.S. 1986. Neurophilosophy. MIT. Cambridge, Massachusetts.
31. CHURCHLAND, P.S. 2002. Brain-wise: Studies in neurophilosophy. MIT. Cambridge, Massachusetts.
32. SINGER, P. 1981. The Expanding circle: Ethics and sociobiology. Farrar, Straus & Giroux. New York.
33. DAWKINS, R. 1976. The selfish gene. Oxford University Press. Oxford, England.
34. DECETY, J. & J.P. KEENAN. 2006. Social neuroscience: A new journal. www.social-neuroscience.com/introduction.asp. Retrieved on July 23, 2006.
35. KREDL, A.C. et al. 2006. The good, the bad and the ugly: An fMRI investigation of the functional anatomic correlates of stigma. Social Neurosci. **1**: 5–15.

36. CHOUCHOURELOU, A. *et al.* 2006. The visual analysis of emotional reactions. Social Neurosci. **1:** 63–74.
37. WITTGENSTEIN, L. 1953. Philosophical Investigations: 3. Macmillan. New York.
38. See FARMER, D.J. 1995. The language of public administration: Bureaucracy, modernity, and postmodernity. University of Alabama Press. Tuscaloosa, Alabama.
39. DECETY, J. & J.P. KEENAN. 2006. Social neuroscience: A new journal. www.social-neuroscience.com/introduction.asp. Retrieved on July 23, 2006.
40. DIAMOND, M.C., A.B. SCHEIBEL & L.M. ELSON. 1985. The human brain coloring book. HarperCollins. New York.
41. See FARMER, D.J. 1997. Derrida, deconstruction, and public administration. Am. Behav. Sci. **41:** 12–27.
42. HABERMAS, J. 1989. The structural transformation of the public sphere: An inquiry into a category of bourgeois society. Trans. Burger, T & Lawrence, F. MIT. Cambridge, Massachusetts.
43. MCDERMOTT, R. *et al.* 2006. What neuroscience has to offer political science. Short course #4. Annual meeting. American Political Science Association. Philadelphia, Pennsylvania.
44. See CIXOUS, H. 1980. The laugh of the Medusa. *In* New French feminisms: An anthology. E. Marks & I. Coutrivron, Eds.: 245–264. University of Massachusetts Press. Massachusetts.
45. See FEINBERG, T.E. & J.P. KEENAN. 2005. The lost self: Pathologies of the brain and identity. Oxford University Press. Oxford.
46. RESTAK, R. 2006. The naked brain: How the emerging neurosociety is changing how we live, work, and love. Harmon Books. New York.
47. MODELL, A.H. 2003. Imagination and the meaningful brain. The MIT Press. Massachusetts.
48. MODELL, A.H. 2003. Imagination and the meaningful brain: 9. The MIT Press. Massachusetts.
49. ROBERTSON, L.C. 2004. Space, objects, minds, and brains: 236. Psychology Press. New York.
50. CHEVALIER, J.M. 2002. Scorpions and the anatomy of time: 164. McGill-Queen's University Press. Canada.
51. CHEVALIER, J.M. 2002. op cit. p. 25.
52. CHEVALIER, J.M. 2002. op cit. p. 26.
53. E.g., MCTAGGART, J.M.E. 1927. The nature of existence. University of Cambridge. Cambridge, England.
54. ATKINS, K. 1996. Of sensory systems and the 'aboutness' of mental states. J. Philos. **93:** 337–372.
55. LEDOUX J. 1996. The emotional brain: The mysterious underpinnings of emotional life. Simon and Schuster. New York.
56. See EARL, P. The legacy of Herbert Simon in economic analysis. Edward Elgar. Massachusetts.
57. DAMASIO, A. 2003. Looking for Spinoza: Joy, sorrow, and the feeling brain: 3. Harcourt. New York.
58. COZOLINO, L.J. 2002. The neuroscience of psychotherapy: Building and rebuilding the human brain. W.W. Norton. New York.
59. PINKER, S. 1997. How the mind works. Norton. New York.
60. ITO, T.A. *et al.* 2006. The social neuroscience of stereotyping and prejudice: Using event-related brain potentials to study social perception. *In* Social Neuroscience:

People thinking about thinking people. J.T. Cacioppo, P.S. Visser & C.L. Pickett, Eds.: 189–208. MIT. Massachusetts.
61. PERSINGER, M.A. 1987. Neuropsychological bases of God beliefs. Praeger. New York. p. x.
62. PERSINGER, M.A. 1987. Neuropsychological bases of God beliefs. Praeger. New York. p. x.
63. WITTGENSTEIN, L. 1953. Philosophical Investigations: 103. Macmillan Press. New York.
64. WITTGENSTEIN, L. 1953. Philosophical Investigations: 105. Macmillan Press. New York.

Fairness and Cooperation Are Rewarding

Evidence from Social Cognitive Neuroscience

GOLNAZ TABIBNIA AND MATTHEW D. LIEBERMAN

The Semel Institute for Neuroscience and Human Behavior, University of California, Los Angeles, Los Angeles, California 90095, USA

> ABSTRACT: To motivate their consumers or employees, corporations often offer monetary incentives, such as cash-back deals or salary bonuses. However, human behavior is not solely driven by material outcome; fairness and equity matter as well. In a recent neuroimaging study, fair offers led to higher happiness ratings and increased activity in several reward regions of the brain compared with unfair offers of equal monetary value. Other neuroimaging studies have similarly shown activation in reward regions in response to cooperative partners or cooperative play. Here, we review these findings and discuss the implications for organizational settings.
>
> KEYWORDS: neuroeconomics; fairness; cooperation; reward; monetary incentives; equity; social factors

INTRODUCTION

Money is widely used as a reward and motivator. Employees are rewarded for good performance by raises in salary or by a bonus, consumers are lured to buy products by cash-back offers and price reductions, and children are coaxed to do unwanted chores by the promise of extra allowance. Although money and other material goods are unquestionably rewarding, in recent years interest has increased in the study of nonmaterial social factors that may also serve as hedonic inputs to individuals' behaviors. These studies have shown that the social context in which material resources are gained also matters. We live in a highly social environment, in which most of the work we do is accomplished through collaboration with others and many of the goods we consume are consumed in the company of others or shared with others. Thus, our labor and the fruits of our labor are differentially satisfying depending on the relative effort exerted and the relative rewards reaped by our peers.

Address for correspondence: Golnaz Tabibnia, The Semel Institute for Neuroscience and Human Behavior, University of California, Los Angeles, 760 Westwood Plaza, C8-532, Los Angeles, CA 90095-1759. Voice: 310-825-9947 (office); fax: 310-825-0812.
golnaz@ucla.edu

The role of money and equity in motivation and welfare has been extensively studied in the past by psychologists, economists, sociologists, and anthropologists, typically through survey methods and behavioral experiments. A number of studies have examined the separate impact of fairness on positive and negative emotions and have found substantial increases in self-rated positive emotions associated with fair treatment, even after controlling for material outcomes.[1-3] In fact, both survey and experimental data indicate that individuals often experience negative emotions if they are the beneficiaries of unfair resource distribution.[4,5] Similarly, voluntary cooperation has been associated with self-reported pleasure and satisfaction.[6,7] Altogether, these studies suggest that fairness and cooperation produce self-reported positive emotions.

Although survey and self-report techniques are important research tools, their value is limited, because participants may not always know or want to disclose the true state of their emotions. Technological advances in neuroimaging, however, have recently allowed for an additional method of studying motivation. Instead of relying on self-report or behavioral measures to gain insight into what people find rewarding, many studies now use functional magnetic resonance imaging (fMRI) to directly peer into the brain and determine which types of incentives activate regions of the brain associated with motivation and reward. In the social cognitive neuroscience approach, neuroimaging techniques are combined with more traditional experimental and survey methods to gain a better understanding of social and affective processes.

In this paper we review studies that employed a social cognitive neuroscience method to investigate the affective impact of fairness and cooperation in collaborative settings. We defined fairness as the equitable distribution of goods or outcomes (e.g., money), and we defined cooperation as doing one's share to maximize public goods rather than working individually to maximize personal goods. In most of these studies, neural activity in each subject was measured during tasks in which the outcome relied on how the subject interacted with a partner. These tasks typically included the ultimatum game, prisoner's dilemma, or trust games. In the following section, we briefly describe each of these tasks. Then, after a brief review of the social cognitive neuroscience approach, we review the findings from neuroimaging studies of fairness and cooperation.

ECONOMIC EXCHANGE GAMES

In the ultimatum game, two players must agree to split a sum of money, known as the stake, or neither player gets anything. The proposer, who is endowed with the stake (e.g., $10), must suggest a way to split it with another player, the responder (e.g., the proposer could offer to give $2 to the responder and keep $8 for himself). If the responder accepts, each player receives the amount allocated by the proposer. If the responder rejects the offer, neither player receives any money. Numerous studies using the ultimatum game have shown that responders do not maximize monetary payoff by accepting every offer; rather, they typically reject unfair offers (<20% of the total stake). These effects occur even when there will be no future interactions with the partner,[8] suggesting that fairness (or unfairness) matters to responders. By examining the responder's brain during presentation of fair or unfair offers, we can gain insight into the type of emotional responses that fairness might elicit.

In the prisoner's dilemma, each of two players independently chooses to cooperate or defect, and each player is paid according to the combination of the two decisions. The four possible combinations are: (1) both players cooperate (CC), (2) player A cooperates and player B defects (CD), (3) player A defects and player B cooperates (DC), or (4) both players defect (DD). The payoffs are arranged such that for player A, DC > CC > DD > CD (e.g., DC = \$3, CC = \$2, DD = \$1, CD = \$0). Critically, no matter how player B responds on a given trial, player A will earn the most if she defects. If player B cooperates, player A earns more by defecting (DC > CC); and if player B defects, player A still earns more by defecting (DD > CD). At the same time, the outcomes are arranged so that the highest earning for the two players combined results from both individuals cooperating (CC + CC > DC + CD > DD + DD). Thus, mutual cooperation is the best strategy for the team collectively, but it requires giving up some personal earnings and potentially a great deal of earnings if the other player defects.

Trust games also tap into cooperation and typically involve two players. The investor is endowed with a sum of money (e.g., \$10) and can either keep it all to herself or turn some or all of it over to the trustee, in which case the trusted money multiplies (e.g., by a factor of three to \$30). At this point, the trustee can either defect and keep the multiplied sum or cooperate and return some (e.g., \$15) to the investor. In single-shot versions of this game, the investor's behavior is a measure of trust, while the trustee's behavior is a measure of trustworthiness and fairness. In iterated versions of the game, both partners' behaviors also measure cooperation.

SOCIAL COGNITIVE NEUROSCIENCE APPROACH

Social cognitive neuroscience[9,10] investigates social psychological phenomena using cognitive neuroscience tools such as neuroimaging and neuropsychological testing of patients with lesions. These tools offer insight into cognitive and affective processes that behavioral or self-report measures alone may not offer. For example, in an fMRI study investigating whether social rejection elicits feelings of pain akin to physical injury, Eisenberger et al.[11] scanned participants who underwent a task during which they were "ditched" by their partners in a ball-tossing game. Compared with nonsocial exclusion (i.e., inability to play because of a computer glitch), social exclusion led to increased activity in dorsal anterior cingulate cortex (ACC), the same brain region that is activated during the psychological distress of physical pain.[12] Self-reported distress after social exclusion correlated positively with ACC activity; however, the main effect of self-reported distress could not be determined because demand characteristics prevented the measurement of self-reported distress after nonsocial exclusion. Thus, not only did fMRI provide a measure of distress that would have been difficult to collect through self-report, it also further elucidated the nature of the distress by revealing common processes underlying social and physical pain.

The social cognitive neuroscience approach relies in part on prior knowledge about functional neuroanatomy. Although a given brain region generally is not exclusively involved in a single process, some patterns of results have emerged from prior research that more strongly implicate certain regions in positive emotions and other regions in negative emotions. The part of the brain most commonly associated with reward is the striatum, including the caudate, and particularly the ventral striatum, a region receiving rich dopaminergic input from the midbrain that is involved in positive reinforcement and reward-based learning.[13,14] The ventral striatum is thought to function together with the amygdala and regions of the orbital and medial prefrontal cortex (PFC) in a reward network,[15,16] with the amygdala coding intensity of reward and the orbitofrontal cortex (OFC) determining valence.[17] A proposed mediolateral distinction in the OFC suggests that medial portions of this region tend to decode rewarding reinforcers, and lateral regions monitor punishing reinforcers.[18] The ventromedial prefrontal cortex (VMPFC) seems particularly involved in preference (e.g., for a preferred brand of drinks).[19,20]

The canonical brain region associated with negative emotional processes, particularly fear, is the amygdala.[21] However, an increasing number of studies now link this region to positive affective processes as well,[22] such as viewing attractive faces.[23] Activity in the anterior insula has also been associated with aversive experiences, such as exposure to a disgusting odor or taste,[24,25] although this region is more generally regarded as the primary sensory cortex for visceral information, including autonomic arousal.[26] The dorsal ACC is another region commonly associated with unpleasant experiences, such as the emotional aspect of physical[12] and social[11] pain. The rostral ACC, on the other hand, has been associated with induced emotions of positive or negative valence.[27]

Notwithstanding the advantages of a social cognitive neuroscience approach, it is important to note that a reverse inference problem exists with studies inferring a cognitive or affective process from neural activation.[28,29] Specifically, because each brain region is involved in more than one process, we cannot confidently infer from the observation of increased signal in a region that activity in that region evoked one mental process rather than another. However, our confidence in the reverse inference could be increased in two ways:

(1) convergence of evidence from multiple techniques and (2) activations in two or more regions thought to underlie the same mental process, particularly if those regions are known to work together in a network.

FAIRNESS IS REWARDING

Numerous behavioral and self-report studies using the ultimatum game have established that people dislike unfair treatment. For example, as stinginess of an offer relative to the stake size increases, a self-reported feeling of contempt also increases, as does the likelihood to reject the offer.[30] Similarly, unfair offers that are rejected tend to elicit activity in the anterior insula, and the more likely a person is to reject unfair offers, the more activity this insula region exhibits.[30,31]

Although evidence suggests that receiving an unfair proposal may be related to negative emotional responses, until recently it was unclear whether fair offers produced positive emotional responses beyond those associated with the monetary payoff that is associated with fair offers. In everyday life, being treated more equitably by another person in financial transactions is typically confounded with better financial outcomes for oneself. To control for monetary payoff, we varied both the offer amount and the stake size across trials,[30] such that the same offer amount could appear as a large percentage of the total stake ($2 out of $4), and therefore fair, or as a small percentage of the total stake ($2 out of $10), and therefore unfair. If fair treatment is experienced as rewarding, then people should report more happiness with a fair offer compared with an unfair offer of the same monetary value. Similarly, brain regions associated with reward should be more active during fair treatment than during unfair treatment, after controlling for monetary payoff. Indeed, we found that fair offers led to higher happiness ratings and increased activity in several reward regions of the brain, including the ventral striatum, OFC, VMPFC, and left amygdala, compared with unfair proposals of equal monetary value.

Fairness can be experienced either directly, by fair behavior from one's partner, or indirectly, when an unfair partner is punished. Punishment of an unfair partner in effect brings about justice and greater equality in outcome. In an fMRI study of the trust game,[32] investors were given the opportunity to punish uncooperative and selfish trustees. Deciding to punish a selfish partner by removing some of his or her earnings increased activity in the caudate nucleus—even though the participant did not gain any money by punishing. Moreover, increased activity in this region was associated with harsher punishments. As the authors explained, given the role of this region in processing accruing rewards for goal-directed actions, these results suggest that people derive satisfaction from implementing justice and maintaining fairness by punishing unfair partners.

This indirect pleasure of fairness was also investigated in a creative study by Singer and colleagues,[33] who studied empathy toward former interaction partners who had played fairly or unfairly. In this study, participants played the ultimatum game with a fair and an unfair proposer. Later, while in the MRI scanner, participants watched as each partner appeared to receive painful stimuli. While viewing fair partners who appeared to be in pain, men and women both exhibited increased activity in insular and anterior cingulate regions, suggesting an empathic response for pain. This finding suggests that people like and are sympathetic toward those who have previously treated them fairly. Interestingly, Singer *et al.* also found that when men (but not women) watched *unfair* proposers receive pain, activity increased in reward regions, such as the ventral striatum. This latter finding shows that the establishment of justice, through punishment of unfair behavior, may elicit positive feelings.

COOPERATION IS REWARDING

The first fMRI study of cooperation, in the trust game, was by McCabe and colleagues[34] who instructed participants to play as the investor in half the games and as the trustee in the other half. Although the study was designed to identify prefrontal regions associated with theory of mind, rather than to link reward with cooperation, it is worth mentioning that the investigators found increased activity in the medial thalamus and right medial frontal pole, during decisionmaking in cooperative players when they played against humans rather than computers. Although neither region is uniquely linked to reward, the thalamus is considered part of the emotion network known as the limbic system, and the right medial PFC, though primarily involved in cognitive integration,[35] has also been associated with approach-related behaviors.[14] These results are not inconsistent with the premise that cooperation has an affective component.

Decety and colleagues[36] were the first to explicitly link cooperation with reward-related neural activity. Rather than using an economic exchange paradigm, the authors used a specially designed computer game in which a participant in the MRI scanner had to arrange a visual pattern following certain rules, in cooperation with another player, in competition with another player, or alone. Compared with working alone, cooperation and competition both led to increased activity in the anterior insula, potentially reflecting increased autonomic arousal. Importantly, cooperation led to more activity in medial OFC than competition, suggesting that cooperation is a rewarding process.

In an innovative fMRI study by King-Casas and colleagues,[37] the brains of investors and fellow trustees were simultaneously scanned, or "hyperscanned," while they played an iterated version of the trust game with each other. Because participants played multiple rounds with one another, the investigators were able to study the development of trust over time, behaviorally and neurally. They found that trustees cooperated depending on their partner's "reputation" or behavior on previous rounds. When an investor was generous following a defection by the trustee, the trustee rewarded this benevolent reciprocity with a larger repayment. Similarly, when an investor was stingy following cooperation by the trustee, the trustee punished this malevolent reciprocity by reducing the repayment. In the trustee's brain, the only region that was more active during benevolent reciprocity than malevolent reciprocity was the caudate nucleus, a region implicated in reward-based learning. Furthermore, the magnitude of this response correlated with the amount repaid by the trustee. The authors interpreted activity in this region as the response to perceived fairness of the partner's behavior, as well as the intention to cooperate and repay benevolent behavior with trust.

Mutual cooperation has been linked with reward-related neural response during other tasks as well. In an iterated version of the prisoner's dilemma in female participants, the ventral striatum, rostral ACC, and medial OFC were activated more by mutual cooperation outcomes than by outcomes of equal monetary payment in a nonsocial context.[38] Consistent with King-Casas et al.,[37] they also found neural overlap between the pleasure of being treated fairly and that associated with the intention to cooperate; activity in rostral ACC and ventral striatum also increased during the part of the trial when participants decided to cooperate, prior to finding out the outcome of the trial. Thus the reward of behaving cooperatively may be intertwined with the reward of receiving cooperative treatment. Rilling and colleagues[39] replicated these results in a subsequent study using the single-shot version of the prisoner's dilemma, in which they found neural activity in VMPFC and ventral striatum to increase with reciprocated and decrease with unreciprocated cooperation.

In an interesting version of the trust game, Delgado et al.[40] influenced investors' decisions by giving them character descriptions of fictitious trustees who were depicted as either noble, neutral, or of questionable moral character (i.e., good, neutral, or bad). Despite equivalent repayment by all trustees, participants tended to trust the good trustees the most. Consistent with previous studies suggesting that cooperation is rewarding, deciding to "share" (i.e., trust) versus "keep" increased activity in the ventral striatum and anterior insula. Interestingly, the opposite comparison did not activate any reward regions, despite the fact that keeping an endowment is a guaranteed monetary payoff. Further analyses indicated that the increased striatal response during share versus keep decisions occurred only with bad or neutral partners, suggesting greater reliance on reward-based learning with ambiguous partners than with partners who have already left a good impression.

This is not to say, however, that being around cooperative and moral people is not rewarding. The pleasure of being exposed to cooperative people was directly studied by Singer and colleagues,[41] who showed participants the faces of partners who had cooperated or defected in multiple rounds of the prisoner's dilemma they had played together earlier. To vary moral responsibility, some partners were introduced as "intentional agents," who freely chose whether to cooperate, and some as "nonintentional agents," who had no choice. Faces of cooperators, regardless of intention, were rated as more likable than neutral faces; and faces of defectors, particularly intentional defectors, were rated as less likable than neutral faces. Viewing faces of intentional cooperators activated bilateral insula, bilateral OFC, bilateral ventral striatum, and left amygdala. Although this study was not optimally designed for examination of responses to faces of defectors, we do know from an earlier study that, as expected, faces of people judged to be untrustworthy activate bilateral amygdala.[42] Thus, positive feelings (and absence of negative feelings) seem not only to be associated with receiving fair treatment and with cooperation, but also with the people who are cooperative and trustworthy.

IMPLICATIONS AND CONCLUSION

Multiple studies have demonstrated that, even without additional monetary gain, fairness or cooperation leads to self-reported, behavioral, and neural evidence of reward. Until recently, studies of the emotional impact of fairness and cooperation relied mainly on behavioral and self-report techniques, which limited ways in which positive emotional experience could be measured. For example, in studies of the ultimatum game, the emotional experience of the responder has often been inferred from his tendency to reject unfair offers; this rejection is thought to reflect unhappiness with unfair offers. However, the opposite side of the coin, happiness as a result of fair offers, has typically been ignored in these studies. Thus, investigations of emotion in economic exchange often focused on the aversive aspects of unfairness and defection, rather than the rewarding aspects of fairness and cooperation.

The tendency for people to prefer equity and resist unfair outcomes and partners is deeply rooted. This "inequity aversion" is so strong that individuals are willing to sacrifice personal gain to prevent another person from receiving an inequitably better outcome.[43] Inequity aversion plays an important role in organizational settings. Perceived inequity in income or exerted effort can dampen employee morale and performance.[6,44,45] Conversely, perceived equity may have the opposite effect and improve employee morale.

Why would humans be built to be sensitive to fairness? It has been suggested that forming secure social bonds is a fundamental human need.[46] Humans have evolved to operate socially, from infancy, when the social connection to parents is critical for survival; to childhood, when learning is accelerated by the transmission of accumulated human knowledge; and to adulthood, when access to food and mating partners depends on social inclusion. Cues that indicate social acceptance may thus be highly rewarding because of the other resources to which they facilitate one's access. Being treated fairly by others may serve as a strong cue of acceptance and thus come to be experienced as intrinsically rewarding in itself.

Consistent with the idea that fairness and cooperation are intrinsically rewarding, the reinforcing effects of fair treatment and cooperation seem to be both ubiquitous and primitive. Fairness preference is evident across cultures[47] and in children,[48] and even capuchin monkeys seem to compare payoffs with peers and react negatively when a peer is rewarded more handsomely for the same effort (see also 49).[50] Recent evidence also suggests that fairness preference may be partly heritable.[51] There is also evidence that rodents prefer cooperation to working in isolation for the same reward.[52] Thus, it is possible that social reinforcers, such as fair treatment and cooperation, are more likely to increase intrinsic motivation, whereas monetary payoff tends to elicit extrinsic motivation. Previous work has shown that increased intrinsic motivation predicts better job performance and satisfaction.[53,54]

Similarly, given that fairness and cooperation lead to increased activity in brain areas associated with reward and positive reinforcement learning, it is conceivable that a work environment imbued with camaraderie and fairness would motivate and mobilize employees to continue the hard work that has been so rewarded. Consistent with this idea, in a behavioral study of the ultimatum game, proposers who reported greater pleasure associated with fairness than with payoffs were more likely than other players to cooperate and give fair offers.[7]

Perceived fairness may also have a profound impact on consumer satisfaction,[55] one of the indicators of a company's health. A recent meta-analysis indicated that, among several predictors of customer satisfaction, equity (fairness judgment in reference to what other consumers receive) was most strongly related to satisfaction.[56]

In short, this review supports the notion that money is not the only motivator. At some level, this is obvious: various maxims have been passed down over centuries warning of the shortcomings of material wealth (e.g., "money can't buy happiness"), and no one would argue that people care about being treated fairly. However, it is rare that issues of fairness and cooperation figure into discussions of promoting organizational productivity and corporate earnings. Nations measure gross domestic product, economists measure consumer confidence, corporations calculate net worth, and employees are keenly aware of their salaries, often with an underlying assumption that these numbers indicate something about public welfare and individual well-being. Surely, these factors play an important part in well-being; however, the fact that fairness and cooperation activate the same hedonic regions of the brain as financial gain is an indication that these factors may merit equal consideration in the structuring of organizational settings.

REFERENCES

1. TYLER, T.R. 1984. The role of perceived injustice in defendants' evaluations of their courtroom experience. Law Society Rev. **18**: 51–74.

2. DE CREMER, D. & H.J.E.M. ALBERTS. 2004. When procedural fairness does not influence how positive I feel: the effects of voice and leader selection as a function of belongingness need. Euro. J. Soc. Psych. **34:** 333–344.
3. HEGTVEDT, K.A. & C. KILLIAN. 1999. Fairness and emotions: reactions to the process and outcomes of negotiations. Social Forces **78:** 269–303.
4. ALESINA, A. et al. 2004. Inequality and happiness: are Europeans and Americans different? J. Public Econ. **88:** 2009–2042.
5. KREHBIEL, P.J. & R. CROPANZANO. 2000. Procedural justice, outcome favorability and emotion. Soc. Justice Res. **13:** 339–360.
6. GÄCHTER, S. & E. FEHR. 2001. Fairness in the labour market? A survey of experimental results. In Surveys in Experimental Economics, Bargaining, Cooperation and Election Stock Markets: 95–132. F. Bolle & M. Lehmann-Waffenschmidt, Eds. Physica Verlag. Heidelberg.
7. HASELHUHN, M.P. & B.A. MELLERS. 2005. Emotions and cooperation in economic games. Brain Res. Cogn. Brain Res. **23:** 24–33.
8. GÜTH, W. et al. 1982. An experimental analysis of ultimatum bargaining. J. Econ. Beh. Organization **3:** 367–388.
9. LIEBERMAN, M.D. 2007. Social cognitive neuroscience: a review of core processes. Annu. Rev. Psych. **58:** 259–289.
10. OCHSNER, K.N. & M.D. LIEBERMAN. 2001. The emergence of social cognitive neuroscience. Am. Psychol. **56:** 717–734.
11. EISENBERGER, N.I. et al. 2003. Does rejection hurt? An fMRI study of social exclusion. Science **302:** 290–292.
12. RAINVILLE, P. et al. 1997. Pain affect encoded in human anterior cingulate but not somatosensory cortex. Science **277:** 968–971.
13. SCHULTZ, W. 2004. Neural coding of basic reward terms of animal learning theory, game theory, microeconomics and behavioural ecology. Curr. Opin. Neurobiol. **14:** 139–147.
14. WAGER, T.D. et al. 2003. Valence, gender, and lateralization of functional brain anatomy in emotion: a meta-analysis of findings from neuroimaging. Neuroimage **19:** 513–31.
15. TREPEL, C. et al. 2005. Prospect theory on the brain? Toward a cognitive neuroscience of decision under risk. Brain Res. Cogn. Brain Res. **23:** 34–50.
16. CARDINAL, R.N. et al. 2002. Emotion and motivation: the role of the amygdala, ventral striatum, and prefrontal cortex. Neurosci. Biobeh. Rev. **26:** 321–352.
17. ANDERSON, A.K. et al. 2003. Dissociated neural representations of intensity and valence in human olfaction. Nat. Neurosci. **6:** 196–202.
18. KRINGELBACH, M.L. & E.T. ROLLS. 2004. The functional neuroanatomy of the human orbitofrontal cortex: evidence from neuroimaging and neuropsychology. Prog. Neurobiol. **72:** 341–372.
19. MCCLURE, S.M. et al. 2004. Neural correlates of behavioral preference for culturally familiar drinks. Neuron **44:** 379–387.
20. DEPPE, M. 2005. Nonlinear responses within the medial prefrontal cortex reveal when specific implicit information influences economic decision making. J. Neuroimaging **15:** 171–182.
21. LEDOUX, J.E. 2000. Emotion circuits in the brain. Annu. Rev. Neurosci. **23:** 155–184.
22. BAXTER, M.G. & E.A. MURRAY. 2002. The amygdala and reward. Nat. Rev. Neurosci. **3:** 563–573.

23. WINSTON, J.S. et al. 2007. Brain systems for assessing facial attractiveness. Neuropsychologia **45**: 195–206.
24. WICKER, B. et al. 2003. Both of us disgusted in my insula: the common neural basis of seeing and feeling disgust. Neuron **40**: 655–664.
25. NITSCHKE, J.B. et al. 2006. Functional neuroanatomy of aversion and its anticipation. Neuroimage **29**: 106–116.
26. CRAIG, A.D. 2002. How do you feel? Interoception: the sense of the physiological condition of the body. Nat. Rev. Neurosci. **3**: 655–666.
27. BUSH, G. et al. 2000. Cognitive and emotional influences in anterior cingulate cortex. Trends Cogn. Sci. **4**: 215–222.
28. POLDRACK, R.A. 2006. Can cognitive processes be inferred from neuroimaging data? Trends Cogn. Sci. **10**: 59–63.
29. SARTER, M. et al. 1996. Brain imaging and cognitive neuroscience: toward strong inference in attributing function to structure. Am. Psychol. **51**: 13–21.
30. TABIBNIA, G. et al. 2007. The sunny side of fairness: Preference for fairness activates reward circuitry (and disregarding unfairness activates self-control circuitry). Psychol. Sci., in press.
31. SANFEY, A.G. et al. 2003. The neural basis of economic decision-making in the Ultimatum Game. Science **300**: 1755–1758.
32. DE QUERVAIN, D.J. et al. 2004. The neural basis of altruistic punishment. Science **305**: 1254–1258.
33. SINGER, T. et al. 2006. Empathic neural responses are modulated by the perceived fairness of others. Nature **439**: 466–469.
34. MCCABE, K. et al. 2001. A functional imaging study of cooperation in two-person reciprocal exchange. Proc. Natl. Acad. Sci. USA **98**: 11832–11835.
35. RAMNANI, N. & A.M. OWEN. 2004. Anterior prefrontal cortex: insights into function from anatomy and neuroimaging. Nat. Rev. Neurosci. **5**: 184–194.
36. DECETY, J. et al. 2004. The neural bases of cooperation and competition: an fMRI investigation. Neuroimage **23**: 744–751.
37. KING-CASAS, B. et al. 2005. Getting to know you: reputation and trust in a two-person economic exchange. Science **308**: 78–83.
38. RILLING, J.K. et al. 2002. Neural basis of social cooperation. Neuron **35**: 395–405.
39. RILLING, J.K. et al. 2004. Opposing BOLD responses to reciprocated and unreciprocated altruism in putative reward pathways. Neuroreport **15**: 2539–2543.
40. DELGADO, M.R. et al. 2005. Perceptions of moral character modulate the neural systems of reward during the trust game. Nat. Neurosci. **8**: 1611–1618.
41. SINGER, T. et al. 2004. Brain responses to the acquired moral status of faces. Neuron **19**: 653–662.
42. WINSTON, J.S. et al. 2002. Automatic and intentional brain responses during evaluation of trustworthiness of faces. Nat. Neurosci. **3**: 277–283.
43. FEHR, E. & K.M. SCHMIDT. 1999. A theory of fairness, competition, and cooperation. Quart. J. Econ. **114**: 817–868.
44. BEWLEY, T.F. 1999. Why Wages Don't Fall During a Recession. Harvard University Press. Cambridge.
45. GREENBERG, J. 1993. The social side of fairness: interpersonal classes of organizational justice. *In* Justice in the Workplace. R. Cropanzano, Ed. Erlbaum. Hillsdale, NJ.
46. BAUMEISTER, R.F. & M.R. LEARY. 1995. The need to belong: desire for interpersonal attachments as a fundamental human motivation. Psych. Bull. **117**: 497–529.

47. HENRICH, J. *et al.* 2006. Costly punishment across human societies. Science **312:** 1767–1770.
48. MURNIGHAN, J.K. & M.S. SAXON. 1998. Ultimatum bargaining by children and adults. J. Econ. Psych. **19:** 415–445.
49. JENSEN, K. *et al.* 2007. Chimpanzees are rational maximizers in an ultimatum game. Science **318:** 107–109.
50. BROSNAN, S.F. & F.B. DE WAAL. 2003. Monkeys reject unequal pay. Nature **425:** 297–299.
51. WALLACE, B. *et al.* 2007. Heritability of ultimatum game responder behavior. Proc. Natl. Acad. Sci. USA **104:** 15631–15634.
52. SCHUSTER, R. & A. PERELBERG. 2004. Why cooperate? An economic perspective is not enough. Behav. Process. **66:** 261–277.
53. BAARD, P.P. *et al.* 2004. Intrinsic need satisfaction: a motivational basis of performance and well-being in two work settings. J. Appl. Soc. Psych. **34:** 2045–2068.
54. LEPPER, M. *et al.* 1973. Undermining children's intrinsic interest with extrinsic rewards: a test of the overjustification hypothesis. J. Pers. Soc. Psych. **28:** 129–137.
55. SWAN, J.E. & R.L. OLIVER. 1985. Automobile buyer satisfaction with the salesperson related to equity and disconfirmation. *In* Consumer Satisfaction, Dissatisfaction and Complaining Behavior. H.K. Hunt & R.L. Day, Eds. Indiana University Press. Bloomington.
56. SZYMANSKI, D.M. & D.H. HENARD. 2001. Customer Satisfaction: a meta-analysis of the empirical evidence. J. Acad. Market. Sci. **29:** 16–35.

Neural Correlates of Corporate Camaraderie and Teamwork

CATHERINE LEVINE

The Miami Project to Cure Paralysis, University of Miami Miller School of Medicine, Miami, Florida 33136, USA

ABSTRACT: Corporate citizenship creates an ethical and professional accountability among the employee, the organization, and the outside market. Teamwork is an essential part of this corporate accountability because it increases communication and confidence within the organization and promotes camaraderie and goal completion. Cognitive neuroscience research has been able to localize socialization to various areas of the limbic system, which includes, among other structures, the hypothalamus and amygdala, and is associated with the prefrontal cortex. These neurocortical areas can be monitored while set tasks are performed experimentally or observed naturally. Within the framework of cognitive neuroscience, one can evaluate the neural architecture involved in various states of organizational behavior. One can then use this framework as an overlay in the corporate environment to track project completion and profitability.

KEYWORDS: cognitive neuroscience; physiological benefits; stress; teamwork; workplace

INTRODUCTION

In corporate culture, the Darwin-like instinct is to work toward one's own professional goals without taking time out for social bonding beyond what is absolutely necessary.[1,2] With the adaptation of an attitude of corporate citizenry fueled by socially conscious business practices and organizational human relations, this instinct can essentially build camaraderie and effective teams.[3–6] Camaraderie in the workplace is often an overlooked area of research and not seen as an innate manifestation of human nature because, after all, how can this bonding behavior with one's peers contribute to increased productivity, increased profits, and even a promotion?[7,8]

Previous work in various milieus of psychology and sociology[9–11] has studied different aspects of positive and negative sensory inputs as they affect the

Address for correspondence: Catherine Levine, The Miami Project to Cure Paralysis, Lois Pope LIFE Center, University of Miami Miller School of Medicine, 1095 NW 14th Terrace, Miami, Florida 33136.
clevine@med.miami.edu

individual and his or her professional performance in the corporate environment.

Also, advanced noninvasive neuroimaging technology, such as positron emission tomography (PET) and functional magnetic resonance imaging (fMRI), has allowed for the localization of activity in various parts of the brain through accompanying changes in cerebral blood flow. These methods can track such changes while the individual is awake and completes given tasks. The correlation between neural activity in distinct parts of the brain during specific behaviors forms the basis of cognitive neuroscience.

Cognitive neuroscience studies have identified the limbic system, which Broca in 1878 termed "le grand lobe limbique," to control decision making, stress regulation, and emotions through the orbitofrontal cortex, hypothalamus, and amygdala, respectively.[12–15] The amygdala is also involved in the sequence of appetitive, also known as positive, conditioning to particular stimuli. Both positive and negative stressors in the workplace will cause a response from the limbic system.[16–18]

Stress, defined as any perturbation of homeostasis, whether emotional or physical, can take place at any time and have various manifestations.[19] The stress system that is activated in the brain and controls neural systems to adjust to the stressful situation are regulated by two main neuroendocrine hormones, corticotropin-releasing hormone (CRH), produced in the paraventricular nucleus of the hypothalamus, and vasopressin (AVP), also produced by the hypothalamus.[14,15] An excess of negative stressors can cause multiple neurochemical imbalances, which in turn disrupts an individual's ability to function to his or her full potential. In fiscal terms, occupational stress costs 10% of the gross domestic product annually in the United States.[19,20]

Correlation of the neurophysiological benefits or even physiological benefits of workplace teamwork first involves evaluating the different types of teams that can be present in a corporate environment and how they are either stressful or beneficial to the individual or organization. A team can be defined as a group of people who are interdependent and have the common goal of achieving a specific task. With this definition, the common goal is the key, whether it is winning a game or marketing a new product. In the corporate environment new challenges are being placed on team members, but these challenges also bring advantages. Because of globalization, there are multicultural and multigenerational participants with various skills in each team. This configuration allows virtual interaction, increased communication, and interdisciplinary knowledge, as well as bringing the challenge of mutual understanding and compromise for achieving the common goal.[21–23]

In his study of teamwork and team building, West identifies three components of team effectiveness. These are task effectiveness, team member well-being, and team viability, all being equally important for the functioning of the team and achieving the common goal. Teams work within a larger social group, and each member needs to be sensitive to the psychological needs of the other members and the skills that each member brings to the group. Here there is an emphasis on deliberate cooperation, and ultimately the team's decisions will either provide gains for the organizational process or hinder it. Both social factors and the type of task presented to the team for completion influence these components.

Task effectiveness deals directly with the objectives of the task. A work or management team needs to define and prioritize each aspect of a task, ensuring that each step is in line with the final goal. The current situation needs to be assessed, and each person's resources can then be used appropriately.

Team member well-being is concerned with the mental health of each member of the team; this concept includes workplace stressors, such as hours worked, or physiological stress, such as increased physical pain (e.g., headache). The well-being of team members also deals with feelings of personal development and work satisfaction. All members of the team must feel that they are contributing fully to the goal. An ongoing communication schema can contribute to achieving feelings of well-being among team members.

Related to the previous two components, the third aspect of team effectiveness is team viability. Ideally, there should be a certain level of probability (undefined) that the team will continue to work together effectively.[24-27]

Teams have different ratings as far as mental health linked with stress. Affective reactions in the workplace, such as job satisfaction, have for several decades been linked to somatic symptoms such as headaches. Spector raises an insightful discussion of stressors in the work environment and how they can be studied. Spector's work emphasized a key pitfall in the study of workplace stress that had manifested not physiologically but psychologically: It is gauged by the subject's perceptions rather than a measured outcome. There may also be elements of reverse causality with these perceptions, such as a negative outcome causing a person to perceive a business environment as stressful.[11] Also, this study accounted for health symptoms as they were related to job stressors through a self-report of nausea, backache, headache, eye strain, and fatigue. Although various correlative studies have been done, one can draw greater insight from long-term (i.e., >10 years) studies where other influential health factors are considered when measuring mental health or physical stress. In a *New England Journal of Medicine* study that tracked participants for more than 20 years, positive mental health did have a statistically significantly positive effect on physical health.[28]

Here I will explore multiple aspects of positive social bonding leading to camaraderie in the workplace, including various benefits to the cooperative and the individual. These benefits include individual gains, such as the reduction of physiological stressors, an increase in internal motivation, job satisfaction, and the building of skill sets and benefits to the cooperative, such as increased performance quality and productivity for the organization,[29,30] which can be implemented in the corporate culture.

ORIGINS OF NEURAL CORRELATIONS WITH ORGANIZATIONAL SOCIAL BEHAVIOR

The theories showing parallels between the body and mind processes and physical action and reaction are not new. Nobelist Gerald Edelman reminds us in *Bright Air, Brilliant Fire* of the seminal studies of French philosopher René Descartes (1596–1650), who believed in the concept of dualism consisting of *res extensa* (extended things) and *res cogitans* (thinking things). Descartes asserted that the pineal gland was where interactions between *res cogitans* and *res extensa* occurred and therefore where the mind and body interacted. Team member well-being would be of continuing concern to Descartes because his seminal studies parallel the goals of modern social cognitive neuroscience. The same is true of Nobelist Roger Walcott Sperry (1913–1994).

With the rise of the study of physiology in the late 19th century, studying correlates between psychology and biology became more feasible, what Edelman describes as "putting the mind back into nature." Edelman also recalls the ideas of the physiological psychologist William James (1842–1910), reminding us that the mind is a "process, not a stuff." This quotation refers to the concept that the mind is more than a physical structure but rather a scheme or arrangement of matter with many capabilities governed by the nervous system. James trained at the University of Leipzig with famed German physiological psychologist Wilhelm Max Wundt (1832–1920), who founded the first psychological laboratory and later the first psychological journal in 1881, *Philosophische Studien.*

One can overlay the work of Jean Piaget (1896–1980), who studied thought processes in children and cognitive development, to various aspects of a successful task effectiveness. For example, each individual is actually evaluated by the team leader before a decision can be made about what role would be best suited for that member to complete his or her portion of the task.[2,31–33]

CORPORATE NEURAL DARWINISM

Just as there is a mapped-out structure in the neural environment, a mapped-out structure in the corporate environment is equally valuable. In emotion research there is currently a drive to understand emotion perception and its relation to neural networks. There is an importance of social bonding in corporate culture, as defined by forming business relationships that are productive in nature on the basis of constructive competitiveness. The innate response in the workplace is to compete with one's peers for the highest sales, the most clients, the best market area, and even time and recognition from upper management. Negative workplace competition can be counterproductive and can be more harmful than beneficial, because in such an environment people spend more time and mental energy on personal failures.[34–37]

Corporate human relations parallels set and plastic structures and networks because human emotions are continuously being affected by environmental stressors. Personal introspection and cognitive appraisal can allow an individual to best handle external stress. Teamwork in turn provides a support system where discourse and problem solving are facilitated, thereby reducing workplace stress.[38,39]

FUTURE DIRECTIONS

Future research includes a continuing analysis of developments regarding the neurophysiological origins of behavior and the beneficial function of integrating teamwork into the corporate environment. These benefits include individual gains, such as the reduction of physiological stressors, an increase in internal motivation, job satisfaction, and the building of skill sets, as well as various benefits to the cooperative, such as increased performance quality, productivity, and profit margin.

Corporate awareness of these positive aspects of camaraderie as a stress reducer and empowerment tool for the individual worker can allow companies to implement tools to promote both teamwork and positive professional relationships in the workplace.

Through an accurate and detailed review of original scientific research in business psychology, organizational behavior, and neurobiology, and implementing innovative research methods in applied social cognitive neuroscience, one can achieve an interdisciplinary appreciation and understanding of this field.

Considerable effort will need to be taken to combine studies of brain activity paired with emotional responses, including the limits and challenges involved with measurement issues of emotion research, such as grading the level of teamwork and job satisfaction, correlated with measurable outcomes, such as performance or learned skills. In this respect, cognitive neuroscience provides a rich environment to pair stimuli with outcome on the corporate level.[40]

Going forward in organizational cognitive neuroscience raises the neurobiological question of the plasticity of neurons, which is also a prominent uncertainty in regenerative neurobiology.[34,41,42] One can only speculate how the knowledge of neural plasticity as it affects behavior will shape the human drive and motivation in the professional setting.

ACKNOWLEDGMENTS

I thank my colleagues at the University of Miami Miller School of Medicine.

REFERENCES

1. BURKE, E.M. 2005. Managing a company in an activist world: the leadership challenge of corporate citizenship. Praeger. Westport, Conn.
2. EDELMAN, G.M. 1992. Bright air, brilliant fire: on the matter of the mind. BasicBooks. New York, NY.
3. CUMMINGS, L.L. & W.E. SCOTT. 1969. Readings in organizational behavior and human performance. R. D. Irwin. Homewood, Ill.
4. GLAZEBROOK, M. 2005. The Social Construction of Corporate Citizenship. The Journal of Corporate Citizenship **17**: 53–67.
5. REECE, B.L. & R. BRANDT. 2005. Effective human relations: personal and organizational applications. Houghton Mifflin. Boston.
6. WADDOCK, S. 2004. Creating corporate accountability: Foundational principles to make corporate citizenship real. Journal of Business Ethics **50**: 313–327.
7. ALLEN, D. 2001. Getting things done: the art of stress-free productivity. Viking. New York.
8. ROBBINS, H., M. FINLEY & H. ROBBINS. 2000. The new why teams don't work: what goes wrong and how to make it right. Berrett-Koehler Publishers. San Francisco.
9. JAMAL, M. 1984. Job stress and job performance controversy: An empirical assessment. Organizational Behavior and Human Performance **33**: 1–21.
10. KELLOWAY, E.K. & J. BARLING. 1991. Job characteristics, role stress and mental health. Journal of Occupational Psychology **64**: 291–304.
11. SPECTOR, P.E., D.J. DWYER & S.M. JEX. 1988. Relation of job stressors to affective, health, and performance outcomes: a comparison of multiple data sources. J. Appl. Psychol. **73**: 11–19.
12. ADOLPHS, R. et al. 1994. Impaired recognition of emotion in facial expressions following bilateral damage to the human amygdala. Nature **372**: 669–672.
13. BROCA, P. 1878. Anatomie comparée des circonvolutions cérébrales: le grand lobe limbique. Rev. Anthropol. **1**: 385–498.
14. DE KLOET, E.R. 2004. Hormones and the stressed brain. Ann. N. Y. Acad. Sci. **1018**: 1–15.
15. DE KLOET, E.R., M. JOELS & F. HOLSBOER. 2005. Stress and the brain: from adaptation to disease. Nat. Rev. Neurosci. **6**: 463–475.
16. BALLEINE, B.W. & S. KILLCROSS. 2006. Parallel incentive processing: an integrated view of amygdala function. Trends Neurosci. **29**: 272–279.
17. MEDFORD, N. et al. 2005. Emotional memory: separating content and context. Psychiatry Res. **138**: 247–258.
18. PATON, J.J. et al. 2006. The primate amygdala represents the positive and negative value of visual stimuli during learning. Nature **439**: 865–870.
19. CHROUSOS, G.P. & P.W. GOLD. 1992. The concepts of stress and stress system disorders. Overview of physical and behavioral homeostasis. JAMA **267**: 1244–1252.
20. MCKENNA, E.F. 2006. Business psychology and organisational behaviour: a student's handbook. Psychology Press. New York, NY.
21. NORMAN, E. 2000. Resiliency enhancement: putting the strengths perspective into social work practice. Columbia University Press. New York.
22. PARKER, G.M. 2003. Cross-functional teams: working with allies, enemies, and other strangers. Jossey-Bass. San Francisco, CA.

23. THIAGARAJAN, S. & G.M. PARKER. 1999. Teamwork and teamplay: games and activities for building and training teams. Jossey-Bass/Pfeiffer San Francisco, Calif.
24. MUCHINSKY, P.M. 1997. Psychology applied to work: an introduction to industrial and orgnizational psychology. Brooks/Cole. Pacific Grove, CA, USA.
25. SHERRITON, J.C. & J.L. STERN. 1997. Corporate culture, team culture: removing the hidden barriers to team success. American Management Association. New York.
26. WEST, M.A. 2004. Effective teamwork: practical lessons from organizational research. BPS Blackwell. Malden, Mass.
27. WEST, M.A. & L. MARKIEWICZ. 2004. Building team-based working: a practical guide to organizational transformation. British Psychological Society: Blackwell Pub. Malden, Mass.
28. VAILLANT, G.E. 1979. Natural history of male psychologic health: effects of mental health on physical health. N. Engl. J. Med. **301:** 1249–1254.
29. BECKER, F.D. & F. STEELE. 1995. Workplace by design: mapping the high-performance workscape. Jossey-Bass Publishers. San Francisco.
30. LEVY, P.E. 2006. Industrial/organizational psychology: understanding the workplace. Houghton Mifflin. Boston.
31. BUCCI, W. 1997. Psychoanalysis and cognitive science: a multiple code theory. Guilford Press. New York.
32. MILLER, G.A. 2003. The cognitive revolution: a historical perspective. Trends Cogn. Sci. **7:** 141–144.
33. SCHULTZ, D.P. 1981. A history of modern psychology. Academic Press. New York.
34. EDELMAN, G.M. 1987. Neural Darwinism: the theory of neuronal group selection. Basic Books. New York.
35. KAHNEMAN, D., E. DIENER & N. SCHWARZ. 1999. Well-being: the foundations of hedonic psychology. Russell Sage Foundation. New York.
36. MASLOW, A.H. & D.C. STEPHENS. 2000. The Maslow business reader. Wiley. New York.
37. PHILLIPS, M.L. & D. MATAIX-COLS. 2004. Patterns of neural response to emotive stimuli distinguish the different symptom dimensions of Obsessive Compulsive Disorder. CNS Spectrums **9:** 275–283.
38. BARONE, D.F., J.E. MADDUX & C.R. SNYDER. 1997. Social cognitive psychology: history and current domains. Plenum Press. New York.
39. LAMBERTON, L.H. & L. MINOR-EVANS. 2007. Human relations: strategies for success. McGraw-Hill/Irwin. Boston.
40. ROSEN, N.A. 1989. Teamwork and the bottom line: groups make a difference. L. Erlbaum Associates. Hillsdale, NJ.
41. EDELMAN, G.M. 1989. The remembered present: a biological theory of consciousness. Basic Books. New York.
42. RAISMAN, G. & Y. LI. 2007. Repair of neural pathways by olfactory ensheathing cells. Nat. Rev. Neurosci. **8:** 312–319.

Business Change Process, Creativity and the Brain

A Practitioner's Reflective Account with Suggestions for Future Research

ROWENA M. YEATS[a,b] AND MARTYN F. YEATS[c]

[a]*Cognitive Evolution Laboratory, Harvard University, Cambridge, MA 02138, USA*

[b]*Psychology Department, Aston University, Aston Triangle, Birmingham B4 7ET, UK*

[c]*Frazier Yeats Associates, Brighton and Hove BN3 7NB, UK*

> ABSTRACT: Resolution of a critical organizational problem requires the use of carefully selected techniques. This is the work of a management consultant: facilitating a business change process in an organizational setting. Here, an account is provided of a practitioner's reflections on one such case study that demonstrates a structure for a business change process. The reflective account highlights certain affective states and social behaviors that were extracted from participants during the business change process. These affective states and social behaviors are mediated by specific neural networks in the brain that are activated during organizational intervention. By breaking down the process into the affective states and social behaviors highlighted, cognitive neuroscience can be a useful tool for investigating the neural substrates of such intervention. By applying a cognitive neuroscience approach to examine organizational change, it is possible to converge on a greater understanding of the neural substrates of everyday social behavior.
>
> KEYWORDS: functional magnetic resonance imaging; business change process; creativity; social behavior; affective states; social cognitive neuroscience; organizations

INTRODUCTION

Management consultants are often approached by senior organizational management teams to channel such groups through a difficult or "wicked"

Address for correspondence: Rowena M. Yeats, Psychology Department, School of Life & Health Sciences, Aston University, Aston Triangle, Birmingham B4 7ET UK. Voice: +44(0) 121 204 3000; fax: +44 (0) 121 204 3696.
yeatsrm@aston.ac.uk

problem.[1,2] Such problems are characterized by their "interconnectedness, complexity, uncertainty, ambiguity, conflict" and by their "societal constraints."[1] One example of a wicked problem concerned a senior management team in place to provide domiciliary care services to older people within a largely rural area of England. The team faced severe budget problems due to cost overruns occurring only part-way into the fiscal year. The primary implication of the continuation of this problem was a possible reduction in preventative services to vulnerable, publicly funded older people living at home. For these older people, a reduction in preventative services typically resulted in early admission to hospital with a consequent increased demand for already scarce resources.

The goal of the management consultant (M.F.Y.) was to facilitate a problem-solving process and, through this process, develop mechanisms to address the cost overrun. This was achieved by encouraging a natural thinking process in the senior management team through utilizing various techniques that extracted, as well as built, a platform for certain social behaviors and affective states to occur. Essentially, this method was intended to allow members of the senior management team to become sensitive to their own thoughts. This would then facilitate goal-oriented behavior using the available information produced by group reflections and decisions about the problem.

This case study is presented to demonstrate a business change process and to highlight the manner in which certain affective states and social behaviors emerge as a result of the techniques used for the business change process. Existing cognitive neuroscientific research into these affective states and social behaviors is then discussed in light of the case study.

THE PROBLEM

A local social care senior management team was allocated a budget of approximately £1.5 m (approx US$3 m). Partway through the fiscal year this budget was approaching a significant overspend.

The Problem Definition

A problem trigger occurs when a combination of events and indicators reaches a response threshold.[3] The trigger is not a problem in itself, but suggests that a problem exists; this, in turn, can lead to a fuller diagnosis. By applying a problem trigger analysis, it is possible to break down and identify the individual components that constitute a negative organizational situation.

The use of a problem trigger analysis assisted the management consultant in the present case study in two ways. First, it enabled clarification that the budget overspend was not the problem—it was merely the symptom. Second, given the extent of this symptom, it highlighted the urgency of further work on problem definition.

THE IMPORTANCE OF TECHNIQUE

To solve organizational problems, clearly defined procedures or problem-solving techniques must be designed to facilitate specific goals or outcomes. Such problem-solving techniques smooth the process of gathering information, mapping situations, generating ideas, and choosing among ideas. One technique, on its own, is generally not enough to solve an organizational problem, given the inherent complex nature of such problems. It is therefore essential for the contribution of any one technique to be viewed as playing its own distinct role, as well as a role within an overall problem-solving process. For example, the problem trigger analysis, as a problem definition technique, indicates that a problem has arisen. However, this is only the starting point—a range of other techniques must be utilized to reach a resolution.

Technique Selection

Within a business change process, it is important to structure the choice of techniques to ensure that problem solving remains the central focus. Structuring this choice can hinge on both established methods and personal intuition.

A four-component model drawn from Backoff and Nutt (1988), Checkland (1981) and Martin (2000) on behalf of The Open University Business School was used to select the techniques for the present organizational problem.[3-5] The first component of the model is *functionality*; this has to do with the identification of the functional requirements for a solution, such performance and fitness for purpose. Second, *innovation* is the need for a solution to be new in some respect; it must be perceived as a change by members of the organization. Third, *feasibility* is the solution's ability to satisfy objective constraints in terms of being technically and organizationally deliverable. Finally, *acceptability* is the solution's ability to meet stakeholder criteria, such as belief systems, cultural acceptability, and consistency of company image.

Individual differences in problem-solving style have been attributed to personal preference for particular stages of the solution.[6] A kind of favoritism among solution stages. For the present business change process to occur intuitively, the value of experimentation and innovation was clear. Techniques intended to channel and develop a full problem description were first chosen by the management consultant.

MANAGING THE BUSINESS CHANGE PROCESS

The management consultant must address logistics, communication, progress control, emotional support, containment, inspiration, and role modeling. In the present case study, a problem-solving group was selected by the management consultant with the help of the overall manager for the service. The problem-solving group comprised the 15 or so senior managers concerned with the assessment for and delivery of domiciliary services for older people within the geographical area. The group session was held offsite in a room with an atmosphere and appearance different from that of the normal working environment. The location of such sessions is of crucial importance and should be selected to promote the idea that this is the place for doing things differently.

In planning and execution, the management consultant allowed room for flexibility to maximize and use the creativity within the management team. An effective creative team generally comprises a blend of characteristics.[7] The blend of styles is important for creative teams. A variety of approaches can be employed to address a given problem, and any tensions generated within the team often result from a mix of inharmonious approaches.

The present business change process was shaped around a set of four principles that can encourage creativity: curiosity, forgiveness, love, and a sense of direction.[3,8] Curiosity allows us to stimulate a need to examine, enquire, challenge, and understand. Forgiveness ensures that curiosity will be uninhibited as the dead ends that are part of all exploration must be accepted. Love allows us to genuinely value the people involved in the problem to provide the scope for confident exploration and learning. Finally, a sense of direction ensures that, overall, work appears to be moving in a meaningful direction.

TECHNIQUE APPLICATION

Story Writing

Story writing is a creative problem solving technique that encourages access to intuitive responses, such as underlying motives, personal agendas, and understandings that might not easily be put into words.[9] Story writing involves creating a story or parable that is clearly fictional but that also has some relationship to the actual circumstances behind the problem.

In the present case study, the management consultant suggested that the participants prepare, in advance, a description of the problem under discussion as a story or a fairytale. Each participant was then asked, as part of the same exercise, to identify his or her own character in the story and then to identify the remaining characters. The purpose of this exercise was to encourage participants to go beyond the traditional framing of the problem, and to think outside the box. This exercise also enabled participants to experience role-taking, as it allowed them to arrive at an understanding of the problem from various points of view. An extensive body of literature exists on the cognitive neuroscience of role-taking, and this is discussed below.

Rich Pictures

The rich pictures technique[5] provides a way to consider the relationships among objects, and thus helps a management consultant gain an understanding of the problem. In this way, rich pictures supplies a useful means of capturing the elements of unstructured situations. The technique was adapted to the present problem-solving session. Thus, the group spent 30 minutes using finger paints and play dough to express, in alternative media, the various aspects of the problem.

During group facilitation sessions, it is of great importance for the management consultant to engage as much as possible in the exercises. The rationale is that colleagues will be more inclined to do something unconventional and unusual in an occupational setting if the facilitator is also seen engaging in the process.

Multiple Redefinition

Multiple redefinition[10] is designed to help users develop imaginative and original redefinitions of the problem and its context via a set of questions that systematically take the participants through different mental modes, such as empathic and analytic. The purpose of using this exercise in the present case study was to build upon the rich pictures exercise[5] and to challenge assumptions and predispositions surrounding the problem. This further encouraged an examination of alternative views of the problem.

Participants were asked to work on their own to complete predefined statements such as, "if I could break all laws of reality (physical, social etc) I would try to solve it by...."

Developing a Balanced View

In the Fishbone Diagram technique,[11] participants draw a horizontal line representing the issue to be discussed. Spurs are then drawn at 45 degree angles, one for every likely cause of the problem. Subspurs are added to represent subsidiary causes. This approach, which is intended to structure the process of identifying possible causes of the problem, has been developed to facilitate a complete and balanced view of the problem, involve the whole group, keep everyone focused on the problem, and show the relative importance of, and interdependencies between, the different parts of the problem.

The significance of this exercise for the present case study was in the definition of the problem. The result of preceding work moved the group forward, from seeing the problem in terms of a budget overspend to perceiving it as a lack of a system for managing resources. As the work progressed through the four techniques, the participants began to break down the problem to its constituent parts—these were discovered to be information technology, the budget, managing expectations, workforce planning, vision and clarity, and the commissioning of preventative services for older people. Once the components had been clarified, they could be thoroughly investigated to bring about resolution of this organizational problem.

Because the business change process is facilitated by highlighting certain social behaviors and affective states, it is reasonable to consider such phenomena in light of relevant cognitive neuroscience research. By identifying the cortical substrates that are implicated in the business change process, it would then be possible to see whether there is overlap with or distinction from networks highlighted in contemporary cognitive neuroscience investigations. Subsequent investigations could then examine whether, and to what extent, activity in these networks is modulated by the specific interventions prescribed by a management consultant. This is important to know because it could facilitate the design of more efficient interventions. Although numerous examples exist of the contributions of cognitive neuroscientific investigations of social and affective processes, the contribution of cognitive neuroscience to the organizational world is less evident.

COGNITIVE NEUROSCIENCE AND THE BUSINESS CHANGE PROCESS

Using a management consultant's reflective account allows the business change process to be broken down into its constituent parts, in this case the principles upon which it was based: curiosity, love, forgiveness, and a sense of direction. Among other components of the business change process were role-taking extracted by the story-writing technique and empathy extracted by the multiple redefinition technique. By taking these elements from this case study, the cognitive neuroscientific approach can then be applied as a powerful tool in this research area[36] and in light of this is discussed below.

Role-Taking, Morality, and the Frontal Lobes

The importance of role-taking within the present business change process case study was demonstrated by its use within a problem-solving technique. Story writing[9] used role-taking to help participants arrive at an understanding of the problem from various points of view. Investigation of the neural correlates involved in role-taking could enhance understanding of the overall neural network involved in the business change process.

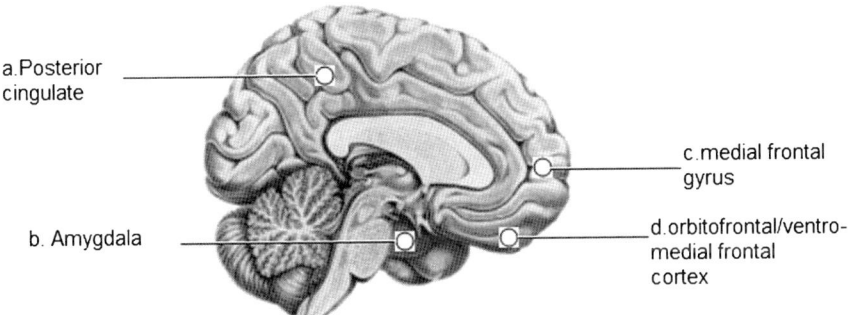

FIGURE 1. Sagittal image of the human brain indicating the proposed regions implicated in the business change process. Adapted from Ref. 15.

Role-taking can be used to make social judgments. Damasio has examined social judgments and their neural basis using patients with neurological injuries.[12,13] The focal damage of these patients was found in the ventral and medial areas of the frontal lobes (see FIG. 1). Damasio has demonstrated that this damage led to the patients' inability to use emotions to guide their intuitive responses. Patients with this type of frontal lobe damage have shown poor performance in tasks thought to replicate ecologically valid decision-making.[14] Tasks related to role-taking and integrating emotion into decision-making, such as intention assigning, have been related to the medial frontal gyrus (FIG. 1) and, in particular, the paracingulate sulcus.[15] These frontal lobe areas appear to be important in integrating emotion and intention assigning; therefore, they may also play a part in role-taking abilities.

Moral judgments also highlight the importance of role-taking. Lawrence Kohlberg's cognitive–developmental approach considers developed moral judgment to be a result of moral reasoning that stems from an understanding of and familiarity with role-taking.[16]

In light of this research, neuroimaging techniques should be used to measure activity in the ventral and medial areas of participants' frontal lobes while they carry out tasks with an occupationally based role-taking focus, along with baseline measurements. Identification of the overlap between role-taking as a social and organizational behavior can then occur.

Empathy and the Anterior Insula

Building on the importance of role-taking within a business change process, empathy has also been described as a key window into organizational behavior. Tudor Rickards's multiple redefinition technique[10] used empathy as one of a set of mental modes extracted from participants to help them arrive at original definitions and alternative views of the problem.

One can appreciate the mental states of others without necessarily engaging personally in this mental state; this ability is reflected in role-taking. However, true empathy is present when one's affective state is identical to that of another individual and is elicited by the observation or imagination of another person's affective state.[17] Empathy seems to take role-taking to the next level.

Neuroimaging techniques, such as functional magnetic resonance imaging (fMRI),[18] reveal functional overlap in brain areas that are activated when participants are exposed to the emotional state of others and when they experience that same emotional state themselves.[17] This suggests that a shared affective neural network is central to our capacity to empathize.

Additional studies of affective neuroscience have focused on the importance of modulation of the empathic state. Confederates acting fairly, when seen as being in pain, elicited empathy-related brain activation in participants in the anterior cingulate cortex and anterior insula.[19] Only male participants displayed a lack of this activation while observing the unfair confederates in pain; instead, seemingly due to the desire for revenge, they showed activation in the nucleus accumbens, an area which has been linked with reward.[19] Investigators found a positive correlation between this activation and the expression of a need for revenge by the male participants. This research not only implicates distinct substrates in the mediation of personal empathy, but also highlights a possible interaction with the experience of social morality.

It can be argued that we evolved empathy as a way to achieve social cohesion and communication.[17] Clearly such a process would have great utility in an organizational setting. Findings here suggest that the anterior cingulate cortex and anterior insula are involved in the empathic state and should be the focus of investigations of this process in a business change intervention. Empathy can help one understand the motivations of others;[20] this suggests that empathy is crucial to the business change process. By understanding the motivations of others, one can help change the organizational behavior of individuals where necessary to make it more advantageous in the work group.

Forgiveness and the Cingulate Gyri

The relationship between empathy and forgiveness remains contentious.[22] Forgiveness, defined in a broad sense as "ceasing to feel angry or resentful toward another",[22] is one of the key principles that encompass the capacity to encourage or discourage creativity in an organizational setting.[3,21] Without forgiveness, the possible outcomes that may arise from curiosity, as one of the four principles that can encourage creativity, may be inhibited and hence may inhibit the business change process.

Along with empathy, forgiveness has been portrayed as playing a central role in social cohesion.[22] Areas of brain activation involved in forgiveness and empathy include the left superior frontal and posterior cingulate gyri (FIG. 1).[22] In one study, patients suffering from post-traumatic stress disorder showed a significant increase in activation engendered within the posterior cingulate gyrus once eradication of their symptoms occurred.[23] Interestingly, a study found activation elicited by both empathy and forgiveness in the left superior frontal gyrus, as well as the orbital frontal gyrus and precuneus. This overlap in the superfrontal regions supports the idea that empathy and forgiveness, as cognitive processes, may share a common component.[22]

An integrated model proposes a three-stage forgiveness process. First, in the motivational stage, a decision of whether forgiveness is suitable is made. Second, if forgiveness is deemed suitable, a level of forgiveness is decided upon, from false to complete forgiveness. Third, intrapsychic and interpersonal challenges are completed; these include awareness in the forgiver that the process of forgiveness has happened.[24]

A model has been mapped to network of cortical regions. The amygdala is at the core of the model because a fear response in the amygdala is activated in response to thoughts regarding the act to be forgiven. A fitting event will then cause the frontal cortex to stifle the amygdala's fear response, which then causes muscular relaxation; this, in turn, indicates to the cortex that forgiveness has occurred. Subsequent memory pathways to the amygdala are inhibited.[25]

Understanding the nature of forgiveness in an organizational setting can act as both prevention and cure; thus, knowledge of forgiveness at a neurological level is extremely beneficial. Ensuring that others know they are in a safe, forgiving environment prevents stifled behavior in a creative setting. A greater understanding of forgiveness, which can be achieved through a social cognitive neuroscience approach, can be translated into the organizational setting to alert individuals to their own behaviors, thus acting as a cure.

Love and the Anterior Cingulate Cortex

From an evolutionary perspective, love is part of a group of affiliative responses, which cohere a social bond.[26] In an organization, love is another mechanism that has the capacity to provide an encouraging environment in which creativity can occur.

The interlocking components of love—the emotional, cognitive, and behavioral aspects—make it one of the most, if not the most, complex affective states.[27] However, it is important to note that love as referred to in the context of creativity is not the romantic love associated with red roses and fireworks, but an affective state of genuine value held for those people around you and the context in which you work. Work on the neural basis for love has focused on romantic and maternal love and again provides the organizational world with a tool from which to base hypotheses and future research.[28]

fMRI studies have shown bilateral activation in the anterior cingulate cortex and (primarily) on the left side of the middle insula, when participants describing themselves as "truly deeply and madly in love" viewed pictures of their loved partners.[27] Data were further analyzed in this study to produce a timeline showing that the anterior cingulate and the insula were differentially activated, suggesting that these areas may play separate roles in the experience of love.[27] Subcortically, the stimuli engendered activation in the caudate nucleus and the putamen, both of which have previously been associated with positive affective states.[27]

The other central form of love that has been investigated at a neurological level is that of maternal love. It is reasonable to assume that love as a means of encouraging creativity may be more similar to maternal love as its components of building an environment in which people feel genuinely valued certainly relate more closely to a warm and caring affect rather than the eroticism more associated with romantic love.[28]

Maternal love, as an attachment-specific affective state, has been investigated using the same methods as for investigations of romantic love; both overlapping and distinctive activation have been found for the two forms of love.[28] Those brain areas found showing coincident activity in response to both states of love are the striatum and, more specifically, the putamen, globus pallidus, and caudate nucleus, as well as the dorsal anterior cingulate cortex and the middle insula. Those areas distinctly activated in response to maternal love were the lateral orbitofrontal cortex (FIG. 1) and the periaqueductal grey area; the areas activated only for romantic love were the dentate gyrus and hippocampus and the hypothalamus. Specific brain areas that have previously been linked to negative affect appeared to be inhibited; for example, the amygdaloid region was deactivated.[27]

Drawing on the distinct and overlapping brain areas activated for maternal and romantic love and investigating the neural correlates of love in a creative sense would confirm whether the latter kind of love produces its own neural signature or one similar to either romantic or maternal love. Grounding the research of the elements involved in the business change process in established cognitive neuroscience will allow for better understanding of the origins of these elements and, as a result, support them in an organizational setting.

Curiosity and a Sense of Direction

Curiosity is fundamental to human behavior, it fuels our need to investigate, to question, and to comprehend. The key to human curiosity is our ability to satisfy it behaviorally through exploration. At both a social and organizational level, exploration is a mechanism that, among other things, provides us with information to make decisions and achieve goals.

Exploratory behavior is linked with exploitation in that we explore a given environment or problem and then choose an option to further exploit it.[29]

Research using an exploratory phase have found increased activation in both the frontopolar cortex and the intraparietal sulcus.[31] These cortical regions have been linked to high-level control and decisionmaking, respectively.[30]

As previously stated, curiosity and its subsequent exploratory behavior is essential to encourage creativity in the work place. However, it is equally important that the energy devoted to this exploratory behavior is channeled appropriately to ensure that it is a constructive pathway to an objective. In creative terms, this is one's sense of direction.

Our ability to stay focused to achieve a goal or objective can be investigated using the motivation and reward processes of the brain as a starting point. Rewards can come in any number of forms, from the more tangible forms (e.g., fruit juice) to more abstract forms (e.g., laughter). Essentially, a reward is anything that produces positive affect, and hence reinforces the behavior that led to its realization.[31]

Specific brain areas are reliably activated in response to reward, including the ventral striatum and nucleus accumbens, the amygdala, and the orbitofrontal cortex. The orbitofrontal cortex appears to connect the reward system with the input of the outside world, as it is here that connections between sensory stimuli and the value produced by the reward seem to occur.[31] Theories have differed with respect to the role of the amygdala. However, a consensus now suggests that the amygdala conveys information on the salience of the stimulus.[31] Activation in the ventral striatum may indicate when mistakes in reward prediction have been made.[31]

Exploration stemming from curiosity and motivation and reward derived from a sense of direction can be seen as key adaptive behaviors. In a business change process, our ability to adapt is what makes the outcome of the process workable. By taking the behaviors from the organizational setting and reducing them, their closest matches in the established world of cognitive neuroscience can be found. This then allows for more effective cognitive neuroscientific investigation, the findings of which can lead to an improved understanding of the behaviors occurring within an organizational setting.

Cognitive neuroscientists work to understand the relationship between the brain and the mind. It would be neglectful of the organizational practitioner not to use this research. However, this is a symbiotic relationship. By using a practitioner's reflective account as an inside window to social behavior occurring in the real world, it will be possible for the cognitive neuroscientist to understand the components that make up this behavior.

REFERENCES

1. MASON, R.O. & I.I. MITROFF. 1981. Challenging Strategic Planning Assumptions. Wiley. UK.

2. RITTEL, H. 1972. On the planning crisis: systems analysis of the "First and second generations". Bedriftsokonomen. Norway.
3. MARTIN, J.N.T. 2000. Managing Problems Creatively. The Open University. UK.
4. BACKOFF, R.W. & P.C. NUTT. 1988. A process for strategic management with special application for the non-profit organisation. Cited in Strategic Planning: Threats and Opportunities for Planners. J.M. Bryson & R.C. Einsweiller, Eds.: 120–144. Chicago.
5. CHECKLAND, P.B. 1981. Systems Thinking Systems and Practice. Wiley. UK.
6. BASADUR, M. 1990. Identifying individual differences in creative problem-solving style. J. Creat. Behav. **24:** 2.
7. BELBIN, R.M. 1981. Management Teams: Why They Succeed or Fail. Heinemann. Oxford.
8. ADAMS, J.L. 1987. Conceptual Blockbusting. Penguin Press. Harmondsworth, UK.
9. VAN GUNDY, A.B. 1988. Techniques of Structured Problem Solving. Van Nostrand Reinhold. New York.
10. RICKARDS, T. 1974. Problem Solving Through Creative Analysis. Gower Press. Aldershot, UK.
11. MAJARA, S. 1988. The Creative Gap. Longman. London.
12. DAMASIO, A.R. 1994. Descartes' Error: Emotion, reason and the human brain. Putman. New York.
13. DAMASIO, H. et al. 1994. The return of Phineas Gage: clues about the brain from the skull of a famous patient. Science **264:** 1102–1105.
14. BECHARA, A. et al. 1996. Failure to respond autonomically to anticipated future outcomes following damage to pre-frontal cortex. Cereb. Cortex. **6:** 215–225.
15. GREEN, J. & J. HAIDT. 2002. How (and where) does moral judgement work? Trends Cog. Sci. **6:** 12.
16. KOHLBERG, L. 1969. Stage and sequence the cognitive developmental approach to socialization. Cited In Handbook of socialization theory and research. D.A. Goslin, Ed.: 347–480. Rand McNally. USA.
17. DE VIGNEMONT, F. & T. SINGER. 2006. The empathic brain: how when and why? Trends. Cog. Sci. **10:** 10.
18. LEE, N. & L. CHAMBERLAIN. 2007. Neuroimaging and Psychophysiological measurement in organizational research: An agenda for research in organizational cognitive neuroscience. This volume.
19. SINGER, T. et al. 2006. Emphatic neural responses are modulated by the perceived fairness of others. Nature **439:** 466–469.
20. PERRY, J. 2001. Knowledge, Possibility and Consciousness. The MIT Press. USA.
21. ADAMS, J.L. 1987. Conceptual Blockbusting. Penguin. Harmondsworth, UK.
22. FARROW, T.F.D. et al. 2001. Investigating the functional neuroanatomy of empathy and forgiveness. Neuroreport **12:** 11.
23. FARROW, T.F.D. et al. 2005. Quantifiable change in functional brain response to emphatic and forgiveability judgements with resolution of post traumatic stress disorder. Psychiatry Res. **140:** 145–53.
24. KAMINER, D. et al. 2000. Forgiveness. Towards an integration of theoretical models. Psychiatry **63:** 344–57.
25. CLARK, A.J. 2005. Forgiveness: a neurological model. Med. Hypoth. **65:** 649–654.
26. CREWS, D. 1998. The evolutionary antecedents to love. Psychoneuroendocrinology **23:** 751–764.

27. BARTELS, A. & S. ZEKI. 2000. The neural basis of romantic love. Neuroreport **11:** 17.
28. BARTELS, A. & S. ZEKI. 2004. The neural correlates of maternal and romantic love. Neuroimage **21:** 1155–1166.
29. COHEN, J.D. *et al.* 2007. Should I stay or should I go? How the human brain manages the trade-off between exploitation and exploration. Philos. Trans. R. Soc. Lond. B. **362:** 933–942.
30. DAW, N.D. 2006. Cortical substrates for exploratory decisions in humans. Nature **441:** 876–879.
31. MCCLURE, S.M. *et al.* 2004. The neural substrates of reward processing in humans: The modern role of fMRI. The Neuroscientist **10:** 3.
32. DIETRICH, A. 2007. Who's afraid of a cognitive neuroscience of creativity? Methods **42:** 22–27.

Cognitive Accuracy and Intelligent Executive Function in the Brain and in Business

CHARLES E. BAILEY

Medical Director, Accurate Clinical Trials, Inc.

ABSTRACT: This article reviews research on cognition, language, organizational culture, brain, behavior, and evolution to posit the value of operating with a stable reference point based on cognitive accuracy and a rational bias. Drawing on rational-emotive behavioral science, social neuroscience, and cognitive organizational science on the one hand and a general model of brain and frontal lobe executive function on the other, I suggest implications for organizational success. Cognitive thought processes depend on specific brain structures functioning as effectively as possible under conditions of cognitive accuracy. However, typical cognitive processes in hierarchical business structures promote the adoption and application of subjective organizational beliefs and, thus, cognitive inaccuracies. Applying informed frontal lobe executive functioning to cognition, emotion, and organizational behavior helps minimize the negative effects of indiscriminate application of personal and cultural belief systems to business. Doing so enhances cognitive accuracy and improves communication and cooperation. Organizations operating with cognitive accuracy will tend to respond more nimbly to market pressures and achieve an overall higher level of performance and employee satisfaction.

KEYWORDS: neuroscience; rational; evolution; executive functioning; psychology; brain; frontal lobes; cognitive; belief systems; cultural; organizational; business; management; leadership

INTRODUCTION

In 1887, physicists Albert Michelson and Edward Morley conceived a brilliant plan to detect the presumed existence of a universal substance known as ether. They speculated that ether would impede light traveling with the turning of the earth more than light traveling at right angles to it. Their failure to detect any difference stunned the scientific world. Einstein explained the failure

Address for correspondence: Charles E. Bailey, Medical Director, Accurate Clinical Trials, Inc., 213 Ridge Rd., Lake Mary, Florida 32746-2709.
cbailey1@cfl.rr.com

by noting that, under the rules of general relativity, the yardstick changed exactly as much as the light beam it measured, rendering the expected difference undetectable.

The theory presented here suggests a similar conundrum in business: As a species, we tend to use inherently inadequate tools to measure the results of our organizational thought and behavior. Lacking awareness of how we use words to think and speak in organizational relationships and situations, and measuring our business success by unquestioned cultural belief systems that we have accepted uncritically, we often fall prey to confusion, emotional turmoil, misunderstanding, and poor communication. This article is based on the conjecture that the components of healthy human mental functioning and evaluations enable more successful, rational business outcomes.[1] "Rational" here refers to behavior, especially cognition, that relies on deliberate evaluation, learning, and informed deliberation, and it is based on cognitive accuracy. Rational cognition is deemed adaptive, pragmatic, practical, flexible, and matched as closely as possible with the present instead of the past. In this view, rationality does not imply finding or knowing a supposed single right answer but rather recognizes that, lacking omniscience, we do best to prepare for a variety of possible outcomes and to readily adapt when things do not go as we would prefer. "In forming opinion about future events, [rational expectations imply] the use of all available information to assess the probabilities of the possible states of the world. More simply, [rational] expectations [are those] that are as correct as is possible with available information."[2] Such flexibility is preferable to "irrationality," used here to refer to behavior, especially cognition, that is rigid and reactive, oriented toward learned rather than learning behavior, and based on belief rather than evidence, that is, operating with old information containing unexamined cognitive inaccuracies.

This article applies the concept of cognitive accuracy as a method for evaluating the accuracy and rationality of thoughts and behaviors in an organizational setting; the primary assumption is that the chief executive has responsibility for the corporate culture as well as business outcomes, acting as the lead evaluator of both his own cognition and that of his team. This method includes three primary components:

- information accuracy—seeking and using objective information based on empirical observation, premise, deduction, conclusions, and testing;
- thought process accuracy—making evaluations and decisions with multivariate terminology, awareness of individual responsibility, and flexibility of thought; and
- time–space or event-level accuracy—connecting and verifying both information and decisions in a time- and context-dependent manner to increase the relative probability of more accurate predictions of current and future outcomes.

Event-level accuracy is especially important in organizations, to ensure accurate integration of policies and behaviors with the constraints of a given moment and place.

BRAIN STRUCTURES, NEUROCHEMICALS, AND RELATIONSHIPS

To understand normal human brain functioning and cognitive accuracy, it is important to understand the mechanisms we use to obtain information, evaluate it, and make decisions. Words and language represent both the largest differences among human populations and the most significant group identifier, forming the basis for relationships and both organizational and individual cultural belief system values. Relationships, including corporate ones, depend on interactions between individuals, and these interactions in turn depend on communication. Faulty, inaccurate communication adversely affects relationships at all corporate levels. This problem usually results from inadequate evaluation and failure to implement rational communication processes by the CEO and management. Unfortunately, " . . . most companies are stuck in outmoded ways of thinking."[3]

Innate Social Mechanisms

We can trace the large variation in socialization among species to the different distribution of oxytocin and arginine–vasopressin receptors and pathways that enable bonding, attachment, affiliative behavior, and the creation of cohesive groups.[4,5] Reward pathways add a positive emotional valence, or value, to bonding and affiliative behavior, mediated (at least in part) by a positive shift in ventral tegmental area dopamine and endogenous opioids.[6] Threats to our social attachments induce a negative limbic valence that may produce jealousy, anger, and violence[6] and may establish dominance hierarchies. This negative valence appears to correlate with increased amygdala activity. Studies show that the stress induced by detachment triggers bereavement-related syndromes, correlated with an increase in stress hormones (corticotropin-releasing factor) and a decrease in brain-derived neuronal growth factor. These changes in turn correlate with increased amygdala activity and decreased volume in the prefrontal cortex (PFC) and hippocampus, with attenuated memory and diminished cognition. These symptoms echo those of anxiety and depression, sometimes leading to anger and aggression.

Like many social species, humans are genetically predisposed to have relationships. For us, however, the innate tendency to bond and affiliate is intimately associated with cultural belief systems, mediated by language.[7,8] We learn the structure and rules of *what* we think and *how* we think from the cultural environment we grow up in. Because cultural belief systems consist largely of language and semantics, they directly affect the thoughts, emotions, and behavior of groups, distinguishing one group from another.[9,10]

Organizational belief systems and groups often overlap or contain subgroups, but a prerequisite set of beliefs usually determines membership. These systems form within business units because of our inherited propensity for bonding and affiliations. We find unique belief systems at all scales: individuals, small groups such as families or affiliations, large groups such as businesses and corporations, and entire societies or states. In business, the rules that they embody for the group regarding thought and behavior are usually passed down through the leadership hierarchy, defining the particular organizational belief system. Because the rules and beliefs directly affect thought and behavior, they also dramatically affect emotions. Because cultural belief systems rely heavily on semantics—the use and meaning of language—one might also conclude that semantics and its usage figure significantly in understanding normal human cognition and interactions.

Knowing this, we can better appreciate the tremendous effect that semantics can have on emotions, behaviors, and perceptions as we evaluate human brain functioning across and within organizations. Semantics directly affects many aspects of human experience—corporate and cultural belief systems, cognition, emotions, behaviors, evaluations, perceptions, affiliations, bonding mechanisms, organizational and social interactions, and even aggressive behavior—so it seems reasonable and appropriate to construct more *naturalistic* organizational structures that recognize, account for, and address these effects rationally.

Subjective Cultural Classifications

Our language structure has many hidden attributes that directly affect our cognition, but they have become so habitual that we use them daily without inspection. These hidden features include unscientific, subjective, and overgeneralized cultural classifications, categorizations, groupings, and labeling. We often express these by using the predicate verb "to be," which allows us to semantically convert any subjective condition into a seemingly objective noun (i.e., we say, "He is a *failure*," instead of saying, "He *failed* at this particular effort"). Cultural labels are often discriminatory, rigidly held, and habitually defended against scientifically derived classifications or alternatives. Accordingly, cultural belief systems also rely on rigid, authoritarian, and sometimes intimidating helping verbs (e.g., *should, must, have to, need to, ought to, got to*). In business, these prescriptive, arbitrary, and cultural artifacts deftly sustain the organizational belief system and exclude rational *choice* and choice–outcome paradigms: They demand a predetermined choice, usually without knowledge or consideration of either the context or the nature of the decisions and outcomes involved. Culturally learned conventions—including either–or, dichotomous cognition—usually automatically preempt multivariate cognitive strategies for evaluations. Even though these automatic habits tend to become embedded in the hierarchical structure, organizations can uncover them with effort and inspection. However, if we do not acknowledge them, we have little chance of finding them.

Evolution and Dominance Hierarchies

An evolutionary model offers some plausible explanations for the relationships between culture and language. If we start with the assumptions that (1) variability and adaptability in the evolution of human social systems depends on dominance hierarchies and (2) survival depends on group functioning, then it makes sense that hierarchies controlled through reinforcement and punishment by dominant individuals or groups of individuals would have been adaptive for survival and reproduction in many species. In human interactions and language, we may still observe the slow evolution of these dominance features, especially in organizational structures.

Unfortunately, dominance hierarchies in humans—characteristic of our genetic inheritance and conditioned by our environment—tend to produce a kind of stodgy rigidity. We are hard-wired for aggression, territoriality, and competition for resources, dominance status, parental–familial–organizational affiliation, defensiveness, and irritability.[11] From individuals to whole cultures, we see language habits—acquired in early development—perpetuating dominance and rigidity. Humans are susceptible to this state because our learning mechanisms (including instrumental learning, modeling, and associative conditioning) depend on language. This learning, supported by language, forms the basic fabric of *what we believe* and *how we think* for most of our lives. Our language processes provide the vehicle for culture, social structure, and dominance, enabling us to operate on a gradient from subjective irrational bias to a more objective rational bias. Organizationally, we tend toward the former, whereas cognitive accuracy offers a way to move closer to the latter. We originally learn these organizational principles from our first "managers" (our parents and caretakers), and such principles tend to give us a subordinate bias.

Cultural Social Inheritance

The beliefs we "inherit" within an organization represent a long line of learned and rigidly held inaccuracies that significantly bias our perception. Becoming aware of the potential inaccuracy of what we know (or think we know) allows us to make corrections and think more critically. We measure cognitive accuracy by the relative distance or gradient between the unexamined, inconsistent, inaccurate, and irrational yardsticks that we have inherited and the established, external, accurate, and rational reference points that we have identified through science. The shorter this distance, the more objectively and rationally we think.

Most people, including business executives and managers, would contend that they do think accurately, rationally, and logically. However, they base their contentions on their own generally inaccurate and irrational frames of reference. For the most part, our individually inherited cultural belief systems significantly bias normal human thought and perception. This bias becomes apparent when compared with a rational reference point or standard (see TABLE 1). Awareness of this irrational bias opens the door to adopting standards that are more accurate and, therefore, have a more reasonable bias.

HUMAN BRAIN MODEL

Neuroscientists sometimes describe normal human brain functioning as a computer model.[12–14] The higher-level executive working memory[15] of the brain's frontal lobes dorsolateral PFC (DLPFC; along with frontopolar, Broca's area, temporal, temporoparietal, and association area *integration*, etc.) may be compared to the computer's random access memory, or RAM.[16] The information used to make decisions compares to the data stored in the computer.[17] The frontopolar cortex appears to play an important role in integration of internal and external appraisals both personally and empathetically with others.[18,19]

Human evolution seems to have added semantics and language on to the lower-level limbic working memory provided by our orbital frontal cortex (OFC). The OFC provides valuable utility calculations[20] while monitoring somatosensory information, emotional valence, relative risk–reward contingencies, and social salience. It also automatically provides bottom-up regulation of the limbic system by using the default semantics and language from our cultural belief system, thus reinforcing the subjective, social, hierarchical, neuroeconomic, and relative psychological values that define our organizational bias.[21,22] If subjective belief systems are edited to operate more accurately (i.e., yielding a more *scientific* belief system), the bias shifts toward the more objective end of the value probability continuum, operating on more rational–cognitive versus emotional–motivational evaluation gradients.[23]

The top-down, higher-level executive functioning of the DLPFC likewise relies heavily on semantics and language to perform critical integration of choice–outcome determinations. Whereas the OFC is limited to a subjective appraisal and read–write capacity, the DLPFC executive functions have an objective *re*appraisal and *edit* capacity. The limbic working memory and the OFC make adjustments relative to reward contingencies, reinforcement, and

TABLE 1. Inaccurate versus accurate rational biases

Inaccurate irrational bias	Accurate rational bias
Faulty rigid assumptions; dogmatic beliefs, unsupported by facts, but stated as unquestionable "truths of the Universe" with questioning prohibited, "superstitious," ritualistic thought and behavior that promotes mind–brain dualism	Rational flexible assumptions stated as theories; hypotheses and conclusions supported by evidence, scientific testing, and mandatory questioning, "scientific," adaptable thought and behavior, mind = brain = mind/brain
Rigid, maladaptive, with lower-level subjective bias	Flexible, adaptive, with higher-level objective bias
Absolute, static bias: certain, "*determinate*," guaranteed	Variable, dynamic bias: uncertain, "*probability*," not guaranteed
Dichotomous cognition limits freedom of executive function	Multivariate cognition expands freedom of executive function
Veridical bias: true and false, either–or, absolute, concrete, black and white; constrictive and restrictive	Associative bias: abstract, gray, gradated; expansive and extensive
Predetermined certainty, all knowing, resulting in decreased frontal lobe requirements: "*afrontal*"	Relative uncertainty, inquisitive, resulting in increased frontal lobe requirements: "*frontal*"
Parental, demanding; adversarial	Adult, requesting; cooperative
Semantic inaccuracy: vague, poorly defined, with overgeneralizations: always, never, every, all, none, etc.	Semantic accuracy: specific, best definition and word use: frequently, infrequently, many, some, few, etc.
Rigid; implies no other choices: I should, I must, I have to, I need to, and I have got to. "*I am obligated*"	Flexible; implies choices; preferential: I prefer, I would rather, I would like to, I choose to. "*It is a choice*"
Tends to ignore inaccuracies of information, of thought process, and of time–space orientation; retroactive, "reactive"	Tends to promote accuracies of information, of thought process, and of time–space orientation; forward-thinking, proactive, "considerate"
Inaccuracies and faulty assumptions promote faulty and inaccurate cause-and-effect conclusions	Accuracies and rational assumptions promote more plausible and more accurate cause-and-effect conclusions
General unawareness of irrational cognitive process "Cultural belief system anosognosia"	General awareness of rational cognitive process and "Cultural belief system awareness"

emotional valence spectra,[24] but the reappraisal and edit function of the executive DLPFC working memory directly contributes to our ability to objectively change and integrate the accuracy of *what* and *how* we think. By comparing internal stored memories with external, rational, up-to-date information, the DLPFC can temper our automatic responses to stimuli to achieve more reasonable objective outcomes,[25] ensuring that the higher-level, objective, executive functioning of the DLPFC will have the *last word* in decision making.[26] The executive of a company also has the last word, and the most successful executives usually make the most rational evaluations before they speak.

Cognitive Processing

The ability of the frontal lobes to use working memory optimally depends heavily on the availability and quality of the process information received from other cerebral regions.[27] The frontal lobes function best with accurate and timely information combined with accurate thought processes—that is, accurate data and the most appropriately flexible software. The software (i.e., how we think) enables the frontal lobes to make executive decisions and to help regulate our emotions and overall homeostasis.[28] Similarly, the executive in an organization has a greater probability of making the most effective decisions with accurate, timely data and flexible thinking.

Process memory (i.e., acquired and developed rules of thinking) directly biases not only how we process internally stored information but also how we perceive environmental information and stimuli.[29] Learned, rigid, *dichotomous* process rules preempt flexibility in our thought processes. As we might expect, *rigid,* inaccurate, irrational process information leads to inaccurate and irrational information processing, and this in turn yields inaccurately biased executive decisions. Faulty, inaccurate, rigid, dichotomous software bias will tend to lead to subjectively biased choices and outcomes, thwarting the *flexibility* offered by higher-order, multivariate executive functioning and thus favoring rigid cultural subjectivity.

HUMAN BRAIN AND COGNITIVE DEVELOPMENT

Where do inaccurate, irrational thought processes come from? How could we have learned our culturally inherited, faulty, inaccurate, irrational thinking without realizing it? Why would we automatically promote this behavior in our organizational culture? A transition from concrete thinking to the potential for abstraction occurs in the frontal lobe development and connectivity as an individual grows from childhood to adulthood. During our development from puberty into young adulthood, our frontal lobes continue to mature with increased connectivity and myelination, especially in the DLPFC.[30] This development contributes to the growing maturity of our decision-making skills (i.e., executive functioning) and heightens our ability for cognitive *awareness*. The frontal lobes are critical in this process.[31] However, the success of this transition depends largely on the foundational structure that we acquired in childhood.

As we grow into adulthood, we increasingly use acquired information as if it were factual, automatically following rigid, dichotomous processing rules that operate outside our awareness. We implicitly assume good–bad relationships between words and reward contingencies learned during our own developmental history. Our decision-making process reflects our cultural bias as we use information filtered through our own subjective personal historical matrix.[32] Organizationally, this takes the form of outdated policies and hierarchical biases that depend more on "how we always did it" than on "what will work best today."

If the process stopped there, we might not face the consequences of irrational thought processes. However, in childhood, we not only learn the concrete thinking of our ancestors but also inadvertently learn cognitive and semantic inaccuracies; faulty assumptions; imagined cause–effect relationships; superstitions; myths; magical thinking[33]; and rigid, culturally biased misperceptions. These elements are handed down from generations of unscientific, misinformed, and (most often) poorly educated elders. We unconditionally absorb rules and information as *truths* without the full benefit of mature executive functions. They tend not to question the factual basis of information, the logic of assumptions, or the reasonableness of conclusions, nor do they have the acquired framework to do so.[34]

As a result, adults often exhibit parent-to-child *authoritarian* characteristics in their thinking and interactions, using irrational demands such as *should, must, have to,* and *need to.* These parental, subjective, dichotomous demands typically "trump" multivariate choices and impede adults from taking responsibility for objective choice–consequence decisions. These parameters form the basis for our primitive management techniques. We learned the principles of subordinate management from parents and caregivers. Even corporate executives well educated in management often continue to use these primitive subordinate rules automatically. The unfortunate result is that employees are "seen and not heard," the recurring theme of childhood. They are afraid to speak up, afraid they will be punished if they tell the emperor that he has no clothes. Executives find themselves surrounded by continuously nodding bobble-heads who cannot accurately assess what is really going on in their own companies. Unfortunately, humans are familiar with dominance and subordination, but this structure fails to promote accurate organizational communication.

Our brains tend to gravitate toward the familiar[35] and away from the unfamiliar.[36] We experience positive rewards, or gratification, by sticking with the familiar, but we experience negative rewards, or amygdala-driven anxiety, for venturing into the unfamiliar. *Familiar* events that deviate little from the mean are assigned a positive valence and a higher *probability* of favorable outcome. *Uncertain events* that deviate significantly from the mean are often assigned a negative value and given a lower probability. This system tends to give *certainty* the upper hand over the perceived ambiguity and lower probability of uncertainty (as illustrated in such sayings as "A bird in the hand is worth two in the bush").

In this sense, the familiar represents comfort, and we become creatures of comfortable habits. Humans often tolerate a great deal of discomfort before they will consider the alternative of "change" (i.e., deviation from the mean). Organizationally, we learn to favor the familiar and generally receive no incentive or training to enhance our cognitive accuracies and help us develop objective, reasonable, and innovative methods for seeking rational alternatives. Indeed, many organizations actually punish attempts to promote cognitive accuracy because it challenges authority and organizational beliefs. This practice usually promotes management styles and rules based on familiarity rather than rational utility or applicability, regardless of what might objectively be in the company's best interest.

Authoritarian Communication

Because of the parent–child environment in which they learned these concepts, most adults continue to use the familiar parental cognitive process in their business interactions. This hierarchical communication is authoritarian, vertical, and one-way (parent to child) rather than cooperative, horizontal, and reciprocal (adult to adult, human to human). These familiar irrational habits from our past usually preempt more reasonable adult–adult communication and block accurate associative reasoning processes, resulting in irrational thought, decision making, and behavior. The parent-to-child irrational thought processes tend to permeate the organizational structure, generally inhibiting reasonable adult-to-adult communication, and this inhibition applies internally (within the individual) as well as externally (in relationships with others).

The strong tendency of humans to gravitate toward the familiar appears to impede adaptive change in business cultures, pulling the entire group backward toward more inaccurate, concrete ways of thinking, making decisions, and behaving.[37] The cultural inaccuracies we encounter in organizations often include an accumulation of past superstitious beliefs that guide corporate behavior and promote ongoing subordination, soothing the human angst of management by establishing pecking orders. Because most organizational information accumulates without the benefit of a scientific framework, we generally lack the critical skills or awareness to assess the information's validity. Our innate affiliative behavior and inherited rigid thinking—now coupled with inaccurate information, unfounded assumptions, and lack of awareness—hinders our progress to more accurate rational thought, behavior, and decision making.

Event-Level Accuracy

Furthermore, we automatically use yesterday's familiar policies and processes to approach today's problems, without a rational method for seeking and incorporating new information (i.e., "We have always done it this way!"). Of course, old knowledge has benefits—some of it derives from valid testing of alternative approaches, and some companies do update procedures periodically to meet changing markets—but new procedural policies are unlikely to substitute for the rational evaluation and dismantling of archaic organizational beliefs. Much of what passes for corporate wisdom no longer addresses how people work today, if it ever did, and as long as it continues to rule the corporate structure, companies will tend to punish the "wrong kind" of innovation, that is, thinking that challenges underlying belief structures, both personal and organizational. If, by sticking with the known, we exclude new and possibly pertinent objective information, our familiar solutions may fail to adequately resolve the problems we face in the present or future. In this state, time and location become disjointed—we operate in the now as if it were identical to the past, creating a cognitive time warp. This rigid time–space distortion plays a role in our irrational bias and appears to be magnified by our rigid, irrational software, thus causing even greater distortions and difficulties.

Conversely, by selecting pertinent, accurate, and current information and processing it with flexible, accurate policies, we shift our time–space orientation to the present, facilitating the most accurate, best-choice, best-outcome decisions. More specifically, we use our frontal lobe executive function and working memory to make the most accurate rational choices by using all available pertinent information. In this way, we make decisions in the present and evaluate plans for the future with greater precision and rational probability. This approach is generally preferable to making irrational choices by using irrelevant information from the past and then using the frontal lobes to retroactively justify and rationalize the decision. Accurate integration of time and space is critical for problem solving and finding the best solution at any given time.[38]

Accurate Evaluations

Without accurate information about the situation at hand, we may decide on a course of action simply because it feels good or promises familiar rewards or because it steers clear of unknown or imagined threats. Research shows that hormones (corticotropin-releasing factor) generated under the stress of dominance and subordination tend to shift our cognition toward lower-level limbic activation of anxiety while limiting higher-order prefrontal cortex functioning. Therefore, we can benefit from applying the knowledge that rational higher-order cognitive functioning can minimize the subordinate organizational structure; minimize emotional stress; and make a significant difference in communication, cooperation, and employee satisfaction.

Irrational Organizational Bias

Present knowledge of normal human brain functioning indicates that humans can choose how and what we think and that we can adapt to new situations more effectively by making better choices. Given this, why would we not choose to manage our organizations with an accurate rational bias with the highest degree of flexibility, incorporating semantic and information accuracy; accuracy of information processing; and accurate, time-appropriate information? Unfortunately, our personal, social, and cultural biases usually prevent us from understanding and using the very information that could enable such a choice.[39]

Because of their inherited belief systems, most humans, including executives, tend to think they *must* be perfect, unblemished and without flaws, that they *must not* be fallible. A blemish or a mistake means that they are no good, unworthy, or deserving of punishment. This absolute rating and labeling blocks recognition of personal fallibility; causes poor acceptance of others as fallible human beings; and promotes unscientific, culturally biased, arbitrary category classifications. This schema leads to rigid and judgmental dogmatic cultural belief systems, bigotry, stereotyping, and blind trust. It also promotes organizational vertical hierarchies with authoritarian, parent-to-child, one-way communication, as well as prolific "shoulding" by management and employees.

"Shoulds" allow management to avoid responsibility for stating and using reasonable communication skills or modeling reasonable interactions between themselves and employees. The use of shoulds promotes retrospective fault finding, blaming, and punishment. Shoulding on employees is akin to not providing adequate instructions, guidelines, or training—typically seen as the responsibility of management—and then blaming subordinates when they fail. Authoritarian managers tend to transfer responsibility for errors "downhill" and backward in time, because the employee did not predict the future accurately, thereby causing an organizational time warp. With this transfer of blame, management can always be right (i.e., "You should not have done it that way!" or "You should have known better!"). This after-the-fact second-guessing perpetuates parental management and does little to prevent the same problem from happening next time.

Rational Organizational Bias

We may characterize business as a series of choices and outcomes. We would like to predict the outcome of a particular choice with some degree of certainty, but doing so depends on understanding the many variables in our ever-changing, *dynamic* world. In such a complicated environment, accurately assessing probable business outcomes by using flexible, multivariate thought-processing and adequately evaluating our choices enhances overall adaptability and subsequent satisfaction by increasing our ability to respond appropriately to the given situation. "Choices can be rational or they can be the outcome of irrational processes."[40] A deliberate bias toward rationality tends to enhance our overall accuracy. This rational bias favors more effective decision making and increases the probability of more reasonable outcomes. On the other hand, an irrational and *static* bias tends to decrease overall accuracy, leading to irrational decision making with fewer reasonable and objective outcomes. The standards for measuring accurate and rational cognitive bias arise in part from the following assumptions:

- *Acceptance of human imperfection enhances information and process accuracy.* We can accurately characterize humans as flawed and fallible—executives included. Accepting our mutual flaws promotes horizontal, human–human, adult communication and reduces inaccurate, absolute, dichotomous, or culturally biased classifications, ratings, and labeling. Such problems occur when we rate the person rather than the behavior.
- *Flexibility enhances information and process accuracy.* Flexibility generally works better than rigidity for the most accurate planning, problem solving, and compromising. Rigid, dichotomous terms such as *should, must,* and *need to* restrict options; multivariate, preferential terms—such as *we would prefer, we would rather,* and *I think it is best for our company*—multiply the possible choices and acceptable rational outcomes. Organizational flexibility allows corporations to achieve open-minded, forward-looking, proactive feedforward/feedback, as well as continuous quality improvement with the best communication. This system promotes monitoring and quickly identifying problems while nimbly adapting new processes and solutions. Businesses realizing that they will not find perfect solutions to problems will learn to operate flexibly and accept reasonable compromise solutions. "The more you keep yourself open for alternative answers to a given problem, the more likely you are to get the best feasible answer to it."[41]
- *Awareness of the relationship between thoughts and emotions enhances information, process, and event-level accuracy.* Organizations succeed best when management takes responsibility for their thoughts, emotions, and behavior (especially for the prevailing organizational belief system). Doing so includes taking responsibility for outcomes, modeling intrapersonal and interpersonal acceptance, and teaching employees that what we humans think can significantly influence our feelings—whether we are aware of the connection or not. Awareness of this relationship enables us to choose the healthiest and most rational thoughts to maximize our emotional and behavioral balance at a given time. Although we might initially react to the situation itself, we generate and sustain our emotional reactions largely by what we think or "believe."[42–44] We tend to sustain the

emotion long after the event through the action of the internal rules and appraisal habits that affect us almost continuously, generally without our awareness or deliberate direction. As Epictetus wrote in the *Enchiridion* in the first century AD, "People are disturbed not by things, but by the views which they take of them." When the boss takes responsibility for his or her own upset, employees will learn to do the same.

Cognitive Awareness

Each of us maintains an internal narrative about our experiences. When something unexpected happens, we might tell ourselves inaccurate, irrational, and overly negative things about the situation, needlessly upsetting and stressing ourselves about it. If instead we choose to describe the situation to ourselves as accurately as possible, we can respond with the most appropriate behavior and most reasonable emotion. Although we all have responsibility for managing our own cognitive accuracy in thoughts, *emotions*, and behaviors, a business leader can also create an organizational climate that rewards such responsibility in employees. Such an environment enhances reasonable behavior and harmony between humans[45] and enables better communication, cooperation, and outcomes.

Correcting Irrational Biases

How do we improve our organizational cognitive accuracy when we receive little or no training for rational information or skills on which to build? How do we use our acquired irrational rigid thought processes to learn how to think rationally and make choices that are more rational? The corporate culture is the responsibility of the chief executive, whose participation is essential for modeling and teaching, team building, rational communication, and cooperation throughout the organization. The boss can still be the boss, but with fewer layers of management and more rational organizational rules, thus ensuring effective, cooperative, two-way communication.

Fortunately, we can replace inaccurate, irrational thinking habits with newer, more accurate, rational associative thought processes. It takes effort and practice to introduce and use new concepts and retool the collective organizational software. Increased accuracy contributes directly to more rational policies, which promote more reasonable outcomes. This result is possible because a rationally biased higher-level executive will have the "last word," both in the brain and in the business.

Implications of Irrational Bias

Irrational biases tend to use floating reference points, whereas more rational biases tend to operate from a stable reference point. How can we explain this apparent paradox? Humans tend to learn, whether directly or indirectly, that *good* is rewarded and *bad* is punished, that *right* is rewarded and *wrong* is punished, and furthermore that parents know what is *right* and what is *wrong*. The problem arises in the organization when we apply these dichotomous constructs to the complexity of frequently changing variables on a day-to-day basis. We perceive the rules for decision making in hierarchal dichotomous or absolutistic terms, such as *should, must, have to, ought to* (e.g., "Either you do that or you will be punished"). This approach creates a problem when the *must* of today becomes the *must not* of tomorrow because some variable or context has changed.

Reference Point Drift

This dichotomous terminology then leads to retrospective judging, fault finding, blaming, and punishing (e.g., "You shouldn't have done that!"). This rationale might work if we had a reliable means for predicting the future; given that we do not, we would do well to find another mechanism. To resolve these apparent discrepancies with reality, we simply move our reference point: We redefine success or modify our recollection of previous failures to cast the current outcome in a better light. By moving the reference point, we can always be right, always be above average, and never make a mistake. We simply move the reference point to undervalue others or overvalue ourselves, and doing so creates the irrational but comforting experience of "self-esteem." We learn this skill in childhood, when we are governed by multiple, subjective, and inconsistent reference points (e.g., from parents, teachers, neighbors, friends, and celebrities). We also learn to easily construct subjectively biased, overgeneralized group classes and use them to denigrate others at will. We can easily overgeneralize or underdefine representative classifications to prove most any point. We can round up or down at will. We have our choice of yardsticks and will usually choose the one that casts us in the most favorable light. We can use one rule to justify and a different rule to vilify any one experience to suit our own beliefs and goals, thereby artificially elevating our self-esteem. Retrospectively, this method works especially well for confirmation bias.

Typical organizations often depend on scapegoats, which allow management to avoid blemishes. Humans blame scapegoats for their own thoughts, emotions, and behaviors. Because we fear being wrong, we simply decide that someone else made us think, feel, or behave a certain way (e.g., "The boss can't be wrong, so the problem must be you," "You made me miss the deadline," "The committee made the wrong decision—I had no choice"). Simply by adjusting the reference point, we easily pass along the blame and judge ourselves not guilty. This system may succeed in bolstering the self-esteem of the blamer, but usually at the expense of anger or guilt from the blamed over his or her demoted self-esteem. Once we pick the scapegoat, we make up after-the-fact explanations and excuses to *justify* our behaviors, refute reality, or recast history. Doing so can have disastrous effects on long-term organizational relationships.

However, we have the resources to counter these (mostly) culturally determined habits by diligent pursuit of cognitive accuracy, even in the face of self-doubt and uncertainty. We can retrain the brain to value rational, probabilistic outcomes; to learn to accept human imperfection in place of self-esteem; and to use accurate information and processing to make decisions about current situations. Each of these practices can eventually enable us to apply the processing abilities of our "new" brain to direct the older, survival-oriented brain structures toward more rational pursuits. We can then shift our focus from subjective, risk–reward evaluations to achieving objective improvement and better outcomes for the future (6, p. 260).

CONCLUSIONS

Accurate, rational thinking in organizational leadership increases flexibility and maximizes appropriate business choices, enhancing achievement of preferred outcomes and minimizing undesirable ones. Fortunately, we can replace or overwrite inaccurate, irrational, parental, absolute thinking by learning and practicing accurate, flexible, rational, and logical thinking, thus improving overall adaptability. We have these rational tools available, but they are often unrecognized, overlooked, or even belittled.

At the turn of the last century, Michelson and Morley found that the act of "measurement" defines what is measured. We tend to calibrate our yardsticks to the business culture in which we find ourselves. Such a yardstick measures only what that culture values and overlooks other potentially beneficial factors. Each culture's yardstick shows *normal*, even though large differences exist between the beliefs and behaviors of various cultures. This approach leaves us prey to the accumulated inaccuracies of our hierarchical structures.

We can also apply cognitive accuracy as a reference point to measure humans across business cultures, and this reference point does not change as you go from one culture to the next. Such a reference point is biased toward objective cognitive accuracy, transcending the inaccuracies of corporate belief systems. Corporate cultures may change, but the yardstick remains the same unless scientific advances and cognitive accuracy are applied to rationally update cultural beliefs. For accurate evaluations, we do best to calibrate our cognitive yardstick with the most accurate, timeliest information, applying it consistently and rationally in the present.

In this article, I have reviewed the intimate connection among semantics, cognition, and the functioning of various brain structures, and I have posited an equally intimate connection from semantics, cognition, emotion, and behavior to how we manage organizations. These later connections suggest an explanation for the persistence of subjective organizational belief systems and their inherent deficiencies in objectivity, accuracy, and flexibility. Can we accept the premise that objective, event-level, accurate processing and information usage yields more satisfactory and reasonable results than rigid, automatic responses based on hand-me-down, imprecise beliefs? If so, it would appear beneficial to orient executive management toward the psychological value of objective relative belief systems, using scientific insights from the tools of cognitive accuracy.

RECOMMENDATIONS AND CONSIDERATIONS

If business leaders try to acquire the skills and habit of cognitive accuracy, their interactions with employees will sustain fewer faulty beliefs and thought processes. Importantly, organizations managed by these adults will have the benefit of cognitive accuracy. Their employees will have more skills for applying cognitive accuracy to address and resolve problems with competent critical thinking, emotional balance, and reasonable behaviors. This foundation will enable these organizations to build on their successes by rationally functioning in the present. It is important that we do not merely shuffle old approaches but instead integrate new rational ideas from organizational neuroscience to provide a vehicle for change.

Our present problems cannot be solved at the level of thinking at which they were created (Albert Einstein, attributed).

REFERENCES

1. BAILEY, C.E. 2006. A general theory of psychological relativity and cognitive evolution. ETC: A Review of General Semantics **63:** 278–289.
2. DEARDORFF, A.V. 2006. Terms of Trade: Glossary of International Economics. World Scientific Publishing Co. Hackensack, NJ.
3. SHAPIRO, S.M. 2001. 24/7 Innovation: A Blueprint for Surviving and Thriving in an Age of Change. McGraw Hill. New York, NY.
4. INSEL, T.R. 2001. A neurobiological basis of social attachment. American Journal of Psychiatry **154:** 726–735.
5. NAIR, H.P. & L.J. YOUNG. 2006. Vasopressin and pair-bond formation: Genes to brain and behavior. Physiology **21:** 145–152.
6. INSEL, T.R. 2001. Op cit.
7. PANKSEPP, J. 1998. Affective Neuroscience: The Foundations of Human and Animal Emotions. Oxford University Press. New York, NY.

8. MITCHELL, J.P., M.F. MASON, C.N. MACRAE, & R.B. MAHZARIN. 2006. Thinking about others: The neural substrates of social cognition. *In* Social Neuroscience, People Thinking about People. J.T. Cacioppo, P.S. Visser & C.L. Pickett, Eds: 63–82. MIT Press. Cambridge, MA.
9. ADOLPHS, R. 2006. What is special about social cognition? *In* Social Neuroscience, People Thinking about People. J.T. Cacioppo, P.S. Visser & C.L. Pickett, Eds: 269–285. MIT Press. Cambridge, MA.
10. DAMASIO, A.R. 2000. A second chance for emotion. *In* Cognitive neuroscience of emotion. R.D. Lane & L. Nadel, Eds: 12–23. Oxford University Press. New York, NY.0
11. WINGFIELD, J.C., I.T. MORE, W. GOYMAN, *et al.* 2006. Context and ethology of vertebrate aggression: Implications for the evolution of hormone-behavior interactions. *In* Biology of Aggression. R.J. Nelson, Ed.: 179–210. Oxford University Press. New York, NY.
12. AVRUTIN, S. 2006. Weak Syntax. *In* Broca's region. Y. Grodzinsky & K. Amunts, Eds: 49–61. Oxford University Press. New York, NY.
13. BENJAFIELD, J.G. 2007. Cognition, 3rd Ed. Oxford University Press. Don Mills, ON.
14. TOATES, F.M. 2007. Biological Psychology, 2nd Ed. Pearson Education Limited. Essex, UK.
15. BADDELEY, A. 2002. Fractionating the central executive. *In* Principles of Frontal Lobe Function. D.T. Stuss & R.T. Knight, Eds: 246–259. Oxford University Press. New York, NY.
16. MESULAM, M.M. 2002. The human frontal lobes: Transcending the default mode through contingent coding. *In* Principles of Frontal Lobe Function. D.T. Stuss & R.T. Knight, Eds: 8–30. Oxford University Press. New York, NY.
17. SCHMALHOFER, F. & C.A. PERFETTI. 2007. Neural and behavioral indicators of integration processes across sentence boundaries. *In* Higher Level Language Process in the Brain: Inference and Comprehension Processes. F. Schmalhofer & C.A. Perfetti, Eds: 161–188. Lawrence Erlbaum Associates. Hillsdale, NJ.
18. DECETY, J. 2007. A social cognitive neuroscience model of human empathy. *In* Social Neuroscience: Integrating Biological Explanations of Social Behavior. E. Harmon-Jones & P. Winkielman, Eds: 246–270. Guildford Press. New York, NY.
19. FERSTL, E.C. 2007. The functional neuroanatomy of text comprehension. *In* Higher Level Language Process in the Brain: Inference and Comprehension Processes. F. Schmalhofer & C.A. Perfetti, Eds: 53–102. Lawrence Erlbaum Associates. Hillsdale, NJ.
20. GLIMCHER, P.W., M.C. DORRIS & H.M. BAYER. 2006. Physiological utility theory and the neuroeconomics of choice. Games and Economic Behavior **52:** 213–256.
21. KAHNEMAN, D., P. SLOVIC & A. TVERSKY. 1982. Judgment under Uncertainty: Heuristics and Biases. Cambridge University Press. Cambridge, MA.
22. PADOA-SCHIOPPA, C. & J.A. ASSAD. 2006. Neurons in the orbitofrontal cortex encode economic value. Nature **441:** 223–226.
23. SCHULTZ, W. & L. TREMBLAY. 2006. Involvement of primate orbitofrontal neurons in reward, uncertainty, and learning. *In* The Orbital Frontal Cortex. D.H. Zald & S.L. Rauch, Eds: 173–198. Oxford University Press. New York, NY.

24. FRITH, C., G. REES, E. MACALUSO & S. BLAKEMORE. 2004. Higher cognitive functions: Mechanisms of attention. *In* Human Brain Function, 2nd Ed. R.S.J. Frackowiak, K.J. Friston, C.D. Frith, *et al.* Eds: 245–268. Elsevier Science USA. San Diego, CA.
25. MESULAM, M.M. 2000. Principles of Behavioral and Cognitive Neurology, 2nd Ed. Oxford University Press. New York, NY.
26. D'ESPOSITO, M. & B.R. POSTLE. 2002. The organization of working memory function in lateral prefrontal cortex: Evidence from event-related functional MRI. *In* Principles of Frontal Lobe Function. D.T. Stuss & R.T. Knight, Eds: 168–187. Oxford University Press. New York, NY.
27. ANDERSON, V., H.S. LEVIN & R. JACOBS. 2002. Executive functions after frontal lobe injury: A developmental perspective. *In* Principles of Frontal Lobe Function. D.T. Stuss & R.T. Knight, Eds: 504–527. Oxford University Press. New York, NY.
28. MALLOY, P.F. & E.D. RICHARDSON. 2001. Assessment of frontal lobe functioning. *In* The Frontal Lobes and Neuropsychiatric Illness. P.S. Salloway, P.F. Malloy & J.D. Duffy, Eds: 125–137. American Psychiatric Publishing.
29. DECETY, J. 2007. Op cit.
30. DENNIS, M. 2006. Prefrontal cortex: Typical and atypical development. *In* The Frontal Lobes, Development, Function and Pathology. J. Risberg & J. Grafman, Eds: 128–162. Cambridge University Press. New York, NY.
31. STUSS, D.T., P.W. TERENCE & M.P. ALEXANDER. 2001. Consciousness, self-awareness, and the frontal lobes. *In* The frontal lobes and neuropsychiatric illness. P.S. Salloway, P.F. Malloy & J.D. Duffy, Eds: 101–109. American Psychiatric Publishing. Washington, DC.
32. HOOKER, C.I. & R.T. KNIGHT. 2006. The role of lateral orbitofrontal cortex in the inhibitory control of emotion. *In* The Orbital Frontal Cortex. D.H. Zald & S.L. Rauch, Eds: 307–324. Oxford University Press. New York, NY.
33. BENJAFIELD, J.G. 2007. Op cit.
34. LEDOUX, J. 2002. Synaptic Self: How our Brains Become who we are. Russell Sage Foundation. New York, NY.
35. BENJAFIELD, J.G. 2007. Op cit.
36. SHAPIRO, S.M. 2001. Op cit.
37. GOETZ, G.T. & T.K. SHACKELFORD. 2007. Introduction to evolutionary theory and its modern application to human behavior and cognition. *In* Evolutionary Cognitive Neuroscience. S.M. Platek, J.P. Keenan & T.K. Shackelford, Eds: 5–19. MIT Press. Cambridge, MA.
38. FUSTER, J.M. 2003. Cortex and mind, unifying cognition. Oxford University Press. New York, NY.
39. BECK, A.T. 1979. Cognitive therapy and the emotional disorders. International University Press. Madison, CT.
40. BENJAFIELD, J.G. 2007. Op cit.
41. ELLIS, A. & R.A. HARPER. 1997. A guide to rational living, 3rd Ed. Melvin Powers Wilshire Book Co. N. Hollywood, CA.
42. OCHSNER, K.N. 2006. Characterizing the functional architecture of affect regulation: Emerging answers and outstanding questions. *In* Social Neuroscience, People Thinking about People. J.T. Cacioppo, P.S. Visser & C.L. Pickett, Eds: 245–268. MIT Press. Cambridge, MA.

43. OCHSNER, K.N., S.A. BUNGE, J.J. GROSS & J.D.E. GABRIELI. 2005. Rethinking feelings: An fMRI study of the cognitive regulation of emotion. *In* Social Neuroscience: Key Readings in Social Psychology. J.T. Cacioppo & G.G. Berntson, Eds: 253–270. Psychology Press. New York, NY.
44. OCHSNER, K.N. 2007. How thinking controls feelings: A cognitive neuroscience approach. *In* Social Neuroscience: Integrating Biological Explanations of Social Behavior. E. Harmon-Jones & P. Winkielman, Eds: 106–133. Guilford Press. New York, NY.
45. GEMBA, H. 2002. Motor programming for hand and vocalizing movements. *In* Principles of Frontal Lobe Function. D.T. Stuss & R.T. Knight, Eds: 127–148. Oxford University Press. New York, NY.

Interviewing Strategies in the Face of Beauty

A Psychophysiological Investigation into the Job Negotiation Process

CARL SENIOR,[a] KARLY THOMSON,[a] JULIA BADGER,[a] AND MICHAEL J.R. BUTLER[b]

[a]*Organizational Cognitive Neuroscience Center, School of Life & Health Sciences, Aston University, Aston Triangle, Birmingham B4 7ET, United Kingdom*

[b]*Organization Cognitive Neuroscience Center, Aston Business School, Aston University, Aston Triangle, Birmingham B4 7ET, United Kingdom*

> ABSTRACT: After the application form is submitted, the interview is the most important method of human resource allocation. Previous research has shown that the attractiveness of interviewees can significantly bias interview outcome. We have previously shown that female interviewers give attractive male interviewees higher status job packages compared their average looking counterparts. However, it is not known whether male interviewers exhibit such biases. In the present study, participants were asked to take part in a mock job negotiation scenario where they had to allocate either a high- or low-status job package to attractive or average looking "interviewees." Before each decision was made, the participant's anticipatory electrodermal response (EDR) was recorded. The results supported our previous finding in that female participants allocated a greater number of high-status job packages to attractive men. Additionally, male participants uniformly allocated a greater number of low-status job packages to both attractive men and attractive women. Overall, the average looking interviewees incurred a penalty and received a significantly greater number of low-status job packages. In general, the EDR profile for both male and female participants was significantly greater when allocating the low-status packages to the average looking interviewees. However, the male anticipatory EDR profile showed the greatest change when allocating attractive women with low-status job packages. We discuss these findings in terms of the potential biases that may occur at the job interview and place them within an evolutionary psychology framework.

Address for correspondence: Carl Senior, Organizational Cognitive Neuroscience Center, Aston University, School of Life & Health Sciences (SW612) Aston Triangle, Birmingham, B4 7ET, United Kingdom. Voice: 0044 0 121 204 4068.
c.senior@aston.ac.uk

KEYWORDS: interpersonal attraction; interviews; social status; employment packages; human resource; social cognitive neuroscience; electrodermal response

INTRODUCTION

Interviews are fundamental to the recruitment and selection process as they allow the employer to "get a feel" for the candidate and decide whether he or she will integrate with the existing workforce.[1,2] Given that such social interaction is an important aspect of human resource decisionmaking, it is important to understand the factors that modulate it.

Clearly, positive traits, such as professionalism, intelligence, and likeability, would benefit the candidate at the job interview,[3,4] and early studies have shown that physically attractive people are also imbued with these positive social traits by others.[5,6] Numerous studies also show that attractive people do fare better than average looking people throughout the hiring process.[7–9] For example, compared with average looking individuals, attractive interviewees are more likely to be offered jobs—unless these individuals sought jobs considered inappropriate for their sex[10,11]—and, once offered the job, attractive candidates are recommended for higher starting salaries.[12,13] A recent study also found that resumes of attractive applicants, which included a photograph, were evaluated more favorably than those of average looking applicants.[14] However, in these studies, attractiveness had a greater effect when the interviewers were presented with average quality resumes; this suggests that, to some extent, other personal qualities may also have some effect on the decision.

There are several explanations for biases during an interview. Consider, for example, the finding that observers selectively attend to attractive people and that both male and female observers are able to more accurately recognize a face that they find attractive.[15,16] Male observers exhibit a specific processing bias toward attractive female faces;[17] and female observers selectively attend to attractive women because such individuals could represent intrasexual competitors.[18,19]

Observers are more likely to agree with an attractive person than with an average looking person regardless of the quality or strength of any argument presented.[20,21] Physical attractiveness also biases help-seeking behavior in social groups: women seek assistance from attractive men more than from their average looking counterparts and will seek even less help from a physically attractive woman.[22,23] However, most previous research reports male responses to attractive women; surprisingly little research has examined female responses to attractive men.

Male attractiveness tends to involve the display of social and physical status.[24] For example, male faces displaying sex-specific cues, such as a lower pupil-to-brow distance and a squarer jaw, elicit judgments of greater social dominance and attractiveness by female observers.[24–26] Studies involving identikit manipulation of male faces have found that features associated with maturity and dominance, such as small eyes, a square jaw, thick eyebrows, and thin lips, are considered to be more dominant looking and more attractive by female observers.[27] However, in another study, baby facial features, such as higher set eyebrows, rounder and larger irises, and narrower chins, were considered attractive.[28] The apparent inconsistencies in judgments of male beauty could have occurred because these studies failed to take note of the menstrual state of the female observers, which has recently been found to modulate female preferences for male faces.[29–31]

High-status or dominant looking men are considered to be attractive by women during the follicular phase of the menstrual cycle, when conception is more likely to occur, compared with the luteal phase.[32,33] This phasic pattern of preferences is an adaptive mechanism ensuring that any offspring benefit from the positive genotypic and phenotypic qualities of a dominant man.[34,35] However, in some instances, women may not be able to get access to high-status, dominant men and, as such, it may in her best interest to allocate her own resources to raise the status of the nondominant male.[36] Indeed, in our previous work, we showed that female interviewers in a mock job negotiation scenario, who were in the follicular phase of the menstrual cycle, gave attractive male "applicants" higher status job packages compared with average looking men.[37]

Status is clearly important and, within the organizational psychology literature, status is well defined as the importance individuals ascribe to others, whether socially, monetarily, or both.[38] Factors that influence the attribution of status include jobs, titles, and salaries, as well as the things those salaries can buy (e.g., material goods, such as clothing and jewelry). Different emblems signify different levels of social status. For instance, a man with a neat and clean appearance, wearing a designer suit and a platinum watch, and driving an expensive sports car will be considered financially secure and will be assigned higher social status than a man with an untidy appearance.[39]

The status of a man is a crucial deciding factor in female mate choice; this has driven the evolution of a corresponding drive for status by men.[34,40] The notion of status, however, is changing at the individual and structural levels of organizations. Recent research has shown that organizational status does indeed facilitate the perception of beauty in the office, and this does not affect only female observers; men may find high-status women to be attractive as well.[41] However, in contrast to female observers, it is not known whether men actively assign high-status cues to attractive women. Either way, the allocation of social status is a complex process and, as such, a set of dedicated neural structures that orchestrate its mediation has probably evolved. By identifying these neural structures, one can begin to examine their role in the mediation of other social processes and understand more about the influence they may have during the interview.

One neural structure implicated in the attribution of status is the ventromedial prefrontal cortex (VMPFC), which is active during the perception of attractive people.[42,43] Furthermore, neuropsychological studies show that this area also plays a role in the representation of social rules and facilitates the influence of emotion on the computation of such rules.[44] Such mentalizing is described in the "somatic marker hypothesis."[45,46]

The somatic marker hypothesis states that stimuli—whether internally or externally generated—initiate either a pleasurable or aversive sensation, and these "somatic markers" serve to guide subsequent decision-making behavior.[47] Functional neuroimaging studies testing the somatic marker hypothesis indicate that the VMPFC is active when one makes an advantageous or preferential choice.[48]

However, the VMPFC can be subdivided further into dorsal and ventral sectors, with each playing a specific role in somatic marker processing. The ventral sector of the VMPFC processes somatic markers that occur when one interacts with someone similar to oneself; in contrast, the dorsal sector is involved when one interacts with someone who is dissimilar.[49] This functional dissociation allows one to infer that people with whom one interacts can experience either the same mental state as one's own or a different mental state.[50,51]

The ability to understand the mental states of others, and to infer that this may be different from your own, could underpin interview-based decisionmaking.[52] By examining the psychophysiological basis of preferential decision-making choices at the interview, one can understand more about the nature of the negotiation strategy and identify when possible discriminatory biases may occur. One way to investigate such processes is by examining the electrodermal response (EDR),[53] which has a long history of use in social and organizational research.[54,55]

Contemporary investigations of the EDR technique have identified the time point at which advantageous decisions are made.[46,56] Patients with specific damage to the VMPFC failed to produce the stereotypical "anticipatory EDR" that is indicative of advantageous or winning strategies in the concurrent gambling task. Convergent support for the role of the VMPFC in advantageous decisionmaking comes from work by Critchley and colleagues, who used functional magnetic resonance imaging (fMRI) to identify the cortical regions orchestrating EDRs.[57,58] These investigators found that EDRs occurring after a stimulus event were largely mediated by the orbitofrontal cortex and insula, whereas anticipatory EDRs, or those occurring when choosing a response, resulted in VMPFC activity.

In the current study, we tested a number of hypotheses. We first asked whether female interviewers would give high-status job packages to attractive male interviewees. Such a finding would replicate our previous work and support the notion that women actively manipulate the environment to optimize the status of attractive men.[37] Considering that high status is considered both attractive and beneficial in the work place, we also examined whether attribution of high status is a sex-specific effect or is evident with both male and female interviewers; in other words, we examined a sex-of-the-interviewer by sex-of-the-interviewee interaction. We also hypothesized that attractive female interviewees would engender a greater EDR response than average looking women in both male and female interviewers, and that attractive male interviewees would engender greater EDRs in female interviewers. However, because of the paucity of literature on the male response to male beauty, we examined the EDR profiles elicited by attractive men in male interviewers in an exploratory, hypothesis-generating manner. Considering the organizational strategies that mediate the attribution of high- or low-status employment positioning, we also examined the psychophysiological profile of such assignments. In light of the role of the VMPFC in the preparation of advantageous decisionmaking, we hypothesized that beneficial interviewing strategies would be associated with greater EDRs in interviewers.

METHODS

Subjects

Nineteen age-matched female undergraduates (mean [MN] = 19 years, range 18–27 years) were asked to participate for research hour credits. We have previously shown that a sample size of 15 is sufficient to reveal significant EDR differences across conditions at the 5% level with test power >80%, so a sample size of 19 should increase test power.[59] All participants indicated that they were free from any kind of hormonal intervention (including the birth control pill), and each experienced a regular 28-day menstrual cycle. At the initial screening, each participant was asked to report the number of days since her last period; from this, the follicular phase (days 9–16) for each participant was calculated.[60] Fifteen male participants were recruited from the same population (MN = 22 years, range 19–30 years). All participants indicated that they were heterosexual, right-handed, and free of a history of psychiatric or neurological disorder or drug or alcohol abuse.

Procedure

Experimental stimuli consisted of 40 photographs of faces, including 10 attractive male faces, 10 attractive female faces, 10 average-looking male faces, and 10 average-looking female faces. Details of the stimulus preparation and rating procedure are provided elsewhere, and details are summarized here.[61] In brief, a corpus of 200 faces (100 male and 100 female), were selected from publicly accessible Internet sources. They were shown to group of 25 male and 25 female heterosexual observers who were asked to determine the attractiveness of each face on a scale of 1 (not very attractive) to 8 (extremely attractive). The stimuli selected for the current study consisted of the top 10 attractive male and female faces as well as the top 10 (i.e., those obtaining the lowest rating) average-looking male and females faces (see FIG. 2).

All participants were told that they were going to take part in a study on human resource management. After providing informed consent, each participant was asked to read a small vignette indicating that he or she was the owner and director of a small company. The vignette indicated that the participant had recently hired a number of personnel and had to decide which of two job packages each "interviewee" would receive. The first employment package consisted of (i) a starting salary of £40,000, (ii) a large company car, (iii) a large private office, (iv) a 40% company discount, (v) 60 days paid annual holiday, and (vi) a spouse-covered pension. The second package consisted of (i) a starting salary of £15,000, (ii) a small company car, (iii) a small shared office, (iv) a 10% company discount, (v) 20 days paid annual holiday, and (vi) an individual-only covered pension. Both employment packages were judged to be of 100% high (first package) or low status (second package) by an independent group of raters recruited from the same population as the experimental subjects (n = 20, MN = 20 years between 18 years and 25 years, including 6 men and 14 women). For the sake of clarity, the terms *interviewer* and *interviewee* will be used throughout this report to describe the research participants and the experimental stimuli, respectively.

All psychophysiological data were recorded with a single Biopac system (Biopac Inc, California). Newprep gel (Weaver and Company, Aurora, CO) was applied to two sites on the distal phalanges of the index and middle fingers of the interviewer's nondominant hand. The interviewer's hand was then placed, palm up, on the table at a comfortable resting distance. Both job package descriptions were placed on the table within easy reading distance, allowing the interviewer to refer to them throughout the experiment.

To mirror real-life organizational settings in which candidates would be interviewed randomly, and to ensure ecological validity, the trials were presented in a computer-generated random order via Superlab software (Cedrus, Inc., CA). To ensure that EDR recordings were taken from a steady physiological state, six average looking faces were shown at the start and data were not collected. Each face was presented individually for 10 s and was separated from the next with a 10-s isoluminant interstimulus interval (ISI). The interviewers were asked to make their responses as quickly—but as accurately—as possible from the onset of the picture (see FIG. 1). At the mid-point of this period, the experimenter clapped and asked the interviewer to sigh deeply. A response from these events ensures equipment integrity. All of the interviewer's job package choices were made via a modified response box where the interviewer was asked to rest his or her response finger on a middle key equidistant from keys A and B, which were used to designate a high- or low-status job package choice. The assignment of keys A and B to the high- or low-status

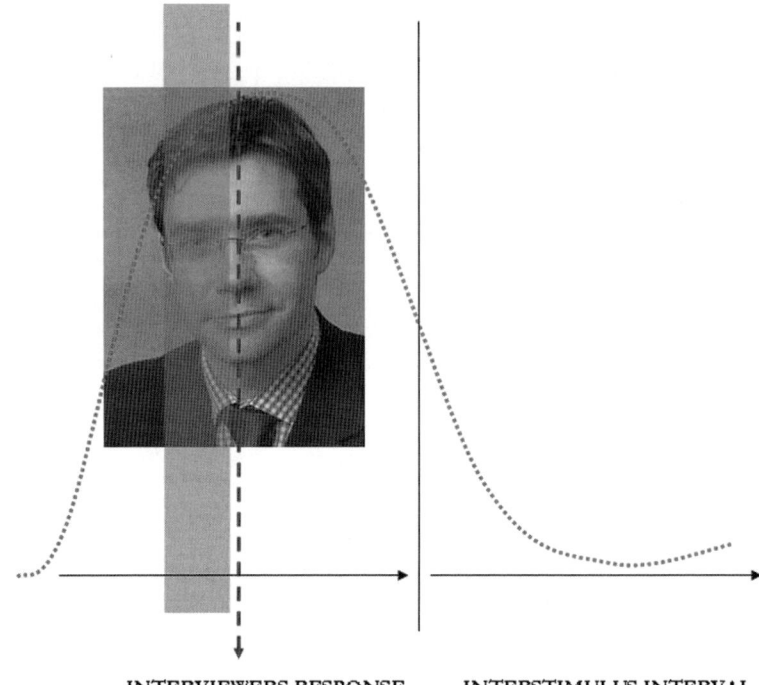

FIGURE 1. Schematic overview of an experimental trial. Each trial consisted of a face presented for 10 s. During this time the "interviewer" was asked to decide which job package (either high- or low-status) to allocate. The dashed line indicates the mean response time to decide which job package to assign to each interviewee, and the dotted line indicates the EDR trace. Each of the faces was separated from the next by a 10-s interstimulus interval (ISI) during which an isoluminant blank screen was presented. No response was made during this period. EDR measurements were taken from a 2.5-s prerseponse period (denoted by the grey bar). The next trial began automatically after the 10-s ISI had elapsed.

package was alternated across runs. Prior to each experimental run, the interviewer was presented with a 5-min blank screen period, during which he or she was asked to sit still and relax.

After testing, all interviewers were presented with the same faces again and were asked to rate the attractiveness of each face (on a scale of 1, not attractive at all, to 8, extremely attractive). Here, they were asked to make their responses on an eight-key number pad, which was configured so that all keys were equidistant from the middle key that was used to initiate each trial. In this rating study, interviewers were asked to make their responses within 10 s. If their responses were made after this period, they were presented with a warning and the trial was repeated.

To examine anticipatory EDRs, overall mean response times to assign both high- and low-status job packages were calculated and used to define a

2500-ms preresponse time window (see FIG. 1). The percentage EDR change from the baseline for each condition was calculated in two steps. First, the lowest point in the baseline period for each subject was added to the rest of that subject's EDR trace; this ensured that subsequent analysis was carried out from a subject-specific baseline. Second, the highest amplitude for each of the four conditions (i.e., attractive men, attractive women, average men, and average women) in the preresponse time window was then used to calculate the percentage difference from the baseline for each condition. The interviewers made no response in the 10-s ISI; this ensured a return to baseline levels prior to the next trial.

RESULTS

Judgments of Beauty

To confirm the presence of a distinct set of attractive and average looking faces, the ratings of beauty for the male and female interviewees were entered into a repeated measures ANOVA with the sex of the interviewee and the classification of attractiveness as within-subject factors and the sex of the interviewers as a between-subjects factor. A highly significant main effect of attractiveness ($F_{1,32} = 597$, $P < 0.001$) confirmed the differences between ratings of attractive faces (MN = 6.5, SE = 1.2) and average looking faces (MN = 2.3, SE = 1.2). Female interviewees (MN = 6.5, SE = 1.5) were judged to be more attractive than their male counterparts (MN = 5.7, SE = 1.5; $F_{1,32} = 78$, $P < 0.001$). Examination of the subsequent three-way interaction ($F_{1,32} = 31.0$, $P < 0.001$) revealed that the ratings given by male interviewers for attractive female interviewees were highest, overall ($t_{32} = 2.65$, $P < 0.05$; male interviewers MN = 7, SE = 0.18 vs. female interviewers MN = 6.2, SE = 0.2). Although the response times to make these ratings were at ceiling level with no differences revealed in any pairings (MN = 2003 ms, SE = 43 ms), these rating data do confirm our pilot work and show that the pictures used were indeed considered to be attractive and average looking by the interviewers in the current study.

Mirroring the analysis of the behavioral responses, the psychophysiological data were analyzed via repeated measures ANOVA with the same factorial design. However, in contrast to the behavioral data, the between-subjects factor did reach statistical significance ($F_{1,32} = 6.93$, $P = 0.01$), with the male interviewers showing a greater EDR change overall (male interviewers MN = 20.0, SE = 2.1 vs. female interviewers MN = 13.09, SE = 1.8). Interestingly, the male interviewers showed a greater EDR change to the average looking interviewees compared with the attractive interviewees (average looking MN = 23.2, SE = 2.4 vs. attractive MN = 17.24, SE = 2.2; $F_{1,32} = 7.28$, $P = 0.01$). The responses in FIGURE 2 show that the differences

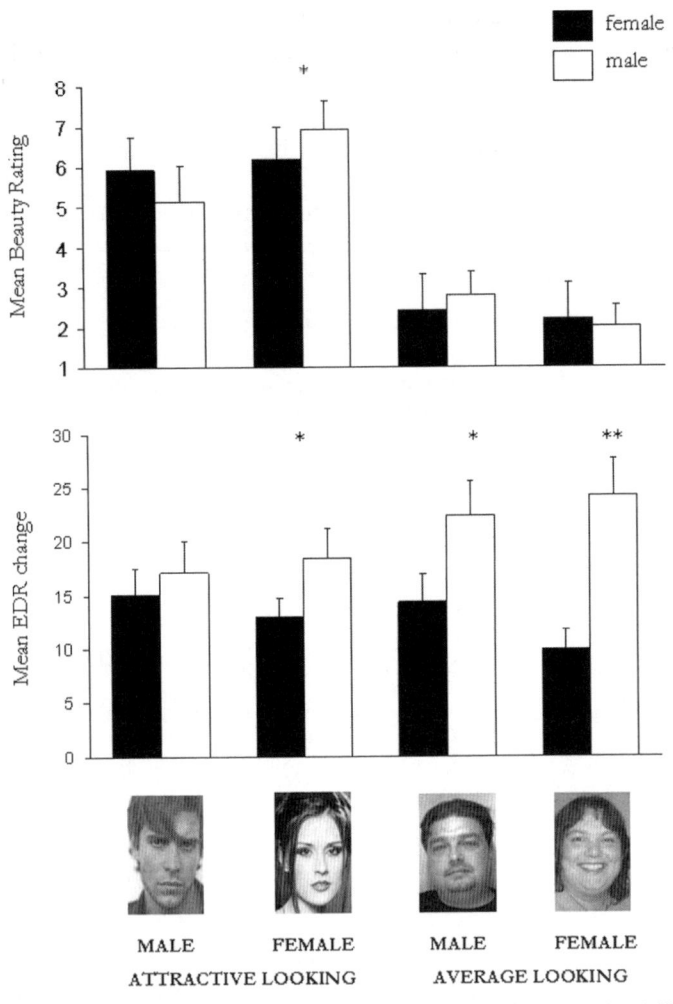

FIGURE 2. Bar chart showing the mean ratings of the attractiveness of the facial stimuli used in this study (*top panel*) and the percentage EDR change when the interviewers were presented with faces from the four conditions (*lower panel*). Examples of facial stimuli are also shown. The average ratings for these specific faces were MN = 6.45, SE = 0.12 and MN = 6.64, SE = 0.48 for the attractive male and female faces, respectively, and MN = 1.95, SE = 0.40 and MN = 1.95, SE = 0.15 for the average looking male and female faces, respectively. Black bars indicate responses to female interviewees, whereas the white bars are the responses to the male interviewees.

between male and female interviewers varied across the conditions. For example, when presented with attractive female faces, EDRs increased for male interviewers but not for female interviewers (male interviewers MN = 18.0, SE = 2.8 vs. female interviewers MN = 13.0, SE = 1.7; $t_{32} = 1.66$, $P = 0.05$).

However, the differences between the male and female responses increased when the interviewers were presented with the average looking men (male interviewers MN = 22.0, SE = 3.2 vs. female interviewers MN = 14, SE = 2.6; $t_{32} = 1.91$, $P < 0.05$) and was greatest when presented with the average female faces (male interviewers MN = 24.2, SE = 3.4 vs. female interviewers MN = 9.9, SE = 1.8; $t_{32} = 3.83$, $P < 0.01$). However, EDRs of male and female interviewers did not differ when they were presented with attractive male interviewees.

Allocation of High- or Low-Status Job Packages

To examine the influence of the attractiveness of the interviewees on the allocation of different types of job packages, an analysis was carried out on attractive and average looking interviewees separately (see FIG. 3A and B). The number of high- or low-status job packages allocated to each interviewee was entered into a repeated measures ANOVA with the sex of the interviewee (male or female) and status of the job package (high or low) as within-subject factors, and the sex of the interviewer (male or female) as a between-subjects factor.

Analysis of the responses to the attractive interviewees revealed an interaction between the sex of the interviewee and the sex of the interviewer ($F_{1,32} = 5.21$, $P = 0.02$). This interaction was driven by the female interviewers allocating more high-status (and fewer low-status) job packages to the attractive men. Although the between-subjects factor failed to reach significance, it did interact with the sex of the interviewee and the status of the job package ($F_{1,32} = 9.54$, $P = 0.004$). To examine this three-way interaction further, subsequent analyses were carried out on the responses for the male and female interviewers separately.

Analysis of the responses from female interviewers revealed that the sex of the interviewee and the status of the job package drove a highly significant interaction ($F_{1,18} = 3.47$, $P = 0.001$). This interaction was driven by the male interviewees receiving more high-status job packages compared to low-status job packages (MN = 6.15, SE = 0.64 vs MN = 3.10, SE = 0.62; $t_{18} = 2.46$, $P = 0.02$). Although the analysis of the responses from the male interviewers failed to reveal significant differences in any pairing, it is interesting to note that their responses were in the direction opposite that of the female interviewers, with more low-status and fewer high-status packages in general assigned to the interviewees.

In contrast to the analysis of the attractive interviewees, the analysis of the average looking interviewees only revealed a main effect of the job package status ($F_{1,32} = 39.35$, $P < 0.001$). This effect was driven by the assignment of more low-status job packages overall (low-status MN = 6.9, SE = 0.3 vs. high-status MN = 2.5, SE = 0.3). In light of the a priori hypothesis concerning the interaction between the sex of the interviewer and the sex of the interviewee, pair-wise contrasts were carried out. Again, the responses from the

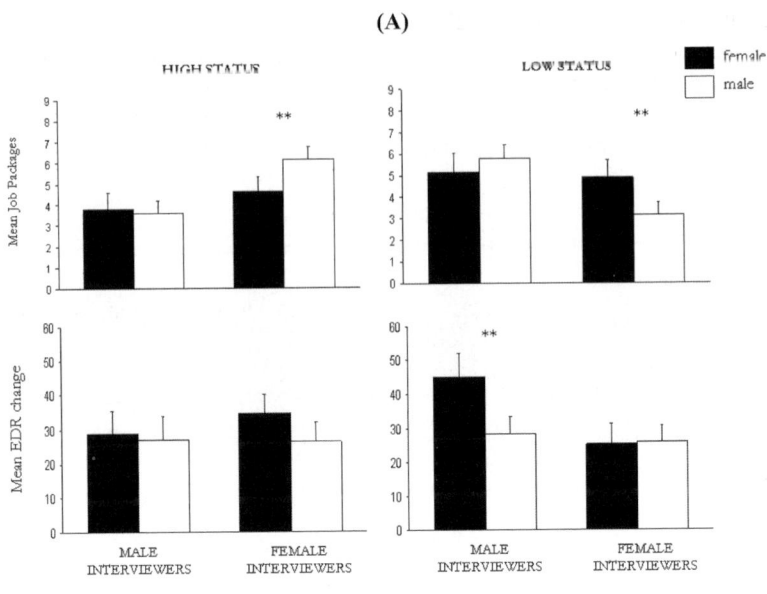
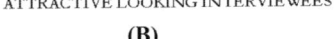
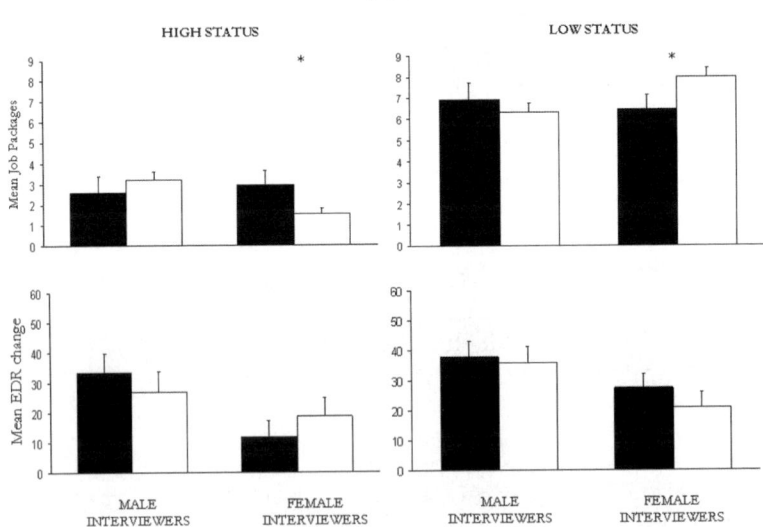

FIGURE 3. (**A**) Attractive interviewees. (**B**) Average looking interviewees. Responses to attractive and average looking interviewees. Bar charts showing the mean and standard error of the number of high- and low-status job packages assigned to either male or female interviewees (*top panel*) and the percentage EDR change that occurred when these job packages were assigned (*bottom panel*). Black bars indicate responses to the female interviewees, whereas white bars are the responses to male interviewees.

male interviewers failed to reach significance. However, for the female interviewers, the pattern of results was in the direction opposite of that revealed for the attractive candidates, with more low-status packages allocated to the average-looking male interviewees compared with the average-looking female interviewees (average looking men MN = 8.0, SE = 0.4 vs. average-looking women MN = 6.4, SE = 0.7).

Analysis of the Electrodermal Response

Separate ANOVAs were carried out to examine the responses to attractive and average looking interviewees. The analysis for the attractive interviewees revealed a highly significant main effect of the sex of the interviewees ($F_{1,32} = 7.99$, $P = 0.008$), with the male interviewees engendering a greater response overall (MN = 33.5, SE = 3.9 vs. MN = 26.5, SE = 3.1). As before, the sex of the interviewer and the status of the job package drove a significant interaction ($F_{1,32} = 5.5$, $P = 0.02$). Examination of this interaction revealed that it was, in fact, driven by a larger EDR change in female interviewers when assigning high-status job packages (high-status MN = 30.4, SE = 4.9 vs. low-status MN = 25.6, SE = 4.9) and a partial greater response in male interviewees ($t_{14} = 1.84$, $P = 0.08$), when assigning low-status packages (low-status MN = 36.6, SE = 5.5 vs. high-status MN = 27.2, SE = 5.5).

Again, the between-subjects factor failed to reach statistical significance; however, the three-way interaction was significant ($F_{1,32} = 4.26$, $P = 0.05$). As before, this interaction was investigated further by analyzing the male and female responses separately. The analysis for the female-only EDR response did not reveal significant differences in any pairing. However, the data from the male interviewers revealed a trend ($F_{1,14} = 3.38$, $P = 0.08$), suggesting that EDR increased when the interviewers allocated low-status job packages compared with high-status packages (high-status MN = 36.6, SE = 4.7 vs. low-status MN = 27.2, SE = 4.3). However, a highly significant main effect of the sex of the interviewee was also revealed ($F_{1,14} = 11.15$, $P = 0.005$), with the male interviewers showing a higher EDR change when assigning low-status job packages to male interviewees (MN = 45.0 SE = 6.0) compared with female interviewees (MN = 28.0, SE = 5.0).

The ANOVA carried out on the EDRs for the average looking interviewees revealed a significant main effect of job package status ($F_{1,32} = 4.30$, $P = 0.05$), with a greater EDR change revealed when the interviewers assigned low-status job packages overall (low-status MN = 30.5, SE = 3.1 vs. high-status MN = 22.6, SE = 3.5).

DISCUSSION

In the present study we tested a number of hypotheses on the influential role of physical beauty on the job negotiation process. To ensure that the stimuli used in the study were distinctly attractive and average looking, the interviewers were asked to rate the attractiveness of all interviewees. These ratings showed a clear distinction between attractive and average-looking interviewees and confirm the distinction found in our pilot study. The stimuli used in this study were thus valid depictions of attractive and average-looking people.

Judgments of Beauty

In a comparison of the ratings assigned by male and female interviewers, only the ratings of the attractive female interviewees differed, with the male interviewers judging them to be more attractive than the female interviewers, again replicating previous work.[62] The ceiling effect observed with the reaction times to make these responses was probably because the interviewers were asked to make their responses within a 10-s time window. In our pilot study we have shown that, when given an unrestricted time period in which to respond, reaction times tend to mirror the rating data, such that subjects take longer to make their responses to attractive faces. Given that beauty may signal the phenotypic and genotypic health of an individual, the fact that male interviewers rate attractive women more highly than female interviewers is probably the result of an adaptive mechanism that facilitates mate choice.[42] However, the fact that female interviewers rated the female interviewees and male interviewees as equally attractive suggests a different process that has been largely ignored in the literature.

Female observers could judge attractive women in terms of intrasexual competitors; however, this does not account for the general in-group bias that female observers exhibit over a range of other cognitive tasks. Recently, Rudman & Goodwin[19] carried out a series of experiments using the implicit attitudes task to fractionate the sex-specific bias and examine its constituent components, namely, gender attitude, gender self-esteem, and gender identity. They found that both male and female participants showed a maternal preference and associated the male gender with negative social aspects such as violence and aggression.[63]

Considered together, these studies suggest that women exhibit more "cognitive balance" than men with regard to their gender, which, in turn, is manifested in the well replicated in-group gender bias reported in many studies.[64] However, the effects of the balance theory are not impervious to other influences and in certain contexts can be obviated.[65] Take, for example the finding by Eagley & Karau[66] that the female-specific in-group bias existed only when women were in female-specific roles. Such "beauty-is-good-only-when-in-its-proper-place" attributions should be considered in light of the present study, where biases at the interview manifested themselves as discriminatory behavior.

The female interviewers' EDRs remained constant when rating the attractiveness of the interviewees. This suggests that, compared with the judgments of their male counterparts, the judgments of women tend to be driven less by emotive content; this, in turn, supports the notion of cognitive balance. In other words, when making assessments about beauty, female observers can make them more rationally. It is worth bearing in mind that, although hormonal fluctuations across the different phases of the menstrual cycle do drive distinct preferences for male beauty,[67] it remains contentious as to whether such cyclic hormonal profiles significantly affect the EDR.[68]

On the other hand, the responses of male interviewers showed a very different pattern of results. Although male interviewers rated the beauty of attractive female faces, their EDRs were greater than the female interviewers' EDRs; this was also the case for the average-looking male and female interviewees. One might assume that the differences between the male and female interviewers across these three conditions is a graduated response. However, the behavioral data, which show a clear difference between the attractive and average-looking faces (see FIG. 2), do not support this assumption, and probably reflect the negative processing observed when participants are shown average-looking faces.[62]

Allocation of High- or Low-Status Job Packages

Examination of the number of high- or low-status job packages allocated to interviewees revealed that female interviewers allocated more high-status job packages and fewer low-status job packages to attractive male interviewees than to average looking men. However, the male interviewers did not differ in the number of high- or low-status job packages they allocated to attractive interviewees of either sex. This finding supports our earlier work and further suggests that female observers actively manipulate the social status of men and are not merely passive observers of such cues.[37] Because the female interviewers all reported to be in the follicular phase of their menstrual cycles, this finding adds to the considerable body of literature on cyclic female preferences.[69]

The suggestion that women manipulate male-specific social information is not without precedent. For example, previous work suggests that paternal investment—the amount of resources a man will invest in subsequent offspring—is positively correlated with the health of both the mother and the offspring; therefore, it is in the best interest of the woman (and her baby) to secure such investment.[70,71] In addition, men invest more resources in children who are similar to themselves.[72–74] In maternity wards, mothers state paternal resemblances with their children and also argue paternal resemblance if the father doubts it.[75] Women also assert paternal resemblance when the man is not the biological father, but the primary caregiver.[76] There is also evidence of matrilineal manipulation of social information such that the female relatives (e.g., aunts) state that the newborn resembles the father more than the mother.[77] Thus, women manipulate social information to secure the resources associated with potential paternity. By manipulating the status of a man, the woman could be assuring potential investment, from which she and any offspring would benefit. Considering that, in the present study, the interviewers were not provided any information as to the qualifications or experience of any of the interviewees, the allocation of high-status job packages could not have been driven by such information.

The responses to the average-looking interviewees were very different from responses to their attractive counterparts. Female interviewers assigned more high-status job packages to the female interviewees and more low-status packages to the men. The male interviewers, on the other hand, allocated more low-status job packages to average-looking interviewees overall, irrespective of the sex of the interviewee. Given that there was no difference in the average number of high-status job packages assigned by either the male or the female interviewers, the female interviewers were punishing the average-looking male interviewees by giving them fewer high-status job packages. Ample evidence suggests that attractive people are favored in the work place, and those who are average looking are at a disadvantage. However, to date, little research has examined the nature of these biases. Here, we show a selective bias with the female interviewers punishing the average-looking male interviewee. The male interviewers, on the other hand, do not show such selectivity and will punish average-looking interviewees irrespective of their sex.

Examination of the Electrodermal Response

When deciding which job package to allocate to the attractive interviewees, the female interviewers showed no change in their EDR profiles. The absence of any differences in the EDRs of the female interviewers is not surprising in light of recent functional neuroimaging studies that found differential activation in areas of the lateral orbitofrontal cortex during emotional processing across the different phases of the menstrual cycle.[78] This region is not thought to play any role in the anticipatory EDRs recorded in the present study. However, the lateral orbitofrontal cortex is involved in the generation of the affective responses, and an event-related EDR paradigm in which the post-stimulus response is analyzed could be used to investigate the nature of such social decisionmaking across the menstrual cycle.[57]

A slightly different pattern of results was revealed when the male interviewers were presented with attractive interviewees. The number of high- or low-status job packages male interviewers allocated to attractive male versus attractive female interviewees did not differ. However, the anticipatory EDR of male interviewers increased significantly when they assigned low-status job packages to attractive female candidates.

The fact that this difference occurred only when assigning low-status job packages ensures that the effect could not have been driven by interpersonal attraction. This EDR difference might reflect advantageous decisionmaking, with the concomitant behavioral response a reflection of that outcome. It is well documented that men tend to be given more resources, such as higher salaries, more holidays, and more promotions, than women.[9] In addition, anthropological evidence from a range of different societies suggests that men do limit access to the resources that would raise the status of women.[79] In an interview scenario, in which every interviewee is to be allocated a job package, an advantageous strategy would therefore be to allocate a greater number of low-status job packages to the attractive women. However, we did not find any difference between the number of high- and low-status packages offered to the attractive interviewees; therefore further studies examining this contention are needed.

The greater EDR change revealed when the interviewers allocated low-status job packages to the average looking interviewees was mirrored by the allocation of a greater number of low-status job packages. This suggests that, in the present study, the average looking interviewees incurred a "career penalty" brought on by their appearance. Furthermore, given the main effect revealed for the EDR analysis, this penalty was probably the outcome of advantageous decisionmaking. Such a social phenomenon has previously been termed the *plainness penalty*, and is observed in a range of careers—not just those for which physical attractiveness would be an obvious asset, such as careers requiring frequent interpersonal contact.[80]

A number of reasons may explain the premium placed on physical attractiveness in the work place, as well as the penalty incurred in the absence of such attractiveness. The central rationale for these social forces is the potential restriction of unmeasured productivity.[81] For example, appearance may affect confidence and the likelihood that potential employees will experience difficulty in communicating with customers or clients. Employees who advertise such potentially negative cues would thus be considered less effective in the work place and would not be promoted frequently.

Indeed, recent research indicates that obese employees, compared to those with normal weight, incurred a wage differential equivalent to approximately 3 years of work experience.[82] However, this bias was found specifically for white female employees, suggesting that a range of social forces may be interacting in the work place. In light of the present study the plainness penalty may be associated with an increase in the anticipatory EDR response.

In the present study, we found evidence of sex-specific preferential behavior in a job interview setting. Female interviewers in the follicular phase of the menstrual cycle assigned more high-status job packages to attractive men. However, the anticipatory EDR profile for the female interviewers showed no difference when assigning any package to male or female interviewees, suggesting that such decisionmaking is not mediated by the

VMPFC. In contrast, the male interviewers did not show a preference for interviewees of a particular sex, and opted instead for allocation of more low-status job packages overall. The highly significant EDR increase when male interviewers gave low-status job packages to attractive female interviewees does imply that the VMPFC may underlie such decisionmaking in this instance.

Although interesting, the results of the present study should be tempered by consideration of a methodological limitation concerning the demarcation of the anticipatory EDR window. This time window may have included the interviewer's motor response involved in selecting a job package, and this—rather than anticipatory cognition itself—could have contributed to the increase in EDRs. This is unlikely to have contributed to the EDR differences across test conditions; however, future work should examine any differential effects of button presses.

Beauty itself is a fluctuating concept, and individual perceptions of who is attractive change from day to day, and even at different points throughout the day. The interviewers in the present study were asked to rate interviewee attractiveness after the EDR data were collected. However, in light of the significant differences between the ratings of attractive and average interviewees shown in FIGURE 2, one can assume that the assessment of beauty, albeit a labile concept, drove the EDR differences.

Although the present study adds to the growing body of literature in applied social cognitive neuroscience, further work examining the overall interaction between the interviewer and interviewee is needed. Both parties at the interview are active members of the social dyad and do not function merely as the transmitter and receiver of social cues. Future studies could examine sex differences in the nature of continued negotiation strategies at the interview, in particular when faced with individuals who have already been allocated high social status.[83]

REFERENCES

1. LOSYK, B. 2003. How to hire the right people. Public Man **85:** 24–26.
2. SHACKLETON, V. & S. NEWELL. 1991. Management selection: a comparative survey of methods used in top British and French companies. J. Occup. Psych. **64:** 23–36.
3. ASHMORE, R.D. & F.K. DELBOCA.1979. Sex stereotypes and implicit personality theory—towards a cognitive-social psychological conceptualisation. Sex Roles **5:** 219–248.
4. FEINGOLD, A. 1990. Gender differences in effects of physical attractiveness on romantic attraction—a comparison across 5 research paradigms. J. Pers. Soc. Psych. **59:** 981–993.
5. DION, K. et al. 1972. What is beautiful is good. J. Pers. Soc. Psych. **24:** 285–290.
6. EAGLY, A.H. et al. 1991. What is beautiful is good, but. . .: A meta-analytic review of research on the physical attractiveness stereotype. Psych. Bull. **110:** 109–128.

7. HEILMAN, M.E. & M.H. STOPECK. 1985. Attractiveness and corporate success: different casual attributions for males and females. J. App. Psych. **70:** 379–388.
8. DICKEY-BRYANT, L. et al. 1986. Facial attractiveness and its relation to occupational success. J. Appl. Psychol. **71:** 16–19.
9. MARLOWE, C.M. et al. 1996. Gender and attractiveness biases in hiring decisions: Are more experienced managers less biased? J. App. Psych. **81:** 11–21.
10. CASH, T.F. et al. 1977. Sexism and "beautyism" in personnel consultant decision-making. J. App. Psych. **62:** 301–310.
11. JAWAHAR, I.M. & J. MATTSSON. 2005. Sexism and beautyism effects in selections as a function of self-monitoring level of decision. J. App. Psych. **90:** 563–573.
12. DIPBOYE, R.L. et al. 1977. Sex and physical attractiveness of raters and applicants as determinants of resume credentials. J. App. Soc. Psych. **62:** 288–294.
13. JACKSON, L.A. 1983. Gender, physical attractiveness, and sex roles in occupational treatment discrimination: the influence of trait and role assumptions. J. App. Soc. Psych. **13:** 443–458.
14. WATKINS, L.M. & L. JOHNSTON. 2000. Screening job applicants: the impact of physical attractiveness and application quality. I.J. Select. Assess. **8:** 76–84
15. MANER, J.K. et al. 2003. Sexually selective cognition: beauty captures the mind of the beholder. J. Pers. Soc. Psych. **85:** 1107–1120.
16. HASSEBRAUCK, M. 1998. The visual process method: a new method to study physical attractiveness. Evol. Hum. Beh. **19:** 111–123.
17. SPRECHER, S. & S. DUCK. 1994. Sweet talk—the importance of perceived communication for romantic and friendship attraction experienced during a get acquainted date. Pers. Soc. Psych. Bull. **20:** 391–400.
18. GUTIERRES, S.E. et al. 1999. Beauty, dominance, and the mating game: contrast effects in self-assessment reflect gender differences in mate selection. Pers. Soc. Psych. Bull. **25:** 1126–1134.
19. RUDMAN, L.A. & S.A. GOODWIN. 2004. Gender differences in automatic in-group bias: why do women like women more than men like men? J. Pers. Soc. Psychol. **87:** 494–509.
20. PALLAK, S.R. 1983. Salience of a communicators physical attractiveness and persuasion: a heuristic versus systematic processing interpretation. Social Cognition **2:** 158–170.
21. DEBONO, K.G. & R.J. HARNISH. 1988. Source expertise, source attractiveness, and the processing of persuasive information—a functional approach. J. Pers. Soc. Psych. **55:** 541–546.
22. NADLER, A. 1980. Good looks do not help: effects of helpers physical attractiveness and expectations for future interaction on help seeking behaviour. Pers. Soc. Psych. Bull. **6:** 378–383.
23. NADLER, A. et al. 1982. Good looks may help: effects of helpers physical attractiveness and sex of helper on males and females help seeking behavior. J. Pers. Soc. Psych. **42:** 90–99.
24. ETCOFF, N. 1999. Survival of the Prettiest: The Science of Beauty. First Anchor Books. USA.
25. SENIOR, C. et al. 1999a. Attribution of social dominance and maleness to schematic faces. Soc Behav & Personality **27:** 331–338.
26. SENIOR, C. et al. 1999b. The perception of dominance from schematic faces: a study using the WWW. Beh. Res Meth. Instrum. Comp. **31:** 341–346.
27. KEATING, C.F. 1985. Gender and the physiognomy of dominance and attractiveness. Soc. Psych. Quart. **48:** 61–70.

28. BERRY, D.S. & L.Z. MCARTHUR. 1985. Some components and consequences of a babyface. J. Pers. Soc. Psych. **48:** 312–323.
29. GANGESTAD, S.W. *et al.* 2002. Changes in women's sexual interests and their partners' mate-retention tactics across the menstrual cycle: evidence for shifting conflicts of interest. Proc. Roy. Soc. B. **269:** 975–982.
30. LITTLE, A.C. *et al.* 2002. Partnership status and the temporal context of relationships influence female preferences for sexual dimorphism in male face shape. Proc. Roy. Soc. B. **269:** 1095–1100.
31. MACRAE, C.N. *et al.* 2002. Person perception across the menstrual cycle: hormonal influences on social-cognitive functioning. Psychol. Sci. **13:** 532–536.
32. SIMPSON, J.A. & S.W. GANGESTAD.1992. Sociosexuality and romantic partner choice. J. Personality **60:** 31–51.
33. LI, N.P. *et al.* 2002. The necessities and luxuries of mate preferences: testing the tradeoffs. J. Pers. Soc. Psych. **82:** 947–955.
34. BUSS, D.M. & M. BARNES. 1986. Preferences in human mate selection. J. Pers. Soc. Psych. **50:** 559–570.
35. SYMONS, D. 1979. The Evolution of Human Sexuality. Oxford University Press. UK.
36. BUSS, D.M. 1989. Sex differences in mate preference: evolutionary hypothesis tested in 37 cultures. *Behav. Brain Sci.* **12:** 1–49.
37. SENIOR, C. *et al.* 2007. The effects of the menstrual cycle on social decision-making. *I. J. Psychophys.* **63:** 186–192.
38. CLEGG, S.R. *et al.* 2006. Power and Organisations. Sage. UK.
39. ARGYLE, M. 1967. The Psychology of Interpersonal Behavior. Pelican Press. UK.
40. SPRECHER, S. *et al.* 1994. Mate selection preferences: gender differences examined in a national sample. J. Pers. Soc. Psychol. **66:** 1074–1080.
41. MARTIN, J.L. 2005. Is power sexy ? Am. J. Soc. **111:** 408–446.
42. SENIOR, C. 2003. Beauty in the brain of the beholder. Neuron **38:** 525–528.
43. WINSTON, J.S. *et al.* Brain systems for assessing facial attractiveness. Neuropsychologia **45:** 195–206.
44. DAMASIO, H. *et al.* 1994. The return of Phineas Gage: clues about the brain from the skull of a famous patient. Science **264:** 1102–1105.
45. DAMASIO, A.R. 1996. The somatic marker hypothesis and the possible functions of the prefrontal cortex. Phil. Trans. Roy. Soc. B. **351:** 1413–1420.
46. BECHARA, A. *et al.* 2005. The Iowa Gambling task and the somatic marker hypothesis: some questions and some answers. Trends Cog. Sci. **9:** 159–162.
47. BECHARA, A. *et al.* 2003. Emotion, decision making and the orbitofrontal cortex. Cereb. Cort. **10:** 295–307.
48. PAULUS, M.P. & L.R. FRANK. 2003. Ventromedial prefrontal cortex activation is critical for preference judgments. Neuroreport **14:** 1311–1315.
49. MITCHELL, J.P. *et al.* 2006. Dissociable medial prefrontal contributions to judgments of similar and dissimilar others. Neuron **50:** 655–663.
50. FRITH, C.D. & U. FRITH. 1999. Interacting minds—a biological basis. Science **286:** 1692–1695.
51. GALLAGHER, H.L. & C.D. FRITH. 2003. Functional imaging of 'theory of mind'. Trends Cog. Sci. **7:** 77–83.
52. JAWAHAR, I.M. & J. MATTSSON 2005. Sexism and beautyism effects in selections as a function of self-monitoring level of decision. J. App. Psych. **90:** 563–573.

53. NAQVI, N.H. & A. BECHARA. 2007. Skin conductance: a psychophysiological approach to the study of decision-making. *In* Methods in Mind. C. Senior, T. Russell & M.S. Gazzaniga, Eds.: 103–123. The MIT Press. USA.
54. AIELLO, J.R. *et al.* 1977. Crowding and the role of interpersonal distance preference. Sociometry **40:** 271–282.
55. WAHLKE, J.C. & M.G. LODGE. 1972. Psychophysiological measures of political attitudes and behavior. Mid. J. Polit. Sci. **16:** 505–537.
56. TRANEL, D. 2000. Electrodermal activity in cognitive neuroscience: neuroanatomical and neuropsychological correlates. *In* Cognitive neuroscience of emotion. R. Lane & L. Nadel, Eds.: 192–224. Oxford University Press. UK.
57. CRITCHLEY, H.D. *et al.* 2000. Neural activity relating to generation and representation of galvanic skin responses: a functional magnetic resonance imaging study. J. Neurosci. **20:** 3033–3040.
58. CRITCHLEY, H.D. *et al.* 2001. Neural activity in the human brain relating to uncertainty and arousal during anticipation. Neuron **29:** 537–45.
59. SIERRA, M. *et al.* 2002. Autonomic response in depersonalisation disorder. Arch. Gen. Psych. **59:** 833–838.
60. ALLIENDE, M.E. 2002. Mean versus individual hormonal profiles in the menstrual cycle. Fertil. Steril. **78:** 90–95.
61. SENIOR, C. *et al.* 2005. You think he's fit and we know it! Social desirability and perception of male beauty. Proc. Brit. Psych. Soc. **13:** 161–162.
62. AHARON, I. *et al.* 2001. Beautiful faces have variable reward value: fMRI and behavioural evidence. Neuron **32:** 537–551.
63. WRANGHAM, R. & D. PETERSON. 1997. Demonic Males: Apes and the Origins of Human Violence. Bloomsbury. UK.
64. HEIDER, F. 1958. The Psychology of Interpersonal Relations. Wiley Press. New York.
65. BROOME, B.J. 1983. The attraction paradigm revisited: response to dissimilar others. Human Com Res. **10:** 137–151.
66. EAGLY, A.H. & S.J. KARAU. 2002. Role congruity theory of prejudice toward female leaders. Psych. Rev. **109:** 573–598.
67. GANGESTAD, S.W. *et al.* 2001. Changes in women's sexual interests and their partners mate retention tactics across the menstrual cycle: evidence for shifting conflicts of interest. Proc. R. Soc., B **269:** 975–982.
68. SIGMON, S.T. *et al.* 2001. The impact of anxiety sensitivity, bodily expectations, and cultural beliefs on menstrual symptom reporting: a test of the menstrual reactivity hypothesis. J. Anxiety Disord. **14:** 615–633.
69. JONES, B.C. *et al.* 2005. Commitment to relationships and preferences for femininity and apparent health in faces are strongest on days of the menstrual cycle when progesterone level is high. Horm. Behav. **48:** 283–290.
70. LANCASTER, J.B. 1989. Evolutionary and cross cultural perspectives on single parenthood. *In* Interfaces in Biology, Sociology and the social sciences. R.W. Bell & N.J. Bell, Eds.: 63–72. Texas University Press. US.
71. HILL, K. & A.M. HURTADO. 1996. Ache Life History: The ecology and demography of a foraging people. Aldine de Gruyter. New York.
72. PLATEK, S.M. 2002. Unconsciousness reactions to children's faces: the effect of resemblance. Evol. Cog. **8:** 207–214.
73. PLATEK, S.M. *et al.* 2002. Reactions to childrens faces: resemblance affects males more than females. Evol. Hum. Beh. **23:** 159–166.

74. BURCH, R.L. & G.G. GALLUP, Jr. 2000. Perceptions of paternal resemblance predict family violence. Evol. Hum. Beh. **21:** 429–435.
75. DALY, M. & WILSON, M. 1982. Whom are newborn babies said to resemble? Ethol. Sociobiol. **3:** 69–78.
76. JAFFEE, B. & D. FANSHEL. 1970. cited in Daly, M., & Wilson, M. 1982 op cit.
77. REGALSKI, J.M. & S.J.C. GAULIN. 1993. Whom are Mexican infants said to resemble? Monitoring and fostering paternal confidence in the Yucatan. Ethol. Sociobiol. **14:** 97–113.
78. PROTOPOPESCU, X *et al.* 2005. Orbitofrontal cortex activity related to emotional processing changes across the menstrual cycle. Proc. Natl. Acad. Sci. USA **102:** 16060–16065.
79. FISHER, H. 1992. Anatomy of love: The mysteries of mating, marriage and why we stray. Fawcett Columbine Press. New York.
80. HAMERMESH, D.S. & J.E. BIDDLE. 1994. Beauty and the Labor Market. Am. Econ. Rev. **84:** 174–194.
81. BIDDLE, J.E. & D.S. HAMERMESH. 1998. Beauty, productivity, and discrimination: lawyers' looks and lucre. J. Labor Econ. **16:** 172–201.
82. CAWLEY, J. 2004. The impact of obesity on wages. J. Hum. Resources **39:** 451–474.
83. SALTER, F. *et al.* 2005. Sex differences in negotiating with powerful males. Hum. Nat. **16:** 306–321.

Neurocognitive Inefficacy of the Strategy Process

HAROLD E. KLEIN[a,b] AND MARK D'ESPOSITO[c]

[a]*Department of General and Strategic Management, Fox School of Business & Management, Temple University*

[b]*Center for Organizational Dynamics, University of Pennsylvania*

[c]*Helen Wills Neuroscience Institute, and Department of Psychology, University of California, Berkeley*

ABSTRACT: The most widely used (and taught) protocols for strategic analysis—Strengths, Weaknesses, Opportunities, and Threats (SWOT) and Porter's (1980) Five Force Framework for industry analysis—have been found to be insufficient as stimuli for strategy creation or even as a basis for further strategy development. We approach this problem from a neurocognitive perspective. We see profound incompatibilities between the cognitive process—*deductive* reasoning—channeled into the collective mind of strategists within the formal planning process through its tools of strategic analysis (i.e., rational technologies) and the essentially *inductive* reasoning process actually needed to address ill-defined, complex strategic situations. Thus, strategic analysis protocols that may appear to be and, indeed, are entirely rational and logical are not interpretable as such at the neuronal substrate level where thinking takes place. The analytical structure (or *propositional representation*) of these tools results in a mental dead end, the phenomenon known in cognitive psychology as *functional fixedness*. The difficulty lies with the inability of the brain to make out meaningful (i.e., strategy-provoking) stimuli from the mental images (or *depictive representations*) generated by strategic analysis tools. We propose decreasing dependence on these tools and conducting further research employing brain imaging technology to explore complex data handling protocols with richer mental representation and greater potential for strategy creation.

KEYWORDS: mental models; strategic thinking; neurocognition; strategic planning; strategy process; cognitive neuroscience; management cognition

Most major corporate and other large organizations engage in the strategy process (also known as a strategic planning process or strategic management process) on a periodic basis, ostensibly for the development of new or revised

Address for correspondence: Harold E. Klein, FSBM 006-00, Temple University, Philadelphia, PA 19122. Voice: 215 204-8883, fax: 215 843-0972.
klein@temple.edu

business strategy. Nevertheless, the application of purportedly rational tools, techniques, protocols, models, or frameworks to the problem of new strategy formation appears to be overwhelmingly ineffectual. Few, if any, organizations actually achieve a new or revised strategy from such efforts. When the genesis of a dramatic change in an organization's objectives and strategies finally is tracked down, it invariably is the result of an informal process that usually is not unrelated to the formal planning effort itself.

This serious failure of formal planning has been well known, if not fully understood, for some time, and was documented more than 25 years ago. Indeed, some reputable scholars in the field recommended at the time that new strategy formation not be attempted through the formal planning process. New or revised strategy had been observed in a variety of large organizations to successfully evolve incrementally independent of the formal planning processes. Hence, these scholars suggested that this was the appropriate way for an organization to adopt a new strategic direction.[1] Currently, there is no evidence that corporations are consciously employing *logical incrementalism* as a means for new strategy formation. Rather, formal strategic planning continues to be an integral activity in most large organizations, employing essentially the same techniques of strategic analysis used a generation ago.[2]

There is some evidence that expectations of the formal strategic planning process have diminished even as it continues to be conventionally practiced. More recently, some major corporations have reoriented the planning process toward addressing specific strategic issues to reach finite decisions.[3] Others have restructured the formal planning protocol to raise awareness concerning the factors and issues management must consider in addressing the more amorphous, less structured strategy formation task, "to build prepared minds that are capable of making sound decisions."[4]

Unfortunately, the strategic analysis protocols at hand—what James March has called *rational technologies*—for "preparing" these minds are sorely lacking.[5] There is little, if any, evidence that the current techniques perform as they are supposed to, namely, by leading to new strategies, inspiring or stimulating the minds of decisionmakers in new strategic directions, or triggering new strategic insights. If anything, the opposite tends to occur: the greater the attempt to "rationalize" the process, the greater the reliance on strategic analysis techniques within the planning system and the greater the attempt to formalize the process; and the greater the formalization of the planning process, the less "out-of-the-box" thinking can be anticipated.[6]

We believe that there is yet a far more fundamental basis for the inefficacy[a] of formal strategic planning efforts, one that goes well beyond

---

[a]The terms *effectiveness* and *efficacy* sometimes are used interchangeably. In some dictionaries, the two are considered synonyms, notwithstanding subtle but real differences in their respective definitions. Effectiveness refers to the *extent* or *degree* to which some activity is performed or accomplished.

behavioral, process, and other explanations. This phenomenon results from profound incompatibilities between the cognitive process—*deductive reasoning*—channeled into the collective mind of strategists within the formal planning process through its tools of strategic analysis (i.e., rational technologies) and the essentially *inductive* reasoning process actually needed to address ill-defined, complex situations. Thus, strategic analysis protocols that may appear to be and, indeed, are entirely logical are not interpretable as such by the processing end of the brain, the neuronal substrate level where thinking takes place. The difficulty lies with the inability of the brain to detect meaningful (i.e., strategy-provoking) stimuli from the mental models (or mental visualizations) evoked by strategic analysis protocols.

In this paper, we focus on what are, arguably, the most ubiquitous strategic analysis techniques, Strengths, Weaknesses, Opportunities, and Threats (SWOT) Analysis[7] and Porter's Five Force Framework (FFF)[8] (see Exhibit 1 for a series of links to SWOT Analysis and FFF definitions and applications). Not only have these approaches been widely used and taught internationally, but these constructs still are foundational to current strategic analysis proposals[9] and pedagogy. Both of these "tools of rational analysis" can be found and recommended (to varying degrees) for use in each of the four top selling strategic management texts, which account for more than half of the market.[10–13] Using these two pillars of strategic planning exercises, we show why strategic response cannot derive directly from performance of such analyses, and why these techniques do not and cannot trigger the creative act of making or revising strategy. The problem lies with the actual and implied cognitive processes conveyed by these techniques, and the *mental model representations* (or "mental imagery") that these evoke in the mind of the decisionmaker.

PLAN OF THE PAPER

First, we discuss the various activities that comprise the rubric of strategic planning. We clarify the key contextual differences between new strategy creation, what we define here as a *strategic situation* (SS), and making *strategic decisions* (SDs). Next, we summarize the perceived major inadequacies of formal strategic planning and analysis technology as conveyed by leading organization scholars as well as the very limited empirical data available on the utility of both SWOT Analysis and the FFF. Then, we identify the cognitive interpretations—what appears in "the mind's eye"—indicated by the structure of these analytical approaches; in other words, the mental imagery evoked by these techniques and how this limits cognitive processing.

Efficacy is an assessment of the *capability* (or *capacity*) of an activity to accomplish an objective or achieve an aim. As we are concerned here with the appropriateness of processes and techniques of analysis, our focus is the latter—what we shall call *neurocognitive efficacy*. Or the lack of it, *inefficacy*.

SWOT & FFF EXAMPLES AND APPLICATIONS...

For Porter's Five Force Frame work...

http://www.quickmba.com/strategy/porter.shtml

http://www.ecofine.com/strategy/Porter%205%20forces.htm

    In practice by consultants:

http://www.metrixmedia.com/5forces.html

http://www.chrisfoxinc.com/strategicOrientation.htm#Strategic%20Planning

    (particularly, click on Strategic Planning. See External Analysis. Note "opportunities and threats," the "O" and "T" of SWOT)

http://caps.uchicago.edu/undergrads/job_search_skills/interviewing/case_interview.html

    U. of Chicago Placement Office tip sheet on interviewing for a consulting job. See "Taking a Case Interview" and note what students are expected to know.

For SWOT...

http://www.netmba.com/strategy/swot/   (Note section on SWOT limitations)

http://www.quickmba.com/strategy/swot/

http://erc.msh.org/quality/ittools/itswot.cfm (even at UNICEF)

http://www.psywww.com/mtsite/swot.html (this is a good one!)

http://scholar.lib.vt.edu/ejournals/JVTE/v12n1/Balamuralikrishna.html

    (Fully applied SWOT in vocational education)

http://www.slideshare.net/rahulogy/textile-industry-in-india-a-swot-analysis

    (At the premier business school in India... note jump to recommendations)

http://www.family-business-experts.com/swot-analysis.html

    (At firms large and ... quite small)

EXHIBIT 1. SWOT and FFF examples and applications.

Next, some key neurobiological concepts that underlie strategic thinking (and *all* thinking) will be presented to explain this mental impasse. And, because thinking and problem solving are inextricably tied to memory, we identify some important neurocognitive aspects of memory activity and mental imagery that are relevant to inductive, strategic thinking. In light of this discussion, we then suggest why SWOT and the FFF, even when used correctly, are not supportive of the creative act of strategy making and how the mental representations these tools evoke must be reinterpreted by the brain to make strategic sense.

DISTINGUISHING THE STRATEGIC SITUATION FROM STRATEGIC DECISIONMAKING

The terms strategy formation, strategic planning, strategic decisionmaking, and strategy selection are used casually, often interchangeably, to denote different contexts and applications. Strategic decisionmaking typically is used to refer to the contexts that are most easily categorized. In such cases, the decision issue in question is reasonably clear—in the important sense that it is commonly understood by decisionmakers—as are the alternatives (or choices) available. Significance alone does not make any particular decision "strategic" in nature. The decision could be in the context of a complex environment in which the external forces normally relevant may be in flux or where some ambiguity may exist in the attributes of the choices; most importantly, the decision could alter the way the company conducts its business (i.e., its strategy). However, the conceit is that common, measurable outcomes can be determined (qualitatively or quantitatively) from each of the choices. Such SDs are tangible and constrained to one immediate purpose or goal (but could have broad company-wide effects), about which there is substantial agreement among involved parties.

Although there is not a universally accepted definition of an SD, there is a sense that, in any one organization, decisionmakers will be in reasonably common agreement as to what constitutes such a decision. A recent examination of strategic decisionmaking effectiveness using different decision processes provides some examples of SDs: a chemical company that enters the sealant business; a company that closes an overseas electronics manufacturing plant; a lighting company that creates a European office; and an electronics company that adopts a new compensation system.[14] From an analytical standpoint, although these decisions were culled from a variety of companies in different industries, they have a number of characteristics in common: (i) extensive past experience and rationality could be brought to bear on the decision process; (ii) nothing is inherently unique about these decisions, however strategically important they might be; (iii) the actions (opening a foreign office, installing a new compensation system, closing a plant, etc.) are themselves generic; and (iv) the factors that would be considered in making such decisions are well known. If not previously addressed by the individual decisionmaker, the factors considered in making the decision could be determined easily by examining the experience of others faced with this same type of decision. In other words, the use of a rational, analytical process—a *deductive reasoning protocol*—would be indicated.

In contrast, we have the SS, a commonplace of corporate-level management in the midst of turbulent environments. Here, the decisionmakers are confronted by a situation[b] at the outset of unknown scope, potentially affecting a large number of organizational decisions, activities, or both. Previously disparate decisions or activities may need to be coordinated and collectively agreed upon. A multitude of relevant extrinsic factors, events, conditions (possibly causally or casually, directly or indirectly related) affecting decisions and activities may need to be addressed or reevaluated because of dramatic changes in a business environment that is in a constant state of flux with no prospect for stability in sight. Nor is it clear which decisions among many specifically need to be addressed or reevaluated immediately, coordinated, or examined in what order or priority. Thus, defining the SS is itself a problem, one arrived at using a good deal of inductive reasoning.

Consider the "War on Terror." Can one, even at this stage, clearly identify the particular decisions—and the specific alternative courses of action—that must be made in response to this "war?" What are the final objectives in fighting this war? Could we define "winning" clearly enough so that we would know if and when this goal has been achieved? Will some adverse set of circumstances for which we have a studied response remain constant long enough for a rehearsed action to be effective? What about some unanticipated terrorist action or other disaster? Which actions need to be taken, or decisions made, immediately? How should the subsequent decisions or actions be prioritized? Which decisions or actions must be coordinated? What ought to be the specific objectives of proposed actions?

At the inception of the Department of Homeland Security, the US federal government released a chart showing 123 federal entities (e.g., agencies, offices, and departments) that were somehow involved in domestic US security and, presumably, in the war as well.[15] Each of these was connected to at least one other security-related organizational unit; a number of entities had several such relationships. This number does not include the thousands of state and local agencies whose resources and mandates similarly are related to some form of homeland security. One can only imagine how much reconfiguration in these arrangements would have to take place when they are confronted by an unanticipated catastrophic event. An ambiguous, complex situation, indeed!

Where does one even start? How does the collective mind of the organizations' decisionmakers, in this case the US government, encompass this situation? This is hardly is a hypothetical situation; one early attempt to grasp the situation was reported in the *New York Times* on April 28, 2004:[16]

---

[b]The term *situation* is used here to convey the lack of distinct boundaries to the problem at hand, where at its initial consideration there is no clear, or even approximate, idea how to formulate, structure, or model the problem—what March characterized as a *complex situation*.[5]

> Soon after the Sept. 11 [2001] attacks, a two-man intelligence team set up shop in a windowless, cipher-locked room at the Pentagon, searching for evidence of links between terrorist groups and host countries.
>
> The men culled classified material, much of it uncorroborated data from the C.I.A.... They recorded and annotated their evidence on butcher paper hung like a mural around their small office. By the end of the year... the men had constructed a startling new picture of global terrorism.

Presumably, these high-level Department of Defense officials had at their disposal the latest, state-of-the-art, rational technologies for addressing the situation. Yet they required more than two months—and, of course, plenty of butcher paper—to assemble their "picture" of the problem.

The War on Terror as an example of an SS is not unique. In fact, it mirrors the corporate strategic planning situation closely. Klein was able to examine the results of a comprehensive strategic planning effort performed within a major electric utility company in the early 1990s—a single company, albeit large, producing essentially one product. This effort was provoked by the passage of federal legislation that effectively would deregulate the electric utility industry during the ensuing decade, thereby completely changing the prospective competitive landscape and the company's existing way of doing business (i.e., the utility's existing strategy). In the span of a decade, the entire electric utility industry would move from being a large group of local, independent, regulated monopolies to a smaller number of consolidated national competitors. This radical industry restructuring would take place concurrently with other major changes in the business environment. Klein found that the company's management identified no fewer than 34 SD issues and activities (e.g., generating capacity, fuel mix, demand side management, transmission type and requirements, central vs. local generation, and pricing) that required reconsideration. A company-wide, extensive environmental assessment, engaging more than 100 company employees supplemented by a variety of outside experts and consultants, yielded about 70 extrinsic factors, forces, and issues that were either directly or indirectly relevant to the aforementioned decisions.[17]

In a similar, but even more extensive, strategy reassessment conducted by an international petroleum company for its US subsidiary, more than 90 SD issues, activities, and functions were identified, along with well over 250 relevant external factors—an even more complex SS. In both the electric utility and petroleum company situations, the initial objectives of their respective planning exercises were not the creation of new strategies, but the identification of which decisions had to be made, the state of the relevant external factors that impinged upon the identified decisions, and the types of action the respective companies could take to moderate prospective adverse events.[18]

EFFICACY OF STRATEGIC ANALYSIS TECHNIQUES—EVIDENCE AND ASSESSMENT

Evidence

Empirical research to establish the efficacy of strategic analysis techniques and their contribution to strategy formation is practically nonexistent. Many studies have examined the *perceived value* of formal planning systems and analytical tools, some with favorable results and others unfavorable. In virtually all of these studies, the measure of value or effectiveness has been subjective (the *ex post facto* assessment either of an observer of the situation under study or of the decisionmaking participants themselves). For example, Sinha's large-sample survey of Fortune 500 companies and their use of formal strategic analysis tools for specific SDs (i.e., strategic programming) found that these tools were positively valued.[19] In contrast, Bresser and Bishop's meta-assessment of the use of formal protocols for strategic planning (i.e., strategy formation) found contradictory results among the empirical studies undertaken.[20]

The utility of rational analytical techniques for addressing specific SDs seemed to be supported, when compared with the use of political processes, in a 1996 study.[14] A more recent, (2003) in-depth examination of corporate-level, strategic planning practice among eight major international oil companies revealed their shift away from strategy formation within the formal planning process (an explicit acknowledgement of the inability of the formal process to generate new strategy). The focus was found to be broad goal setting and consideration of major specific SDs. Strategic planning was devolved to individual divisions. In this research effort, as with virtually all others attempting to measure or otherwise evaluate the worth of formal planning processes and rational techniques, the raw data were personal assessments—the views and experiences of managers who participated in the planning process under study.[21]

Remarkably, it appears that only one extensive, systematic examination exists of the actual results of a standardized application of a strategic analysis tool or technique. Hill and Westbrook gained access to the results of the formal strategic planning efforts of 20 UK manufacturing companies. Thanks to a UK government-funded effort to encourage and facilitate the use of rational planning and decisionmaking practices, a series of professional consultants were teamed with the managements of 14 of the 20 companies to assist them in conducting a formal strategic planning process, following exactly the same protocol. One step, in each case, was the performance of a SWOT Analysis. In their examination of the strategic planning results, Hill and Westbrook did not find a single company among the 20 for which the SWOT results were used *at all* in subsequent steps of the planning exercises. They concluded that the use of SWOT Analysis should be discontinued.[22]

Porter's (1980) FFF has not faired much better. The operational difficulties in applying the framework were identified soon after its publication,[23] and these weaknesses have not been resolved.[24] Both techniques, it has been argued, convey no notion of a temporal dimension in competitive dynamics, induce cross-sectional thinking, are vague as to the application of results even within the purported analytical framework, and have no discernable relevance for strategy implementation. To date, no study has been performed, comparable to that of Hill and Westbrook's, that examines the effectiveness of the FFF. This is surprising—and dismaying in light of its stellar position within the strategic management firmament.

Assessment

More than a decade ago, Mintzberg conducted what is, perhaps, the most extensive and thoughtful examination of the causes for failure of formal strategic planning systems and strategic analysis techniques. He concluded that planning is an *analytical* exercise, but strategy creation is *synthesis*. Strategy will derive from other, more *informal* activities, but not from the process itself, which is more appropriate for *strategic programming*—the "codification, elaboration and conversion" of strategies into detailed, implementable plans. The clearer a stated strategy—what you want done and essentially how you ought to do it—the greater the likelihood that it can and will be implemented.

Mintzberg concluded, apparently correctly, that strategy is the product of "right-side of the brain" thinking, and analysis (which he deemed *planning*) is a "left-side of the brain" activity. Hence, corporate planners should revert to a facilitating function and act as catalysts for some "black box" whence strategy will emerge (where the black box is presumably the collective mind of the corporate strategic managers). Clearly, different thinking processes are involved in analysis and synthesis.[25]

Others have come to similar conclusions.[26] Most recently (2006), James March, a founder of the field of organizational science, has seriously questioned the very utility of "the core technologies of strategic management." That is, the strategic analysis techniques at the heart of strategic planning processes, what March variously refers to as *rational technologies*, *techniques of model-based rationality*, or *analytical tools*. He concludes that there is no evidentiary basis for believing that these supposed analytical techniques are capable of addressing complex strategic problems. It is useful to mention March's summarization of the difficulties that contribute to the "misspecification of situations," diminishing the applicability of strategic analysis techniques: (i) uncertainty about the attributes of the situation; (ii) causal complexity—the many interdependencies among situation variables; (iii) confound of measurability and importance—the tendency of analysts to give more weight to measurable variables than more-difficult-to-measure ones; (iv) preference ambiguity—the indeterminacy of values and utilities of action; (v) interpersonal trade-offs—the difficulty of determining combinatorial preferences of situation participants; and (vi) strategic interaction—the causal interdependency of action–reaction among organizations. March notes the apparently total confidence of strategic management scholars in the ultimate utility of rational analytic techniques for addressing a complex SS and offers a concise description of this phenomenon: "The Heroism of Fools."[5]

STRATEGIC ANALYSIS TECHNIQUES APPLIED—IN THE MIND'S EYE

The formalized steps in the comprehensive strategic planning rubric (or the strategic management or the strategy process) are well known and have been accepted for decades as a variant of the rational decisionmaking model. The nomenclature may vary, but the essentials of the steps are the same: (i) set organizational objectives; (ii) conduct an environmental assessment (internal to the organization and external to it); (iii) form or revise a strategy; (iv) implement a strategy through such actions as organization structure redesign, resource allocations for operational programs, complementary management information and other internal systems development, adjustment of the organization's reward system, etc.; (v) enact strategic control by monitoring and analyzing feedback of the organization's performance in relation to its goals; and, finally, (vi) take timely corrective action in response to observed deviations in desired performance. In situations where it is obvious to the collective management that the organization is confronting major external environmental change, and where the likelihood is high that the organization will need to revise significantly its existing strategy or devise a new one if it is to survive, the environmental assessment step is performed first, in place of objective-setting.

Surprisingly, the essential tools of strategic analysis that are used in each of the steps have not changed materially during the last 20 years or so. Often, the most critical step in the formal strategic planning process—the environmental assessment step, which provides the stimulus or impetus for strategic response—is comprised largely of the FFF, variants of a SWOT Analysis, or both (see Exhibit 1).

The essence of the FFF is conveyed visually by means of the five-force diagram, in which "industry rivalry" is at the hub, surrounded equidistantly by the four external "forces" impacting the industry; visually, the FFF is a hub–force with four spokes, or forces. Each of the latter four rather general forces (i.e., the power of buyers, the power of suppliers, the threat of substitute products, and the threat of new entrants) is, in turn, comprised of a series of more specific forces, easily from 5 to 10 or more. Thus, the force, "supplier power" might comprise: (i) supplier concentration; (ii) importance of volume to supplier; (iii) differentiation of inputs; (iv) impact of inputs on cost or differentiation; (v) switching costs of firms in the industry; (vi) presence of substitute inputs; (vii) threat of forward integration; and (viii) cost relative to total purchases in industry. Any robust FFF for an industry could have 25 to 30 or more individual forces impinging on the "industry rivalry" force (the hub) which, itself, comprises 10 or so industry attributes.

The most commonly encountered variant of a so-called SWOT Analysis is a series of verbal statements organized into four distinct groups, classified according to the sense of the SWOT acronym (i.e., a series of simple or annotated statements listing strengths, another listing of weaknesses, and so on). The relevance of any list item is not usually stated explicitly; nor is there indication visually or otherwise of any interdependency or connection of items within a list or among lists. Hence, the SWOT representation simply consists of four lists with varying degrees of detail for each item.

MENTAL VISUAL REPRESENTATION OF SWOT AND FFF CONSTRUCTS

From a cognitive perspective, both approaches have important similarities despite apparently different representations. Both SWOT and the FFF convey the notion of a number of issues, variables, or forces *simultaneously* and *mutually exclusively* affecting something: the former implied, usually the "corporation"; the latter quite explicitly, the "industry." In the case of SWOT, four sets of items are developed, where each item either is descriptive of the organization (in the case of Ss and Ws) or relevant to the organization (in the case of Os and Ts).

One can only surmise, but with some confidence, how the mind frames the problem conceptually in statement form, *the propositional mental (verbal) image* or its visualization, *the depictive mental (visual) image*.[27] For both tools, the structure of relationships (or lack thereof) is clearly explicit. In recognition of the vagaries of SWOT, at times the strengths and weaknesses might be individually arrayed opposite the opportunities and threats, creating four sets—SOs, WOs, STs, and WTs—this has been termed a *TOWS Analysis*.[28] This reconfiguration of the four sets of items into two pairwise sets purportedly overcomes the deficiencies of the SWOT Analysis. But does it? With the TOWS arrangement, depending on the richness of the imagination or recall in generating the original SWOT lists, one is confronted by a set of apparently mutually exclusive paired items of indeterminate number (each application would yield different results and pair relationships). A responsive strategy would have to be created for each pair. No protocol is provided to address these multiple paired relationships.

The FFF need not be imagined, as the construct always is presented pictorially as a hub with four spokes, arranged in the appearance of the face of a compass. Similarly, SWOT simply consists of four lists, sometimes shown in vertical sequential order and other times depicted in a four-quadrant square with the strength list opposite the weakness list and, below, the opportunity list opposite the threat list. As indicated above, the relevance (i.e., rationale) for any one item's presence on any of the four lists can only be inferred as there is no explicit indication from the visual representation itself.

Exhibit 2 provides generalized representations of the propositional and depictive mental images of both SWOT and the FFF. Schematic A should be recognizable as the general case of the FFF, except that it is here shown with six nodes (or "forces") connected to a central node, or hub ("industry rivalry" in the case of the FFF). Schematic B is a list of nodes, all commonly connected to another node; this might be an interpretation of, say, the "strengths" of the firm, where the firm is the single node to which the other six are connected. A comprehensive visualization of SWOT might be four such lists. It should be evident that both Schematics A and B are identical structurally, both from a propositional and depictive standpoint!

In essence, these propositional and depictive mental images (Exhibit 2, Schematics A, B) are the verbal and diagrammatic analogues, respectively, of a linear, multiple regression equation, but without coefficients and with a vague dependent variable (the corporation or the industry). And that might very well be the mental model evoked in the mind of an economist. Someone else, such as a business analyst, indoctrinated in the applicability of the FFF, more likely would envisage a bicycle wheel arrangement. But, again, analytically these are one and the same problem constructs.

ARRIVING AT A MENTAL DEAD END—THE FUNCTIONAL FIXEDNESS PROBLEM

There are two difficulties with the SWOT and FFF representations: (1) they do not jibe with reality; and (2) the mind cannot possibly process these problem representations as given (i.e., depictive schematics A or B in Exhibit 2). Neither the SWOT nor the FFF representation conveys any temporal or serial quality of the arrayed forces, factors, or issues.[29,30] All forces, in fact, do not act simultaneously, nor are these mutually exclusive of one another; they are highly interdependent and, often, causally related but not in a quantitatively describable fashion. And, while an econometric model exercised on a computer can handle multiple factors simultaneously (given the appropriate input data), the human mind, at the conscious level, does not and, more importantly, cannot execute that task.[c]

[c]That is, for high-level cognitive tasks (e.g., strategic thinking). We routinely do two things at once, but not two complex cognitive tasks where each demands our individual attention. One can hold a conversation while driving a car, the latter a highly complex cognitive task but one that, over time, can become automatic. But holding a conversation while watching television is difficult for most people to do; we end up switching our attention between these two activities in serial, sequential fashion.

A & B ALL EIGHT FAC TORS/NODES SIMULTAN EOUSLY AND/0R COMMONLY IMPACT OR CREATE ANOTHER NODE

C TWO PAIRS OF NODES MUTUALLY INDEPENDENT OF EACH OTHER IMPACT OR CREATE TWO OTHER NODES. THE RESULTING TWO NODES IMPA CT OR CREATE ANOTHER NODE

PROPOSITIONAL MENTAL IMAGES

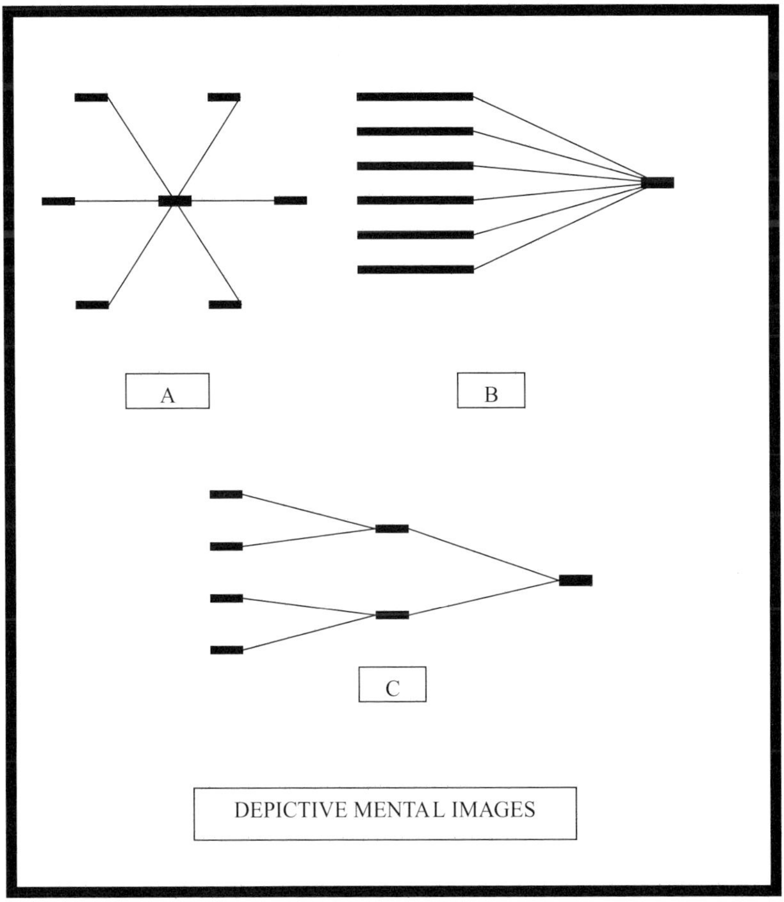

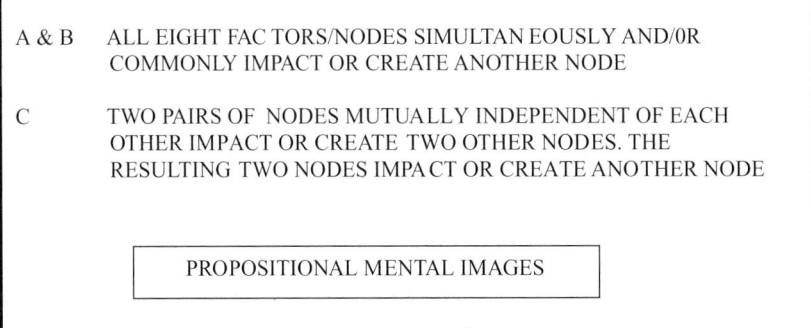

EXHIBIT 2. Generalized mental imagery of SWOT and FFF: depictive and propositional.

Exacerbating the cognitive problem is the use of the terms "analysis" with SWOT (i.e., "SWOT Analysis") and "model" with the FFF, where the FFF is referred to loosely as the "Five Force *Model*" as opposed to the "Five Force *Framework.*" Porter himself has been careful to make the distinction between the attributes of a model and a framework. The latter is conceived of as a more robust construct in theory building, inclusive of more variables, and more complex. It does not need to meet the criterion of application, as it is not intended for that purpose. A model has fewer variables, is less comprehensive, and is more appropriate for hypothesis testing.[31] But when the FFF is dubbed the "Five Force Model" does it not suggest to the planner that an analytic application is called for? And does it not also create the expectation of simultaneous consideration of the relevant forces affecting the industry? In the case of SWOT lists, does "analysis" imply that the variety of positive and negative organization attributes (strengths and weaknesses, respectively) need to be considered in responding to the positives and negatives of the prospective environment (opportunities and threats, respectively) or collectively considered in developing a company strategy?

Here, the semantics (the propositional representation) and the visualization (the depictive representation) together channel the brain toward attempting an analytical, *deductive* solution. Additionally, there is the reinforcing effect of being exposed repeatedly to the notion that the use of SWOT or the FFF is an "analysis" that will lead to strategic revelations. The ubiquitous nature of SWOT and the FFF in business school classrooms and in planning practice would seem to assure their status as what cognitive psychologists refer to as *frames* or *scripts*—routines, heuristics, and memorized procedures for addressing particular problems.[32] Figuratively, and perhaps literally speaking, these mental constructs have been "hard-wired," into the psyche of the strategic analyst and decisionmaker.

But what can the mind do with these mental models? The FFF provides no clue as to how to handle the identified forces, either in relation to each other or to the industry. In the case of SWOT, the problem of model construction is worse still, as there is no dependent variable, however ambiguous, upon which to focus the items in each of the SWOT lists, and there are no constraints on what can be included or omitted from these lists.[30] Other versions of SWOT, such as TOWS, that attempt to add some structure and simplification (i.e., S–W or O–T pairwise constructs), only add a different type of ambiguity to the problem: Are the pairwise relationships mutually exclusive? If they are not, how are they related? How can these relationships be expressed in an objective manner? And what does one do with these anyway?

Obviously, something useful. A recent (2006) assessment of the "big ideas" in strategic thinking—those that have stood the test of time and practice—identified four "new, sharper analytical tools that help managers make better sense of their markets, competitors, and industries." SWOT and the FFF (referred to as "industry structure") were included along with "product life cycle" and "market segmentation."[2] But recall that the UK study, the only empirical assessment of the actual use of SWOT analysis results as inputs to strategy formation, found no indication that the SWOT lists were used subsequently in the identification or creation of new or revised strategy. Neither SWOT nor the FFF provide any further problem-solving heuristics beyond the potential trigger to memory embedded in the list items themselves. Hence, the output from these two "analyses"—essentially lists—in some manner act as extrinsic stimuli, raising different problem-solving heuristics to the conscious level; alternatively, these analyses are mentally discarded and the problem addressed anew.

From a neurocognitive perspective, SWOT or the FFF sets up an insoluble problem for the brain—a mental dead end. There are no instructions, no protocol, and no practiced analytical approach provided; each application is unique. There is no prescribed way, and no script in the analyst's mind, to examine simultaneously two or more of the five forces and their multiple components or the dozens of items on the SWOT lists. If the analyst is fixated on the mental model evoked by the FFF or SWOT, there is no way for the brain to proceed (recall the criticism above).

What appears to result is the *functional fixedness* effect,[33] or mental fixation:[34] unless what is construed as an analytical problem is mentally reconfigured, it cannot be solved.[35] If, indeed, functional fixedness is taking place (it can only be inferred from observation alone), the original mental model (i.e., the FFF or SWOT) is more or less discarded. In the absence of any further analytical guidance, the mind presumably falls back on prior experience (i.e., memory) in dealing with such situations. In laboratory functional fixedness experiments, once a subject is shown how to reframe the problem, the subject most often can solve it easily.[d] But in such controlled experiments, there always is a correct and finite solution. It is possible to measure the exact time it takes to reach a solution under both conditions, or whether a solution is reached at all.[34,36] There are no comparable objective measures with the application of SWOT or the FFF. There are no generalized follow-on protocols extant for coping with the various FFF-generated forces or the items on SWOT lists.

In effect, every strategy formation exercise is a novel one, requiring, anew, the integration of prior knowledge and experience with new extrinsic stimuli

---

[d] A classic functional fixedness experiment is to provide a subject with a box of matches, a candle, and a tack. The problem is to affix the lit candle to a wall. If the match box itself is seen as one of the objects that can be used in solving the problem, then the solution is readily obtained: empty the box of the matches; tack the box to the wall, creating a shelf; light the candle with one of the matches; and place the lit candle on the side of the box protruding from the wall. If the subject doesn't see the box as a separate object to be used, but simply as a container for the matches, either the problem will not be solved or it will take materially longer. Hence, the term functional fixedness or mental fixation: a subject is "fixated" on the function of an object, in this case a match box, and does not consider an alternative use for it. Once the subject is made aware that the box itself may be used in performing the task, it is quickly completed.

that trigger associations in the mind of the strategist. It should be expected that novices in the use of these "analytical tools" would have difficulty in their application. However, continued exposure to examples of their application (as in the classroom through case studies), along with practice in attempting to apply the tools themselves, appears to provide egress from the encountered mental dead ends, a process that might appear seamless to the observer.

Consequently, for the SWOT or FFF results to prove useful in the subsequent strategy formation step (as they appear to be, given the iconic status of these tools), some unobserved thought process, or change in thought process, must be taking place. Those who begin their analyses with the SWOT or FFF mental image would need to reconfigure their mental model of the problem, something they would learn to do almost unconsciously. The more astute (or experienced) among us, having frequently confronted this kind of problem before, intuitively (from implicit memory) reconfigure it to address each factor or force individually or in some simple combination.[37,38] The even more intelligent, perhaps, might clump related factors before beginning their analysis, or explicitly search for some common threads or linkages among the various factors or forces. The problem might be reconfigured along the lines of Schematic C in Exhibit 1, where the implications of the interrelationship of two factors are considered in relation to the results of two other interdependent factors.

Depending on the kind of representations evoked in the brain, different associations will elicit different configurations of prior knowledge which, in turn, will activate different parts of the brain and, hence, different memories.[39] Ultimately, given the multiple factors in the initial condition and others triggered from memory, an inductively derived reasoning process should emerge. In contrast, if an individual remained fixated on trying for a dead-end analytical solution where there is not one, brain activation patterns should be different, perhaps occurring within brain regions that support deductive reasoning.[40]

RELEVANT NEUROCOGNITIVE FINDINGS WITH RESPECT TO THINKING AND MEMORY

Investigations in cognitive neuroscience have yielded explanations of how thinking and memory work (the two are wholly interdependent phenomena), and how these processes come about. Findings of these investigations provide further explanations for the inefficacy of SWOT and the FFF for new strategy creation and the importance of mental visualization in making sense of a complex SS. SWOT and the FFF are little more than lists of issues, forces, or factors to consider in the complex task of strategy formation. In effect, these are extrinsic inputs to the brain. Without further instruction on how to proceed, the mental visualization evoked by the SWOT Analysis (i.e., lists) or the FFF (i.e., the hub-and-spoke diagram with "the industry" or "industry rivalry" at the center) becomes important and determines the mental model driving the solution attempt.[41] Individuals will address these SWOT and FFF lists differently from one another. Each item, individually or in some combination, will activate different types of memory and, consequently, different areas of the brain. For example, instructions to address items sequentially or in a certain order will trigger different activation patterns.[42] An attempt to address two or more tasks simultaneously excites different brain regions and produces different activation patterns than performing the same two tasks sequentially.[43] Also, mental performance for engaging in two or more tasks simultaneously will drop compared to the performance for engaging in either task alone. The frontal lobes of the brain are engaged under such conditions in an attempt to coordinate and allocate sufficient attentional resources to handle concurrent tasks successfully; these brain regions are also important for selecting among competing choices in solving problems. However, two tasks that require recruitment of similar areas of the brain will compete for limited resources, and absolute successful performance will be difficult unless the subject can be trained extensively to create a more automatic routine.[44,45]

Regardless of whether these factors are addressed individually or clumped, the four impacting forces or their components in the FFF and the larger number of strengths, weaknesses, opportunities, and threats would each (individually or in small groups) be dealt with mentally in a *serial* fashion. There is no getting away from it: to proceed, mental processes that differ from those conveyed by the original representations must be followed.

It has been known for some time that even simple tasks, such as scanning our memory for information to be recalled, are performed in a serial fashion.[46] For example, subjects that are asked to recall a single letter from a remembered list of six letters will take longer to recall the letter than if the remembered list was three letters. In perceptual tasks, searching for a target within a vast of array of similar targets also is performed in a serial fashion.[47] Simultaneous stimuli are processed less efficiently by the brain than are the same stimuli provided in sequential fashion.[48] Thus, it seems counterintuitive, from a neuroscientific perspective, that a human presented with a difficult problem would be able to simultaneously process all aspects of the factors involved in coming up with a solution, say, to a multivariate strategic problem in a manner analogous to a computer's performance of a multiple regression.

We summarize below some of the key incompatibilities between relevant memory attributes and strategic analysis tools.

- Memories that are the basis of new ideas, solutions, and creations (i.e., strategic options) are spurred by some trigger or association (these rarely come about through a mental leap from nothingness); the trigger is all-important. Hence, the more vague the trigger, the less likely it is that some meaningful association will come about. In its most common representation, SWOT exists without relevance for any particular aspect of the

organization for which it is performed. When SWOT list items are paired, as they often are when using some variant of a TOWS construct, one has, yet again, a mutually exclusive set of more complex relationships (e.g., a strength arrayed against a weakness).
- Memory is wholly dependent on circumstance; it is not static and does not exist without relation to a stimulus. (A stimulus to memory may come from within the brain itself, exemplified by the common experience of something just having "popped" into one's head, seemingly without any extrinsic input.) Even the slightest variant in the stimulus can lead to a different fragment of memory surfacing to the level of consciousness—this may, in turn, serve as the stimulus that elicits some new memory (i.e., a new idea synthesized from existing or reconfigured memory fragments). The FFF representation suggests mutual exclusivity of each of the forces, more than likely resulting in diminished consciousness-raising within the mind of the strategist.
- Data and information derived from data tend to be clustered (or clumped) within the mind based on some commonality(s); the composition of a memory cluster is situation-specific and can change materially even with the slightest alteration in situation (i.e., stimulus). Neither the FFF nor SWOT representations even remotely encourage the notion of joint consideration of forces or factors (i.e., mutual exclusivity).
- Multiple stimuli presented concurrently actually cause lower measurable activation patterns within the brain than do the same stimuli presented in serial fashion. Hence, the representations themselves immediately reduce strategic thinking efficiency.
- Finally, at the highest level of consciousness, when we are confronted by complex, nonroutine cognitive tasks, the brain is mainly a serial processor. It is only at lower levels of consciousness—what has been called the *preconscious* or, further down, the subconscious levels—that the brain exhibits parallel processing capabilities. Hence, the more complex the strategic decision issue and the more factors that must be taken into account, the greater the necessity for mapping out a more serial protocol with explicit triggers to provoke a creative response on the part of the strategic decisionmaker.

This provides a rationale for de-emphasizing the use of SWOT results in strategy formation processes, even once this analysis has been accomplished comprehensively. Indeed, it could be hypothesized that the more strengths, weaknesses, opportunities, and threats are elicited, the less will be the utility in so doing. A similar case can be made regarding the FFF. Without any further protocol or heuristic for handling only the four general forces impinging on the industry, their effects cannot be systematically evaluated. If strategic management texts continue to promote these tools for strategic analysis, caveats concerning the cognitive weaknesses of these techniques ought to be included (as some texts already do), if for no other reason than to reduce the frustration and ego-deflating effect on students (and planners) who are expected to produce strategy from such analytical results.

THE IMPORTANCE OF MENTAL IMAGERY

The capacity to reason through a complex problem is enhanced by its visualization (i.e., mental model), either in depictive or propositional form.[49] In collaborative circumstances particularly, the condition most prevalent in organizations, a commonly shared understanding of the initial problem situation is of critical importance to effective decisionmaking. It has been shown that agreement at the outset of the initial situation and the final goals—the mental model of the situation—is even more important in effective decisionmaking than the ensuing problem-solving protocol followed.[50] In particular, when the initial condition is that of a complex dynamic system, an ability to grasp the system's causal structure and the interdependencies of causative factors improves one's ability to exercise overall system control.[38] The important role of mental image representation (i.e., the construct of a problem as it appears within the brain) in determining the efficacy of high-level, problem-solving heuristics or protocols has been explored extensively at the behavioral level.[51,52] Mental imagery has been found to be a significant factor in determining the quality of the solution for structured problems[53] and, more recently, in more creative problem solving.[49] It also has been shown that the choice of problem-solving protocol derives from the envisaged mental representation; more importantly, it can bypass the functional fixedness phenomenon.[53]

In The War on Terror SS provided above, defining the initial conditions was the subject of the *ad hoc* search process (recall the locked room with butcher paper adorning the walls) described in the *New York Times*. Although the locked room does not suggest much interest in sharing understanding of the situation, procedurally the attempt to develop a visualization of this complex problem was laudable. A shared understanding of the initial conditions and goals certainly is unattainable without a recognition of the need to search for such an understanding in the first place.

When used as the basis for the environmental assessment step in the planning process or an industry structure analysis, the SWOT or FFF lists, respectively, define the initial situation. There is no complementary problem-solving protocol and there is no further meaningful indication of interdependencies or causal relationships among the SWOT list items or FFF forces. No analyzable mental model can ensue from these depictions. It would seem that the functional fixedness effect is all but assured.

FINAL THOUGHTS

To date, virtually all decisionmaking studies—whether in cognitive psychology, cognitive neuroscience, neuroeconomics, or economics—have been premised on the existence of alternative decisions, where the problem is a matter of choice. Indeed, a recent issue (May 2007) of the Annals focused on "Current Trends in Decision Making."[54] Decision making was defined as "the processes by which animals (and humans) choose between competing actions on the basis of the expected value, or utility, or their consequences," thus, more or less encompassing the SD, but certainly not the SS problem.

The "unstructured" decision situation *per se*, where some cognitive process must occur to arrive at decision options, is virtually uncharted territory.[55] Instead, the focus has been on understanding how the brain functions in essentially deductive decisionmaking contexts.[40] Even in neurocognitive experiments, where choices exist but are ill-defined and adaptive decisionmaking is called for, the brain activity detected is very different from what would occur in clear choice contexts.[56] Brain activity when confronted by the SS should differ substantially from both ill-defined and clear choice contexts. It is questionable how much understanding has been gained in cognitive and neurocognitive research that is applicable to the SS.

The correct identification of the obstacles to the use of techniques such as SWOT and the FFF for understanding and analysis of complex situations cannot be overstated. Extensive pedagogy at all levels of education rests on similar types of mental models. In decisionmaking in virtually every domain of human activity, one can conceive of using SWOT Analysis[e] or one of its variants, notwithstanding its known limitations. The FFF is similarly ubiquitous internationally.

The degree to which mental imagery plays a role in furthering decisionmaking in a highly complex, more ambiguous SS has not been explored and, most likely, cannot be explored through controlled behavioral studies (as employed in the above cited research). The functional fixedness/mental fixation phenomenon, for example, can only be inferred from behavioral experiments alone.

Until very recently, the idea of distinguishing among patterns of brain activity associated with different kinds of high-level thinking would have been inconceivable. Now, with dramatically improved brain imaging techniques, brain activation patterns triggered by even subtle syntax changes in speech (for example, a change in the tense of a sentence) can be discerned; implicit and explicit learning activity can be identified;[57] the efficacy of brain activity in switching between tasks has been deciphered;[43] and the distinct brain regions engaged in the performance of simultaneous and sequential tasks have been determined,[43] among other brain mapping advances. Recent brain map-

---

[e]If one had any doubts as to the universality of SWOT Analysis, one could type the term into an Internet search engine in quotation marks and wade through the resulting 1,860,000 websites. Add to "SWOT Analysis" any object, activity, or place, and it is likely that someone, somewhere in the world, has performed a SWOT Analysis on it. An Internet search for "Five Force Framework" or "Five Force Analysis" with anything that could be considered a business or industry yields similar results.

ping studies examining the occurrence of insight in problem-solving activity have been able to discern the functional fixedness effect.[34]

It is necessary to examine brain activation triggered by the attempted application of different strategic analysis protocols. It should be possible to examine brain activity during the application of strategic analysis techniques to the creative act of strategy formation. The identification of appropriate and ineffective visual representations of complex situations, the extrinsic stimuli that facilitate cognition, is the first necessary step to improving the strategy-formation process.

REFERENCES

1. QUINN, J.B. 1980. Strategies for Change: Logical Incrementalism. Irwin. Homewood, IL.
2. ALLIO, R.J. 2006. Strategic thinking: the ten big ideas. Strategy & Leadership. **34**: 4–13.
3. DEAN, J.W. JR. & M.P. SHARFMAN. 1996. Does decision process matter? A study of strategic decision-making effectiveness. Academy of Management J. **39**: 368–396.
4. KAPLAN, S. & E.D. BEINHOCKER. 2003. The real value of strategic planning. MIT Sloan Management Review **Winter**: 71–76.
5. MARCH, J.G. 2006. Rationality, foolishness and adaptive intelligence. Strategic Management Journal **27**: 201–214.
6. LENZ, R.T. & M.A. LYLES. 1985. Paralysis by analysis: is your planning system becoming too rational? Long Range Planning **18**: 64–72.
7. STEINER, G.A. 1979. Strategic Planning, What Every Manager *Must* Know: A Step-By-Step Guide. The Free Press, Division of Macmillan Publishing Co., Inc. New York.
8. PORTER, M.E. 1980. Competitive Strategy. Free Press. New York.
9. GHEMAWAT, P. 1999. Strategy and the Business Landscape. Prentice Hall. Upper Saddle River, NJ.
10. HILL, C.W.L. & G.R. JONES. 2008. Essentials of Strategic Management. Houghton Mifflin Company. Boston, MA.
11. HUNGER, J.D. & T.L. WHEELAN. 2007. Essentials of Strategic Management. Fourth Ed. Pearson, Prentice Hall. Upper Saddle River, NJ.
12. IRELAND, R.D. *et al.* 2006. Understanding Business Strategy, Concepts and Cases. Thomson South-Western. Mason, OH.
13. THOMPSON, A.A., JR. *et al.* 2006. Strategy: Core Concepts, Analytical Tools, Readings. Second Edition. McGraw-Hill Irwin. New York, NY.
14. DEAN, J.W. JR. & M.P. SHARFMAN. 1996. Does decision process matter? A study of strategic decision-making effectiveness. Academy of Management J. **39**: 368–396.
15. MITCHELL, A. 2001. Disputes erupt on Ridge's needs for his job. New York Times, 4 November 2001. 1.
16. RISEN, J. 2004. How pair's finding on terror led to a clash on shaping intelligence. New York Times, 28 April 2004. 1.

17. KLEIN, H.E. & J.R. VETTER. 1991. Designing scenarios for planning & decision-making: a demonstration of the SPIRE approach. *In* Proceedings: Eighth Electric Utility Forecasting Symposium, The Foundation of Planning. Electric Power Research Institute: 50-1–50-12.
18. KLEIN, H. & W.H. NEWMAN. 1980. How to use SPIRE: a systematic procedure for identifying relevant environments for strategic planning. Journal of Business Strategy **1:** 32–45.
19. SINHA, D.K. 1990. The contribution of formal planning to decisions. Strategic Management Journal **11:** 479–492.
20. BRESSER, R.K. & R.C. BISHOP. 1983. Dysfunctional effects of formal planning: two theoretical explanations. Academy of Management Review **8:** 588–599.
21. GRANT, R.M. 2003. Strategic Planning in a turbulent environment: evidence from the oil majors. Strategic Management J. **24:** 491–517.
22. HILL, T. & R. WESTBROOK. 1997. SWOT analysis: it's time for a product recall. J.Long Range Planning **30:** 46–52.
23. O'SHAUGHNESSY, J. 1984. Competitive Marketing. Allen & Unwin. Boston.
24. SPEED, R.J. 1989. Oh Mr. Porter! A re-appraisal of *Competitive Strategy*. Marketing Intelligence & Planning **7:** 8–11.
25. MINTZBERG, H. 1994. The Rise and Fall of Strategic Planning: Reconceiving Roles for Planning, Plans, Planners. Free Press. New York.
26. SCHWENK, C.R. 1984. Cognitive simplification processes in strategic decision-making. Strategic Management Journal **5:** 111–128.
27. KOSSLYN, S.M. 1994. Image and Brain: The Resolution of the Imagery Debate. The MIT Press. Cambridge, MA.
28. WEIHRICH, H. 1982. The TOWS matrix—a tool for situational analysis. Long Range Planning **15:** 60.
29. BOURGEOIS, L.J. *et al.* 1999. Strategic Management, A Managerial Perspective, II. Dryden Press Series in Management. Dryden Press. Fort Worth, TX.
30. HABERBERG, A. 2002. Swatting SWOT. Strategy 9/02.
31. PORTER, M. 1991. Towards a dynamic theory of strategy. Strategic Management Journal, Special Issue: Fundamental Research Issues in Strategy and Economics **12:** 95–117.
32. SCHANK, R.C. & R.P. ABELSON. 1977. Scripts, Plans, Goals and Understanding. Erlbaum. Hillsdale, NJ.
33. DUNCKER, K. 1972. On Problem Solving. Greenwood Press. Westport, CT.
34. MAI, X.-Q. *et al.* 2004. "Aha!" effects in a guessing riddle task: an event-related potential study. Human Brain Mapping **22:** 261–270.
35. REISBERG, D. 1997. Cognition. W.W. Norton. New York.
36. KERSHAW, T.C. 2004. Insight problems: further evidence for the importance of non-dot turns in the nine-dot problem. J. of Experimental Psychology: Learning, Memory, and Cognition **30:** 3–13.
37. SIMON, H.A. 1962. The architecture of complexity. *In* Proceedings of the American Philosophical Society. **106:** 467–482.
38. SCHOPPEK, W. 2004. Teaching structural knowledge in the control of dynamic systems: direction of causality makes a difference. *In* Proceedings of the 26th Annual Conference of the Cognitive Science Society.
39. MIYASHITA, Y. 2004. Cognitive memory: cellular and network machineries and their top-down control. Science **306:** 435–440.

40. GOEL, V. 2005. Cognitive neuroscience of deductive reasoning. *In* Cambridge Handbook of Thinking & Reasoning. K. Holyoak & R. Morrison, Eds. Cambridge University Press. New York.
41. JOHNSON-LAIRD, P.N. 1983. Mental Models. Harvard University Press.
42. POLDRACK, R. & P. RODRIGUEZ. 2003. Sequence learning: What's the hippocampus to do? Neuron **37:** 891–893.
43. DREHER, J.-C. & J. GRAFMAN. 2003. Dissociating the roles of the rostral anterior cingulated and the lateral prefrontal cortices in performing two tasks simultaneously or successively. Cerebral Cortex **13:** 329–339.
44. D'ESPOSITO, M. *et al.* 1995. A neural basis of the central executive system of working memory. Nature **378:** 279–281.
45. BADDELEY *et al.* 1997. Dual task performance in dysexecutive and nondysexecutive patients with a frontal lesion. Neuropsychology **11:** 187–194.
46. STERNBERG, S. 1966. High-speed scanning in human memory. Science **153:** 652–654.
47. TREISMAN, A. & J. SOUTHER. 1985. Search asymmetry: a diagnostic for preattentive processing for separable features. Journal Experimental Psychology **114:** 285–310.
48. KASTNER, S. 1998. Mechanisms of directed attention in the human extrastriate cortex as revealed by functional MRI. Science **282:** 108–110.
49. KNAUFF, M. 2007. How our brains reason logically. Topoi **26:** 1–165.
50. THALEMANN, S. & G. STRUBE. 2004. Shared knowledge in collaborative problem solving: acquisition and effects. *In* Proceedings of the 26th Annual Conference of the Cognitive Science Society. K.D. Forbus *et al.* Eds. Lawrence Erlbaum Associates. Mahwah, NJ.
51. COOPER, L.A. 1990. Mental representation of three-dimensional objects in visual problem solving and recognition. J. Experimental Psychology. Learning, Memory and Cognition **16:** 1097–1106.
52. KOSSLYN, S.M. 1991. A cognitive neuroscience of visual cognition: further developments. *In* Mental Images in Human Cognition. R.H. Logie & M. Denis, Eds. North-Holland. Amsterdam.
53. ANTONIETTI, A. 1991. Why does mental visualization facilitate problem-solving? *In* Mental Images in Human Cognition. R.H. Logie & M. Denis, Eds. North-Holland. Amsterdam.
54. BALLEINE, B.W. *et al.* 2007. Introduction to Special Issue of the Annals of the New York Academy of Sciences **1104:** xi–xv.
55. FELLOWS, L.K. 2004. The cognitive neuroscience of human decision making: A review and conceptual framework. Behav. Cogn. Neurosci. Rev. **3:** 159–172.
56. WALTON, M.E. *et al.* Adaptive decision making and value in the anterior cingulated cortex. NeuroImage **36**(Supplement 2): T142–T154.
57. AIZENSTEIN, H.J. *et al.* 2000. Complementary category learning systems identified using event-related functional MRI. J. Cognitive Neuroscience **12:** 977–987.

Being Fed Up

A Social Cognitive Neuroscience Approach to Mental Satiation

ANDREAS MOJZISCH AND STEFAN SCHULZ-HARDT

Georg-August University Goettingen, Goettingen, Germany

ABSTRACT: Being fed up with something is a prevalent and fundamental human experience. Although the relevance of mental satiation, that is, the process of becoming fed up with an action, is highly acknowledged in organizational psychology, almost no empirical research has examined this concept. In this article, we take a social cognitive neuroscience approach to mental satiation. By building on and extending the classic work of Lewin and Karsten, we propose a new model of mental satiation that focuses on the cognitive, motivational, and neural processes underlying mental satiation. Our model starts with the assumption that repeated performance of an action undermines one's need for competence and hence leads to a loss of intrinsic motivation. We then distinguish between two phases of the satiation process: The first phase is characterized by a loss of intrinsic motivation to perform the action. The second phase starts when the intrinsic motivation has vanished and volitional control is required to continue the action. We predict that the loss of intrinsic motivation in the first phase of the satiation process is correlated with a *decrease* in activity in brain regions associated with positive hedonic experience, such as the nucleus accumbens, the ventral pallidum, and the medial orbitofrontal cortex. In contrast, the growing aversion toward the action during the second phase of the satiation process is predicted to be correlated with an *increase* in activity in brain regions associated with unpleasant affect and volitional control, such as the amygdala, the anterior insula, and the anterior cingulate cortex.

KEYWORDS: being fed up; mental satiation; intrinsic motivation; social cognitive neuroscience; organizational psychology

INTRODUCTION

We are all familiar with the experience of being fed up with something. Over the course of his shift, a man working as a quality-control technician for

Address for correspondence: Dr. Andreas Mojzisch, Georg-August-University Goettingen, Institute of Psychology, Economic and Social Psychology Unit, D-37073 Goettingen, Germany. Voice: +49/551/39-13566; fax: +49/551/39-13570.
mojzisch@psych.uni-goettingen.de

an automotive company becomes more and more irritated because he has to do the same work all day long. A researcher who has always been enthusiastic about chemistry is fed up with it because she is tired of running the same statistical analyses each day. A psychologist working in a human resources department is fed up at the end of the day after conducting an endless stream of job interviews.

Obviously, the concept of mental satiation is of both high theoretical and high practical relevance for organizational behavior. As illustrated by the examples above, the feeling of being fed up with one's work is not restricted to blue-collar workers employed in jobs characterized by short cycle times and monotonous demands but can occur in almost all jobs. Importantly, mental satiation may result in a decrease in performance, may spill over beyond the task (to structurally similar tasks), and may culminate in an early "exhaustion of the occupational will."[1] Indeed, there is evidence that mental satiation is associated with disengagement from work.[2] Although the relevance of mental satiation is highly acknowledged in industrial psychology and although preventing mental satiation at the workplace is a major objective of the international standard ISO 10075, this concept has motivated hardly any empirical research and has escaped the interest of experimental psychology and cognitive neuroscience. As a result, the cognitive and neural mechanisms mediating the experience of being fed up are largely unknown.

More generally, the concept of mental satiation refers to an important, but rather underappreciated, aspect of organizational behavior, that is, the feelings experienced during performing an action. Recently, there has been a growing interest in the issue of affect at the workplace.[3] However, this research typically focuses on mood states or on subjective well-being at the workplace in general and not on the affective experience associated with performing a particular task. Thus, affective experience during work is still largely neglected in organizational theories of work motivation. However, recent advances in psychology and cognitive neuroscience make it evident that understanding motivation at the workplace without considering affective experience is incomplete.[4,5] Furthermore, previous work in organizational research has largely ignored the waxing and waning of human motivation during the performance of an action. In stark contrast, the concept of mental satiation refers to the question why we lose interest in performing an action and may even experience a growing aversion toward it if it must be repeatedly performed over a long period. Hence, the concept of mental satiation calls particular attention to the dynamic aspect of human motivation.

In this article, we take a *social cognitive neuroscience approach* to mental satiation. Social cognitive neuroscience combines the tools of cognitive neuroscience with questions, theories, and phenomena from various social sciences, including social psychology, motivational psychology, organizational behavior, and political science.[6] The tools used to study these topics include functional magnetic resonance imaging (fMRI), positron emission tomography

(PET), neuropsychological lesion techniques, transcranial magnetic stimulation (TMS), event-related potentials (ERP), and single-cell recording.

In the following, we first delve into the classic work of Karsten[7] and Lewin,[1] who introduced the concept of mental satiation almost 80 years ago. Building on and extending this work, we then describe a new model of mental satiation that focuses on the motivational, cognitive, and neural processes underlying this phenomenon. Our model starts with the assumption that repeated performance of an action undermines one's need for competence and therefore leads to a loss of *intrinsic motivation*. We then distinguish between two phases of the satiation process: The first phase is characterized by a loss of intrinsic motivation. The second phase starts when the intrinsic motivation to perform the action has vanished and volitional control is required to continue the action. We hypothesize that the loss of intrinsic motivation in the first phase of the satiation process is correlated with a *decrease* in activity in brain areas associated with positive hedonic experience. In contrast, the growing aversion during the second phase is predicted to be correlated with an *increase* in activity in brain structures associated with unpleasant affect and volitional control.

MENTAL SATIATION: THE BEGINNING

The concept of mental satiation is based on Lewin's field theory, according to which psychological needs, in the same way as physiological needs, include states of hunger, satiation, and oversatiation. The state of hunger is transformed into the state of satiation through actions that satisfy the need; in doing so, the soliciting nature of these actions changes from a positive to a neutral state. If one continues the actions beyond the point of satiation, the result is oversatiation.

In a series of experiments, carried out during 1924 and 1926, Karsten investigated the symptoms occurring during the process of mental satiation. In a prototypical experiment, participants were asked to repeatedly read a short poem or to repeatedly draw small vertical or horizontal strokes on a sheet of paper. Participants were instructed to repeat the task until they were completely fed up with it. The experiments were arranged in two different ways: Either the experimenter gave absolutely definite instructions—forbidding any outside preoccupation (such as playing with objects on the table or singing) and forbidding any large alterations in the structure of the task (e.g., drawing circles instead of strokes, singing instead of reciting poetry)—or the participants were given complete freedom in carrying out the task, without being restricted by the experimenter in any way.

Karsten[7] described various symptoms occurring during the process of satiation. First and most prominently, participants often did not continue to do the task exactly as they had been instructed or as they had first performed it but instead altered the task. For example, in poetry reading the tempo was varied or the emphasis was changed; particular sections were no longer said out loud but were whispered. Interestingly, more subtle forms of variations occurred even if participants were explicitly forbidden to alter the structure of the task. Second, many participants started to work carelessly and inaccurately, causing their performance to deteriorate. A third symptom was the distraction of attention from the task. Participants no longer concentrated on their prescribed task but started a new activity while performing the prescribed task with minimal attention. For example, while drawing strokes a participant started to whistle a song. Karsten concluded that mental satiation results from the interplay of three conditions: repeated performance of an action, ego involvement, and no advancement despite continual effort.

The theoretical obscurity of Karsten's[7] satiation concept is evident in these three conditions. After all, in these conditions two processes are entwined, which may lead to comparable symptoms but which are entirely different with regard to the underlying psychological processes: One may lose interest in an action over a given period because it is repetitive (first condition). One may also lose interest in an action because one does not reach a goal or one does not obtain the desired result (third condition). The more meaningful the action is for the individual (second condition), the more intense both processes become. Nonetheless, both processes are different from each other: In the first case, boredom is the result; in the second case, frustration. Frustration may also be the outcome even if the action had no repetitive character; similarly, boredom may also be the outcome irrespective of the results of the action. In the secondary literature, too, this ambiguity in the satiation concept turns up in various explanations of mental satiation.[8]

Moreover, Karsten[7] also mixed up the subjective experience associated with satiation (e.g., the feeling of aversion and irritation) with its behavioral consequences (e.g., a deterioration in performance) and the self-regulation mechanisms aimed to slow the satiation process (e.g., distracting one's attention from the task). Finally, neither Karsten nor Lewin succeeded in providing a concise model to develop specific predictions regarding the causal variables and the mediating mechanisms of mental satiation. The absence of such a model complicates systematic research into the concept of mental satiation and its practical applications, for example, within organizations.

THE REVISED MODEL OF MENTAL SATIATION

On the basis of Karsten's[7] and Lewin's[1] original work, Schulz-Hardt, Rott, Meinken, and Frey developed a revised model of mental satiation.[9] In the following, we will build on and extend this revised model of mental satiation. For our model, we take a broad concept of actions as the basis, which includes intentional activities on different levels of abstraction. Here the action is what individuals understand of their doing at a particular moment, that is, the representation of their own behavior.[10] For example, a woman who is working at a kindergarten could represent her work as "reading fairy tales aloud," "entertaining the children," "fostering the children's creativity," or "cultivating the next generation of authors." Thus, individuals can have different representations of what they are doing at the moment, and these representations may be either relatively specific or relatively abstract.

In the following, we refer to a prominent distinction between different types of motivation on the basis of the different reasons or goals that give rise to an action, that is, to the distinction between *intrinsic* and *extrinsic motivation*.[11,12] Intrinsic motivation refers to doing something because it is inherently interesting or pleasurable, whereas extrinsic motivation refers to doing something because it leads to a subjectively valued outcome that can be separated from the action. The woman in the example above may be motivated to work in the kindergarten because she enjoys playing with children or because she is paid for it.

By referring to the distinction between intrinsic and extrinsic motivation, we define mental satiation as the loss of intrinsic motivation during the repeated performance of an action. If, because of extrinsic motivation, an action is continued although the intrinsic motivation has vanished, oversatiation occurs, which is accompanied by a growing intrinsic aversion to the action. Hence, we distinguish between two phases of the satiation process: The first phase is characterized by a loss of intrinsic motivation to perform the action. The second phase starts when the intrinsic motivation has vanished and volitional control is required to continue the action.

What are the neuroanatomical correlates of the loss of intrinsic motivation during the first phase of the satiation process? Drawing on recent neuroscience research, we propose that the loss of intrinsic motivation is correlated with a decrease in activity in brain areas representing hedonic experience, such as the nucleus accumbens, the ventral pallidum, and the medial orbitofrontal cortex. In the following, we will take a closer look at each of these brain regions.

Changes in Brain Activity during the First Phase of the Satiation Process

Intrinsic motivation refers to doing something because it is inherently pleasurable. Thus, to say that a pianist loses her intrinsic motivation to play a particular piece means that she no longer experiences pleasure while playing it. This definition leads us to the intriguing question of how hedonic experience is represented in the brain.

Interestingly, dopamine, the neurotransmitter traditionally made responsible for mediating hedonic experience, recently turned out to be neither necessary nor sufficient for generating pleasure.[13] For example, the intensity of liking expressions in the rat (as measured by facial affective expressions) is changed neither by suppression nor by activation of mesolimbic dopamine systems.[14] Similarly, activation of dopamine transmission by an amphetamine injection into the nucleus accumbens of rats fails to increase "liking." In human subjects, dopamine receptor antagonists typically do not suppress the pleasure ratings of amphetamine.[15] Thus, despite the traditional view, dopamine is not a pleasure neurotransmitter in the sense of mediating hedonic experience.

So which brain circuits actually underlie hedonic experience? According to a growing body of evidence, a family of chemicals known as the opioids play an important role in mediating hedonic experience. Opioids, such as enkephalin, endorphin, and dynorphin, act on the same receptors as opiate drugs such as morphine or heroin. Opioids seem to activate a circuit deep inside the brain that overlaps with the dopamine system. Specifically, two brain structures have emerged as likely candidates to mediate hedonic effect: the nucleus accumbens and the ventral pallidum.[16] Both structures are located within the ventral forebrain, share reciprocal projections with one another, and are embedded within larger mesocorticolimbic reward systems. Opioid activation in the nucleus accumbens has been linked to both positive heroin reward and affective relief from pain.[17,18] In rats, hedonic reactions to a sucrose taste, which is normally liked, vanish after ventral pallidal lesions. Consistent with this finding, a recent neuropsychological case study showed that a human patient with selective damage involving the ventral pallidum suffered from depressed mood and severe anhedonia.[19]

A third brain region that has turned out to be a strong candidate for mediation of hedonic experience is the medial orbitofrontal cortex.[20,21] Activity in the medial orbitofrontal cortex has been found to increase or decrease in line with the level of pleasure that people report feeling during or after drinking, eating, or sensing a touch.[22,23] Furthermore, activation in the orbitofrontal cortex and the ventral striatum has been shown to correlate with highly pleasurable responses (so-called shivers-down-the-spine responses) elicited by music.[24] Of particular relevance for our model, the medial orbitofrontal cortex seems to play a key role in "selective satiety," which refers to the effect that individuals who have been fed to satiety on one food still find other foods rewarding. The brain mechanism underlying this effect has been investigated in an fMRI study in which hungry participants were first scanned while being presented with two food-related odors (banana and vanilla).[25] Thereafter, participants were taken out of the scanner and given a banana lunch. After having eaten the banana lunch to satiety, the participants were placed back in the scanner, and the odor conditions were repeated. The results show that activation of the orbitofrontal cortex decreased in response to the odor of the food eaten to satiety (banana) but not in response to the odor of the food that had not been eaten (vanilla). Although transferring these results to the domain of mental satiation may be premature, the findings indicate that the orbitofrontal cortex tracks changes in the reward value of stimuli.

The Need for Competence as a Basis for Intrinsic Motivation

Having delineated the brain regions proposed to be associated with the decrease in intrinsic motivation, we now turn to the question of why prolonged repetition of an action decreases intrinsic motivation. To this end, we will first briefly elaborate on the evolutionary underpinnings of the intrinsic motivation system.

In accordance with the evolutionary approach in motivation research,[26] we assume that motivation systems are phylogenetic answers to evolutionary demands concerning the fitness of the organism. In this context, the main purpose of the intrinsic motivation system is that the individual rehearses patterns of behavior and acquires knowledge, the use of which is proven only later. That is, the intrinsic motivation system serves the "acquisition of competence" for the individual. According to White,[27] individuals often engage in activities simply to experience efficacy or competence. Similarly, in their *self-determination theory*, Deci and Ryan refer to the "need for competence" and argue that human beings have a need to competently interact with their environment to reach goals and fulfill needs.[28] Thus, the internal drive to be effective, or competent, develops as the individual explores his or her environment and continually learns and adapts. The idea that the need for competence forms the basis for intrinsic motivation is supported by early experiments showing that positive feedback enhanced intrinsic motivation compared with no feedback and that negative feedback decreased intrinsic motivation compared with no feedback.[29,30] Moreover, there is evidence showing that felt competence mediates the effects of positive versus negative feedback on intrinsic motivation.[31] However, from an evolutionary point of view, competence development is the ultimate cause but not the proximal trigger of intrinsic motivation. The child at play is doing things for fun, not to develop his competence in dealing with the world.

The idea that the need for competence forms the basis for intrinsically motivated behavior helps explain why prolonged repetition of an action leads to a loss of intrinsic motivation. Assuring oneself of being able to perform the same piano étude for more than 10 years is unlikely to result in a feeling of efficacy or competence. Rather, to experience efficacy a pianist needs to feel able to perform more and more difficult études or to continually extend his or her repertoire. Hence, for intrinsic motivation to occur, an incongruence is required between person-related characteristics (e.g., level of skill) and environmental characteristics (e.g., task demands). The reduction of such incongruence may take place, for example, by acquiring knowledge or skills. Intrinsic motivation is at its peak when the individual overcomes optimal incongruencies, or *optimal challenges*. Optimal means that the level of challenge that is subjectively experienced when engaging in an activity is positively balanced with the perceived skills that one has for that task.[32,33]

Apparently, repeated performance of an action reduces the incongruencies between person-related characteristics and environmental characteristics because the action becomes overly familiar and is, in turn, no longer challenging. That is, performing an action that has already been performed a thousand times before is no longer challenging for an individual because there are no more incongruencies between person-related and environmental characteristics. Hence, we propose that prolonged repetition of an action undermines the individual's need for competence and therefore reduces the intrinsic motivation to perform the action.

Mental Satiation and Action Representation

In view of the above, every action should be satiated or oversatiated if repeated continually. But people repeat certain actions constantly without becoming victims of satiation processes. For example, a football player kicks the ball several hundred times during training—why is he not totally fed up with kicking the ball? At this point, the aforementioned concept of action becomes important: As long as kicking the ball is not represented as an action for this player—that is, he does not regulate kicking the ball on a conscious level—there is no repeated performance of the action and, hence, the action will not be satiated. Therefore, automated activities (e.g., walking) are not satiated unless they are performed consciously. That is, mental satiation should be eliminated (or at least slowed) if the action is not consciously represented.

More specifically, we distinguish between two ways of not consciously representing an action: First, one can slow down or even eliminate mental satiation by shifting one's attention away from the primary task, either toward a new task or toward internal information unrelated to the task at hand (e.g., remembering past events or imagining future events). Thereby, the task at hand is performed as a largely unconscious action while devoting oneself to a new main action. A painter and decorator may not become fed up with painting all day long if she lets her mind wander, for example, imagining meeting her friends in the pub in the evening, or if she focuses on another task, such as listening to the radio. Thus, we propose that shifting one's attention away from the task at hand serves as an effective mechanism to counter mental satiation. This prediction is in line with an observation already made by Karsten[7]: If the participants in her experiments shifted their attention from the prescribed task toward another task (e.g., whistling a song while drawing strokes), mental satiation was eliminated.

The precondition for being able to successfully distract one's attention from the performance of an action, that is, familiarity with the action resulting from frequent repetition (effect of practice), is the same precondition that also leads to mental satiation. The more familiar someone becomes with performing a particular action, the less attention is required to control task performance.

Hence, the possibility to counterregulate mental satiation by distracting one's attention from performing an action increases simultaneously with the loss of intrinsic motivation during task performance. Interestingly, this is the natural course of developmental processes: A baby who joyfully takes his or her first steps loses interest to the same extent as he or she masters walking. At the same time, walking becomes so automatic that it no longer requires online attentional control and therefore cannot be (over-) satiated. If the conscious control of the action recedes as the familiarity of the action increases, mental satiation does not pose a problem. Yet mental satiation may become a problem if there is a high degree of familiarity with the action, but nonetheless the action is consciously controlled. This constellation occurs under different conditions: (1) The attention cannot be shifted away from the task because the task requires constant attentional control. For example, conducting a large symphonic orchestra is hardly possible without continuously paying attention to the music and the different parts of the orchestra. (2) In principle, the task does not require constant attentional control; however, if the task were performed automatically, there could be errors, an outcome that the individual could not afford. A professional pianist may be able to play a well-practiced piece without much conscious thought; yet if she is performing in a concert in front of thousands of people, she will constantly focus on the music to deliver a flawless performance.

The second way of not consciously representing an action consists of integrating the action into a superior context that defines a new action. This method explains why the painter and decorator from our examples above may not become fed up with dipping the brush into the paint several hundred times a day. As long as she represents her action not as "dipping the brush into the paint" but as "refurbishing the house," she is less likely to become fed up. Hence, we propose that mental satiation is slowed or even eliminated if the action is represented on a hierarchically higher level. This idea builds upon *action identification theory*, which holds that any action can be identified in many ways, ranging from low-level identities that specify how the action is performed to high-level identities that signify why or with what effect the action is performed.[10] Identifying what one does in high-level terms is proposed to distract attention from the repetitiveness of the action.

Although neuroscientists have largely neglected the distinction between concrete and abstract representations of actions, recent evidence suggests that representations of the value of actions become more abstract as we move from posterior to anterior medial frontal cortex.[34] One path for future studies could be to investigate whether activating more anterior regions of the medial frontal cortex—when thinking about a particular task—slows down mental satiation.

In summary, we propose that the satiation process can be slowed or even eliminated if the action is not consciously represented either because the attention is shifted away from the task at hand or because the action is represented on a hierarchically higher level.

Changes in Brain Activity during the Second Phase of the Satiation Process

The second phase of the satiation process starts when the intrinsic motivation to perform the action has vanished. If an action must be continued even though the intrinsic motivation to perform it has vanished, unpleasant affect is likely to occur and volitional control is required to fight competing action tendencies. This is, generally, what people mean when they say they are "fed up" with their work.

In the following, we propose that the growing aversion during the second phase of the satiation process is correlated with an *increase* in activity in brain regions associated with unpleasant affect and volitional control, such as the amygdala, the anterior insula, and the anterior cingulate cortex.

First, the amygdala has been implicated as a key component of the neural circuit involved in the detection of emotional significance and particularly in the generation of negative affective states. It responds quickly to apparent danger and potentially threatening situations and hence serves as an alarm of sorts.[35,36] The amygdala has been involved in the response to fearful vocalizations,[37] to visual presentations of threatening words,[38] to unpleasant olfactory[39] and gustatory[40] stimuli, and in the memory of emotional episodes.[41,42] Amygdala lesions in humans reduce autonomic reactivity to a variety of stressful stimuli.[43] Furthermore, bilateral amygdala lesions in humans not only affect emotional responses to innate unconditioned emotional stimuli but also interfere with the response to cognitive information that has acquired properties that automatically elicit emotional responses, for example, emotional responses to losses of money.[44]

A second brain structure that has been associated with negative emotional states is the anterior insula. Anterior insula activation is consistently seen in fMRI studies of pain and distress, hunger and thirst, and autonomic arousal. Moreover, this region also appears to be involved in the evaluation and representation of specific negative emotional states, particularly in the representation of anger and disgust.[45] Lesions of the anterior insula in humans have been shown to markedly impair both the recognition of facial and vocal signals of disgust and the subjective experience of disgust.[46] Interestingly, an fMRI study investigating the neural underpinnings of the response to fair and unfair offers in the Ultimatum Game observed that activity in the anterior insula associated with the receipt of an unfair offer and that this activity predicted participants' subsequent decision to reject the offer.[47] Therefore, the anterior insula, compared with the amygdala, might be involved in more context-dependent aversive representations.[48]

A third brain structure that may be implicated in the second phase of the satiation process is the anterior cingulate cortex. Although the specific function of this brain structure is controversial, there is a growing consensus that the anterior cingulate cortex serves as an interface integrating interoceptive, cognitive, and motivational states with states of bodily arousal.[49,50] On the one hand, the anterior cingulate cortex has reciprocal corticocortical connections with the lateral prefrontal cortex, supporting its proposed role in cognition. On the other hand, the anterior cingulate cortex projects to subcortical brain regions associated with homeostasis and autonomic control, including the hypothalamus, periaqueductal gray matter, and pontine gray matter. Evidence from fMRI and PET studies implicates the anterior cingulate cortex in cognitive processes involving executive control and attentional demand. A meta-analysis of more than 100 PET studies concluded that the activity of the anterior cingulate cortex increases with task difficulty or mental effort.[51] Activity in the anterior cingulate cortex has also been related to error detection, response inhibition, attentional selection, and strategy formation.[52,53] In addition to its involvement in cognitive functions, activity in the anterior cingulate cortex is also strongly associated with affective and bioregulatory processes, including respiration,[54] nociception,[55] and autonomic arousal states.[56,57] In particular, activity in the dorsal anterior cingulate cortex is related to sympathetic modulation of heart rate during an effortful cognitive task.[49] With regard to mental satiation, we hence propose that the heightened arousal and irritation often experienced during oversatiation is mediated by activation of the anterior cingulate cortex.

Interestingly, others have argued that the anterior cingulate cortex plays a key role in willed action control and self-regulation.[50,58] In line with this notion, patients with lesions of this brain region typically have severe problems with overcoming inertia when spontaneously initiating actions or with resisting the interfering effects of competing action tendencies.[50] Hence, we argue that the anterior cingulate cortex is strongly associated with the volitional control required to continue an action despite being fed up with it. Or perhaps this brain region also plays a more general role in mental satiation. Thus, according to a recent hypothesis, the anterior cingulate cortex represents the intrinsic values of actions and, hence, is needed to update or represent the value of the action itself.[59]

In summary, we propose that increasing activity in the amygdala and the anterior insula is associated with the growing aversion to the action. In contrast, we propose that activity in the anterior cingulate cortex is correlated with heightened arousal and the amount of volitional control required to continue the action, despite being fed up with it.

Oversatiation and Autonomous Self-regulation

If an action is continued even though the intrinsic motivation to perform it has vanished, the action conflicts with the individual's need for competence. The more often the action is repeated beyond the point of satiation, the stronger this conflict becomes. To be able to continue the action (despite being fed up with it), one needs volitional control. Volitional control refers to the ability to stick to an intention and to shield it against competing action tendencies.[60] The excessive operation of volitional control processes can explain the occurrence of negative affect, intrusive thoughts, and anger during the phase of oversatiation.

If so, however, how can we explain that not all people suffer from symptoms of oversatiation (i.e., feelings of irritation, stress, and anger), despite having to perform a highly repetitive job 8 hours a day? The answer to this question lies in how people volitionally control their behavior. According to Personality Systems Interactions (PSI) theory,[61] a general framework that seeks to explain human action control and personality functioning, shielding an intention against competing action tendencies does not necessarily lead to negative affect. Only if a self-suppressive mode of volitional control is used (characterized by "dictatorial" enforcement of explicit intentions against emotional preferences and needs) are negative affect and intrusive thoughts likely to arise. This self-suppressive mode of volitional control is associated with external control (e.g., "The supervisor wants me to work overtime"). In contrast, if an autonomy-oriented mode of volition is implemented (defined as a flexible, efficient, and nonrepressive control of one's own affective states), individuals have no difficulty sticking to the task. Importantly, PSI theory argues that the implementation of this autonomy-oriented mode of volitional control depends on the degree to which individuals integrate a goal into their self-system (e.g., identify with the task).

Transferring this line of reasoning to the domain of mental satiation yields an interesting prediction: If people identify with the values of an action (i.e., the values associated with the action are in congruence with the self), and therefore implement an autonomy-oriented mode of volitional control, they will have no difficulty sticking to the task and will experience no symptoms of oversatiation. For example, a psychologist who must conduct job interviews all day long may experience no symptoms of oversatiation if she identifies with her job and is committed to her company.

Moreover, the personality disposition of action versus state orientation moderates this effect.[62,63] This disposition captures individual differences in self-regulation under stress. Individuals who are action oriented are skilled at intuitive affect regulation. By contrast, state-oriented individuals have weak intuitive affect regulation skills and hence are vulnerable to ruminations and hesitation, especially under stress. We thus predict that symptoms of oversatiation are more pronounced in state-oriented than in action-oriented individuals, particularly if these people do not identify with the task at hand.

Although there have yet to be studies investigating the neural correlates of different modes of volitional control, it is tempting to speculate that the distinction between the self-suppressive and the autonomy-oriented mode of volitional control is paralleled by a neural distinction of lateral and medial prefrontal cortex.[64] Thus, if goals are externally dictated, they seem to be presented laterally. In contrast, if goals are derived from sources internal to

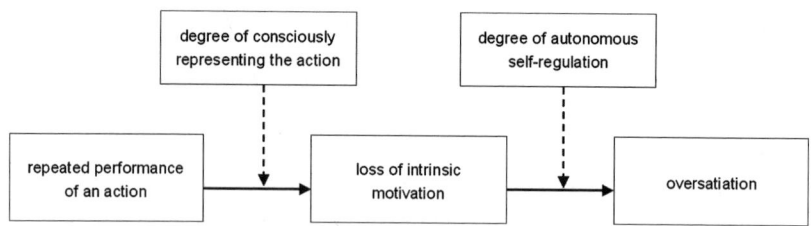

FIGURE 1. The process of mental satiation.

the actor, they are more likely to be represented medially. This assumption, however, is highly speculative.

In summary, we propose that if people identify with the values associated with the action and hence implement an autonomy-oriented mode of volitional control, they will have no difficulty sticking to the task and will experience no symptoms of oversatiation. The personality disposition of action versus state orientation moderates this effect.

RESEARCH AGENDA

In the following, we formulate five hypotheses that summarize our model of mental satiation and constitute a research agenda for advancing our understanding of the psychological and neural mechanisms underlying mental satiation. The first three hypotheses (i.e., the hypotheses regarding the psychological mechanisms and moderating variables of mental satiation) are illustrated in FIGURE 1.

Hypothesis 1: Repeated performance of an action leads to a loss of intrinsic motivation because it reduces the incongruence between person-related and environmental characteristics and, as a consequence, undermines the need for competence.

Hypothesis 2: Mental satiation can be slowed or even eliminated if the action is not consciously represented.

Hypothesis 3: If people identify with the values associated with an action and hence implement an autonomy-oriented mode of volitional control, they will experience no symptoms of oversatiation.

Hypothesis 4: In the first phase of the satiation process, the loss of intrinsic motivation is correlated with decreasing activity in brain structures mediating hedonic experience, that is, the medial orbitofrontal cortex, the nucleus accumbens, and the ventral pallidum.

Hypothesis 5: In the second phase of the satiation process, activity in the amygdala and the anterior insula is correlated with the growing aversion to the action, whereas activity in the anterior cingulate cortex is correlated with heightened arousal and the amount of volitional control required to continue the action.

CAVEATS, CONCLUSION, AND FUTURE PERSPECTIVES

In contrast to other consequences of strain at work, such as mental fatigue or monotony, mental satiation is an uncharted area of scientific investigation. With our revised model of mental satiation, we hope that we have succeeded in showing that the questions of why people become fed up with their work and which work characteristics moderate this process deserve future research effort. Obviously, many aspects of our model are highly speculative. Thus, our model should not be considered a finished product but rather as a starting point for research in both social cognitive neuroscience and organizational sciences.

Regarding the neurobiological aspects of our model, one must keep two caveats in mind. First, complex psychological or behavioral concepts, such as mental satiation, do not map into single regions of the brain. Localization is more likely to occur at lower levels of organization (e.g., the processing of color information in visual cortex). Therefore, our assumption that the two phases of the satiation process can be mapped to the activation or deactivation of specific brain regions may be overly simplified. Second, neuroimaging data cannot reveal the causal role of brain regions for a particular cognitive process. In the best case, neuroimaging data can tell us whether a given brain region is active during a cognitive process. However, we cannot exclude that the cortical activity associated with a cognitive process in a neuroimaging study is epiphenomenal, that is, not contributing to that process in a *causal* way. Therefore, caution is needed when inferring from cortical activity as measured in a neuroimaging study.[65,66]

Whatever the neural mechanism, an important implication of our model is that mental satiation is a double-edged sword. On the one hand, mental satiation can be considered an evolutionary adaptive mechanism protecting us from doing the same thing over and over again despite no further improvement in our skills. Thus, the growing aversion may serve as a signal either to switch to a new action or to withdraw one's attention. On the other hand, we often encounter situations in which we are not able or cannot afford to switch to another action or withdraw our attention, for example, in the workplace. Hence, mental satiation can impose severe strain on individuals and, in the long run, may lead to burnout.[2]

We envision several aspects that merit further research. First, albeit that monotony and mental satiation are more or less correlated with each other, future research should clearly distinguish between these two concepts. In particular, although both monotony and mental satiation are likely to result from a high degree of repetitiveness of work, mental satiation is predicted to result from demanding tasks that do not allow the attention to be withdrawn from the task, whereas monotony typically results from work underload, that is, from conditions in which workers are employed in jobs beneath their abilities. Previous research on work monotony has typically neglected the idea that work underload and repetitive work pose different work demands. Moreover, research on work monotony has ignored mental satiation.

Second, future studies are needed to better understand the mechanisms mediating mental satiation. For example, from a theoretical point of view it would be interesting to examine whether the conscious representation of doing the same things over and over again is a causal prerequisite of mental satiation. Imagine a woman working on an assembly line who is fed up with her job. If you ask her why she is fed up with it, she will probably tell you that it is because she has to do the same things all day long. Hence, intuitively, the conscious representation of doing the same things time after time may be an important prerequisite of mental satiation. However, mental satiation might also occur automatically and without conscious processing. According to our model, people may lose their intrinsic motivation to perform an action because repeating the action reduces incongruencies between person and environmental characteristics and hence undermines one's need for competence. Thus, it is at least theoretically possible that we may become fed up with performing an action even if we do not have a conscious representation of having previously performed the action.

A third avenue for future research is to take a closer look at interindividual differences in mental satiation. Albeit speculatively, we propose that interindividual differences in the speed of mental satiation are associated with the personality trait of novelty seeking. According to Cloninger et al.,[67] novelty seeking represents a tendency toward frequent exploratory activity and intense excitement in response to novelty. People with a high level of novelty seeking have a strong desire to seek new ways of doing things and new challenges. Therefore, such people may become fed up with repeatedly performing the same action more quickly than do individuals with a low level of novelty seeking. Extending this line of research, it would be interesting to examine the neuronal and neurogenetic basis of interindividual differences in mental satiation. Recently, human brain imaging studies have related the function and structure of the anterior cingulate cortex to the novelty dimension of personality.[68,69] Furthermore, there has been extensive research on the genetic background of novelty seeking and the cortical response to novelty.[70,71] Although the evidence is somewhat inconsistent, this research provides a promising starting point for investigating the neuronal and neurogenetic basis of interindividual differences in mental satiation.

Fourth, from a more practical point of view, it is crucial to investigate whether predictions derived from theories on organizational stress can be transferred to mental satiation. For example, research emanating from Karasek's job demand–job control model[72] has investigated the idea that the combination of high demands and low decision latitude is most detrimental to people's health and well-being. Decision latitude here refers to employees' having a high degree of decision authority and control over managing work tasks. Specifically, the job demand–job control model predicts that decision latitude acts as a buffer against the negative consequences of high demand, reducing its effect on subjective strain and cardiovascular disease. Although the empirical evidence supporting this buffer hypothesis is mixed,[73] examining whether one can transfer the predictions derived from the job demand–job control model to the domain of mental satiation would be interesting. For example, a workplace characterized by the combination of high demands and high decision latitude should provide a challenging atmosphere that counteracts the loss of intrinsic motivation during repeated performance of an action. Testing this hypothesis is an important area for future research.

Preventing mental satiation at the workplace has become a major part of the international standard ISO 10075. However, without a profound knowledge of the psychological mechanisms underlying mental satiation, workplace interventions designed to prevent mental satiation stand on shaky ground. Therefore, research is urgently needed to examine the mediating mechanisms and the moderating factors of mental satiation. We hope that our model helps to inspire the next steps on this way.

ACKNOWLEDGMENTS

This work was supported by a grant from the German Science Foundation (Deutsche Forschungsgemeinschaft [DFG]), project MO 1717/1-1. We are grateful to Anne Tomaschek, Bernd Kaderschabek, Frank Vogelgesang, Leo Schilbach, Peter Richter, and Thomas Schultze for helpful discussions on the topic of this article.

REFERENCES

1. LEWIN, K. 1928. Die Bedeutung der psychischen Sättigung für einige Probleme der Psychotechnik [The significance of mental satiation for some problems of psychotechnics]. Psychotechnische Zeitschrift **3**: 182–188.
2. DEMEROUTI, E. *et al.* 2002. From mental strain to burnout. Eur. J. Work Org. Psychol. **11**: 423–441.
3. BRIEF, A.P. & H.M. WEISS. 2002. Organisational behaviour: Affect in the workplace. Ann. Rev. Psychol. **53**: 279–307.
4. DAMASIO, A.R. 1994. Descartes' error: Emotion, reason, and the human brain. Avon Books. New York.
5. EREZ, A. & A.M. ISEN. 2002. The influence of positive affect on the components of expectancy motivation. J. Appl. Psychol. **87**: 1055–1067.
6. LIEBERMAN, M.D. 2005. Principles, processes, and puzzles of social cognition: An introduction for the special issue on social cognitive neuroscience. Neuroimage **28**: 745–756.
7. KARSTEN, A. 1928. Psychische Sättigung. Psychol. Forschung **10**: 142–254.
8. VERNON, M.D. 1969. Human motivation. University Press. Cambridge, CA.

9. SCHULZ-HARDT, S. *et al.* 2001. Ein weiterentwickeltes Modell psychischer Sättigung [A revised model of psychic satiation]. Psychol. Rundschau **52:** 141–149.
10. VALLACHER, R.R. & D.M. WEGNER. 1987. What do people think they're doing? Action identification and human behavior. Psychol. Rev. **94:** 3–15.
11. DECI, E.L. & R.M. RYAN. 1985. Intrinsic motivation and self-determination in human behavior. Plenum Publishing Co. New York.
12. RYAN, R.M. & E.L. DECI. 2000. Self-determination theory and the facilitation of intrinsic motivation, social development, and well-being. Am. Psychol. **55:** 68–78.
13. BERRIDGE, K.C. 2007. The debate over dopamine's role in reward: the case for incentive salience. Psychopharmacology **191:** 391–431.
14. PECIÑA, S., K.C. BERRIDGE & L.A. PARKER. 1997. Pimozide does not shift palatability: separation of anhedonia from sensorimotor suppression by taste reactivity. Pharmacol. Biochem. Behav. **58:** 801–811.
15. BRAUER, L.H. & H. DE WIT. 1997. High dose pimozide does not block amphetamine- induced euphoria in normal volunteers. Pharmacol. Biochem. Behav. **56:** 265–272.
16. PECIÑA, S., K.S. SMITH & K.C. BERRIDGE. 2006. Hedonic hot spots in the brain. Neuroscientist **12:** 500–511.
17. GREENWALD, M.K. *et al.* 2003. Effects of buprenorphine maintenance dose on mu- opioid receptor availability, plasma concentrations, and antagonist blockade in heroin- dependent volunteers. Neuropsychopharmacology **28:** 2000–2009.
18. ZUBIETA, J.K. *et al.* 2005. Placebo effects mediated by endogenous opioid activity on mu-opioid receptors. J. Neurosci. **25:** 7754–7762.
19. MILLER, J.M. *et al.* 2006. Anhedonia after a selective bilateral lesion of the globus pallidus. Am. J. Psychiatry **163:** 786–788.
20. KRINGELBACH, M.L. 2005. The human orbitofrontal cortex: Linking reward to hedonic experience. Nat. Rev. Neurosci. **6:** 691–702.
21. KRINGELBACH, M.L. & E.T. ROLLS. 2004. The functional neuroanatomy of the human orbitofrontal cortex: evidence from neuroimaging and neuropsychology. Prog. Neurobiol. **72:** 341–372.
22. SMALL, D.M. *et al.* 2001. Changes in brain activity related to eating chocolate: from pleasure to aversion. Brain **124:** 1720–1733.
23. DE ARAUJO, I.E. & E.T. ROLLS. 2004. Representation in the human brain of food texture and oral fat. J. Neurosci. **24:** 3086–3093.
24. BLOOD, A.J. & R.J. ZATORRE. 2001. Intensely pleasurable responses to music correlate with activity in brain regions implicated in reward and emotion. Proc. Natl. Acad. Sci. USA **98:** 11818–11823.
25. O'DOHERTY, J. *et al.* 2000. Sensory-specific satiety-related olfactory activation of the human orbitofrontal cortex. Neuroreport **11:** 893–897.
26. BUSS, D.M. 1995. Evolutionary Psychology: A New Paradigm for Psychological Science. Psychol. Inquiry **6:** 1–30.
27. WHITE, R.W. 1959. Motivation reconsidered: The concept of competence. Psychol. Rev. **66:** 297–333.
28. DECI, E.L. & R.M. RYAN. 2000. The "what" and "why" of goal pursuits: Human needs and the self-determination of behavior. Psychol. Inquiry **11:** 227–268.
29. BOGGIANO, A.K. & D.N. RUBLE. 1979. Competence and the overjustification effect: A developmental study. J. Pers. Soc. Psychol. **37:** 1462–1468.

30. DECI, E.L. 1971. Effects of externally mediated rewards on intrinsic motivation. J. Pers. Soc. Psychol. **18:** 105–115.
31. VALLERAND, R.J. & G. REID. 1984. On the causal effects of perceived competence on intrinsic motivation: A test of cognitive evaluation theory. J. Sport Psychol. **6:** 94–102.
32. JACKSON, A.S. & M. CSIKSZENTMIHALYI. 1999. Flow in sports: The keys to optimal experiences and performances. Human Kinetics. Champaign, IL.
33. NAKAMURA, J. & M. CSIKSZENTMIHALYI. 2002. The concept of flow. *In* Handbook of positive psychology. C.R. Snyder & S.J. Lopez, Eds.: 89–105. Oxford University Press. Oxford.
34. AMODIO, D.M. & C.D. FRITH. 2006. Meeting of minds: the medial frontal cortex and social cognition. Nat. Rev. Neurosci. **7:** 268–277.
35. DAVIDSON, R.J. & W. IRWIN. 1999. The functional neuroanatomy of emotion and affective style. Trends Cogn. Sci. **3:** 11–21.
36. PHILLIPS, M.L. *et al.* 2003. Neurobiology of emotion perception I: The neural basis of normal emotion perception. Biol. Psychiatry **54:** 504–414.
37. PHILLIPS, M.L. *et al.* 1998. Neural responses to facial and vocal expressions of fear and disgust. Philos. Trans. R. Soc. Lond. B. Biol. Sci. **265:** 1809–1817.
38. ISENBERG, N. *et al.* 1999. Linguistic threat activates the human amygdala. Proc. Natl. Acad. Sci. USA **96:** 10456–10459.
39. ZALD, D.H. & J.V. PARDO. 1997. Emotion, olfaction, and the human amygdala: Amygdala activation during aversive olfactory stimulation. Proc. Natl. Acad. Sci. USA **94:** 4119–4124.
40. O'DOHERTY, J. *et al.* 2001. Representation of pleasant and aversive taste in the human brain. J. Neurophysiol. **85:** 1315–1321.
41. CAHILL, L. *et al.* 1996. Amygdala activity at encoding correlated with long-term, free recall of emotional information. Proc. Natl. Acad. Sci. USA **93:** 8016–8021.
42. CANLI, T. *et al.* 2000. Event-related activation in the human amygdala associates with later memory for individual emotional experiences. J. Neurosci. **20:** 1–5.
43. LEE, G.P. *et al.* 1998. Clinical and physiological effects of stereotaxic bilateral amygdalotomy for intractable aggression. J. Neuropsychiatry Clin. Neurosci. **10:** 413–420.
44. BECHARA, A. *et al.* 1999. Different contributions of the human amygdala and ventromedial prefrontal cortex to decision-making. J. Neurosci. **19:** 5473–5481.
45. CALDER, A.J., A.D. LAWRENCE & A.W. YOUNG. 2001. Neuropsychology of fear and loathing. Nat. Rev. Neurosci. **2:** 352–363.
46. CALDER, A.J. *et al.* 2000. Impaired recognition and experience of disgust following brain injury. Nat. Neurosci. **3:** 1077–1078.
47. SANFEY, A.G. *et al.* 2003. The neural basis of economic decision making in the Ultimatum Game. Science **300:** 1755–1758.
48. SEYMOUR, B., T. SINGER & R.J. DOLAN. 2007. The neurobiology of punishment. Nat. Rev. Neurosci. **8:** 300–313.
49. CRITCHLEY, H.D. *et al.* 2003. Human cingulate cortex and autonomic control, converging neuroimaging and clinical evidence. Brain **126:** 2139–2152.
50. PAUS, T. 2001. Primate anterior cingulate cortex: Where motor control, drive and cognition interface. Nat. Rev. Neurosci. **2:** 417–424.
51. PAUS, T. *et al.* 1998. Regional differences in the effects of task difficulty and motor output on blood flow response in the human anterior cingulate cortex: a review of 107 PET activation studies. Neuroreport **9:** R37–47.

52. CARTER, C.S., M. BOTVINICK & J.D. COHEN. 1999. The contribution of the anterior cingulate cortex to executive processes in cognition. Rev. Neurosci. **10:** 49–57
53. GEHRING, W.J. & D.E. FENCSIK. 2001. Functions of the medial frontal cortex in the processing of conflict and errors. J. Neurosci. **21:** 9430–9437.
54. LIOTTI, M. *et al.* 2001. Brain responses associated with consciousness of breathlessness (air hunger). Proc. Natl. Acad. Sci. USA **98:** 2035–2040.
55. BÜCHEL, C. *et al.* 2002. Dissociable neural responses related to pain intensity, stimulus intensity, and stimulus awareness within the anterior cingulate cortex: a parametric single-trial laser functional magnetic resonance imaging study. J. Neurosci. **22:** 970–976.
56. FREDRIKSON, M. *et al.* 1998. Functional neuroanatomical correlates of electrodermal activity: a positron emission tomographic study. Psychophysiology **35:** 179–185.
57. CRITCHLEY, H.D., C.J. MATHIAS & R.J. DOLAN. 2001. Neural activity in the human brain relating to uncertainty and arousal during anticipation. Neuron **29:** 537–45.
58. POSNER, M.I. & M.K. ROTHBART. 1998. Attention, self-regulation and consciousness. Philos. Trans. R. Soc. Lond. B. Biol. Sci. **353:** 1915–1927.
59. RUSHWORTH, M.F.S. *et al.* 2007. Contrasting roles for cingulate and orbitofrontal cortex in decisions and social behaviour. Trends Cogn. Sci. **11:** 168–176.
60. KUHL, J. 1996. Who controls whom when "I control myself"? Psychol. Inquiry **7:** 61–68.
61. KUHL, J. 2000. A functional-design approach to motivation and self-regulation: The dynamics of personality systems interactions. *In* Handbook of self-regulation. M. Boekaerts, P.R. Pintrich & M. Zeidner, Eds.: 111–169. Academic Press. San Diego, CA.
62. KUHL, J. 1994. Action versus state orientation: Psychometric properties of the Action Control Scale (ACS-90). *In* Volition and personality: Action versus state orientation. J. Kuhl & J. Beckmann, Eds.: 47–59. Hogrefe & Huber. Goettingen, Germany.
63. DIEFENDORFF, J.M. *et al.* 2000. Action-state orientation: Construct validity of a revised measure and its relationship to work-related variables. J. Appl. Psychol. **85:** 250–263.
64. LIEBERMAN, M.D. 2007. Social cognitive neuroscience: A review of core processes. Ann. Rev. Psychol. **58:** 259–289.
65. CACIOPPO, J.T. *et al.* 2003. Just because you're imaging the brain doesn't mean you can stop using your head: A primer and set of first principles. J. Pers. Soc. Psychol. **85:** 650–661.
66. KOSSLYN, S.M. 1999. If neuroimaging is the answer, what is the question? Philos. Trans. R. Soc. Lond. B. Biol. Sci. **354:** 1283–1294.
67. CLONINGER, C.R., D.M. SVRACIC & T.R. PRZYBECK. 1993. A psychobiological model of temperament and character. Arch. Gen. Psychiatry **50:** 975–990.
68. GALLINAT, J. *et al.* 2007. Association between cerebral glutamate and human behaviour: the sensation seeking personality trait. Neuroimage **34:** 671–678.
69. PUJOL, J. *et al.* 2002. Anatomical variability of the anterior cingulate gyrus and basic dimensions of human personality. Neuroimage **15:** 847–855.
70. EBSTEIN, R.P. 2006. The molecular genetic architecture of human personality: beyond self-report questionnaires. Mol. Psychiatry **11:** 427–45.
71. KLUGER, A.N., Z. SIEGFRIED & R.P. EBSTEIN. 2002. A meta-analysis of the association between DRD4 polymorphism and novelty seeking. Mol. Psychiatry **7:** 712–717.

72. KARASEK, R.A. 1979. Job demands, job decision latitude, and mental strain: Implications for job redesign. Admin. Sci. Quart. **24:** 288–308.
73. VAN DER DOEF, M. & S. MAES. 1999. The Job Demand-Control (-Support) model and psychological well-being: a review of 20 years of empirical research. Work Stress **13:** 87–114.

Research Possibilities for Organizational Cognitive Neuroscience

MICHAEL J.R. BUTLER AND CARL SENIOR

Organisational Cognitive Neuroscience Center, Aston University, Birmingham B4 7ET, United Kingdom

> ABSTRACT: In this article, we identify research possibilities for organizational cognitive neuroscience that emerge from the papers in this special issue. We emphasize the intriguing finding that the papers share a common theme—the use of cognitive neuroscience to investigate the role of emotions in organizational behavior; this suggests a research agenda in its own right. We conclude the article by stressing that there is much yet to discover about how the mind works, especially in organizational settings.
>
> KEYWORDS: research possibilities, organizational cognitive neuroscience and organization studies

Time present and time past
Are both perhaps present in time future,
And time future contained in time past.

—T.S. Eliot (1888–1965): *Four Quartets*, "Burnt Norton, I"[1]

INTRODUCTION

The study of organizational cognitive neuroscience has a short history, but a promising future. In this special issue we have sought to illuminate the variety of perspectives that distinguished international scholars already have used to explore this new field. Most of the contributors identify a possible research agenda emerging from their work. We encourage the reader to follow those suggestions, and we will not review them here. Instead, we suggest research possibilities from the holistic perspective we have as editors of the special issue.

This special issue is divided into three sets of contributions, each of which has a different perspective on the emotional aspects of organizing work relationships. The first set of papers provides a methodological approach to

Address for correspondence: Michael J. R. Butler, Aston Business School, Aston University, Aston Triangle, Birmingham B4 7ET United Kingdom. Voice: +44 (0) 121-204 3053 (Direct/Voicemail), +44 (0) 121-204 3257 (Group Administrator/Voicemail); fax: +44 (0) 121-204 3327.
m.j.r.butler@aston.ac.uk

organizational cognitive neuroscience; nevertheless, these papers have affective insights about the workplace. The second set of papers explores the importance of positive emotions in the workplace, and each succeeding paper becomes more applied in its discussion as the authors seek to relate cognitive neuroscience to organizational well-being. The third set of papers explores how the workplace can become a toxic environment.

We suggest research possibilities for organizational cognitive neuroscience that emerge out of the three sets of contributions. However, we examine the intriguing finding that all three sets of papers promote the use of cognitive neuroscience to investigate the role of emotions in organizational behavior; the emergence of this common theme suggests a research agenda in its own right.

COGNITIVE NEUROSCIENCE AND ORGANIZATIONAL WELL-BEING

We deliberately made the call for papers as wide as possible to explore ongoing research in the field of organizational cognitive neuroscience. The papers we selected for publication, which broadly reflect what we received, share in common the goal of linking cognitive neuroscience with organizational well-being. This allies the emergence of organizational cognitive neuroscience to another emerging new field—compassion.

Attention to compassion in organizations is relatively recent, although discussions of the concept span both time and discipline.[2] Frost *et al.* provide a brief overview of the intellectual history of the idea and draw on four literatures: religious, philosophical, medical, and innate human instinct.[3] They argue that possessing the innate instinct for compassion biologically underpins the religious and philosophical literatures. It is on this last point that compassion, organizational cognitive neuroscience, and the papers in this special issue all converge, discovering what innate instinct means for people in organizations.

In more detail, Frost *et al.* define compassion as a three-part process: noticing another's suffering, feeling empathy for the other's pain, and responding to the suffering in some way.[3] They then offer three distinct theoretical lenses through which to view compassion: interpersonal work, narrative, and organizing.

Interpersonal work is that which happens in the space between two people.[4] Its success is a product of the joint qualities and behaviors of the people involved and consumes both cognitive effort and emotional energy.[5] Such work would not be done unless it had a benefit, for example, helping a colleague who has been berated by a boss so the colleague can carry on and is productive.[6] Narrative highlights that lived experience is captured, stored, and told as stories.[7] People express what they know and how they feel in organizations through stories; in other words, people use stories and narrative to make sense of their organization.[8] Organizing is a process of social accomplishment that requires active coordination across actors that gives rise to complex, nonlinear processes in the organization. These processes might take the form of networks of contact that give shape to complex processes.[3]

Here, we suggest a fourth theoretical lens—organizational cognitive neuroscience—that can be deployed to research all three parts of the compassion process. Many of the papers in this special issue are grouped around interpersonal work; it is possible to deepen the research on interpersonal work and also to expand into narrative and organizing.

RESEARCH POSSIBILITIES EMERGING FROM THE SPECIAL ISSUE

As noted, this special issue is divided into three sets of contributions, each of which takes a different perspective on the emotional aspects of organizing work relationships. The three sets of papers are used to identify research possibilities.

The first set of papers provides a methodological approach to organizational cognitive neuroscience; from these papers, two research streams emerge. The first is the need for greater conceptual clarification: What do we mean when we use the label *organizational cognitive neuroscience*? A new field will not become accepted or established unless scholars working in that area have a language and a set of methods that allow them to communicate with each other. A shared narrative will then encourage more scholars to venture into this area.

The second research stream is the need to develop innovative methods so that future special issues in this area include data-rich contributions and, more importantly, so that evidence-driven contributions engage more with the practice of organizing. In other words, are staff to be brought into the research laboratories or can the laboratory be taken out to the workplace? This also raises the issue of turning current research findings into practical tools with which to develop business and management.

The second set of papers explores the importance of positive emotions in the workplace. In this special issue, organizational well-being is focused on three topics: fairness, cooperation, and corporate camaraderie as a business change process. More work needs to be done on these topics; in addition, the discussion about compassion suggests alternative directions for fruitful research.

One key research area related to interpersonal work is the investigation of variability in the expression of organization well-being across different work settings and, indeed, variation across different cultures, especially given the growth of the globalized economy. This also concerns narrative: How do different work settings and different cultures represent their stories about interpersonal work? In terms of organizing, the question is whether different work settings and cultures create appropriate processes to voice well-being?

The international perspective is important. The editors have noted that all of the contributions have come from the developed world—the UK, Europe, and the USA. However, organizational cognitive neuroscience should not be geographically limited because it addresses research questions fundamental to all humans.

The third set of papers explores how the workplace can become a toxic environment. This special issue focuses on four concerns: identifying cognitive inaccuracies and then finding strategies to improve decisionmaking, overcoming gender bias in the job negotiation process, challenging the faddish application of two popular tools because they do not facilitate creativity, and recognizing mental satiation with a repeated action.

Although historically psychological and organizational research has demonstrated a strong bias toward understanding negative or detrimental conditions rather than positive or virtuous ones,[9] it is still important to understand such conditions so that they can be minimized or eliminated. This is especially true for the paper on the application of popular business tools, because the tools concerned, Strengths, Weaknesses, Opportunities, and Threats and Porter's Five Force Framework,[10] are taught in virtually all business and management schools and, as a consequence, are widely used in real settings.

Again, more work must be done to address the concerns highlighted in this special issue. Here we have highlighted the importance of researching the presupposed benefits of a tool used in learning and teaching. There are many more concerns to be addressed, which can easily be identified as we go through our daily routines; talk to family, friends, and colleagues; or consume the media. One particular area for future work will be burnout, or how to help the helper, an area that is already recognized in the caring professions.[11]

CONCLUDING REMARKS

Pinker echoes the scope of the research ideas outlined above by pointing out that we do not understand how the mind works, certainly not well enough to design utopia or to cure unhappiness.[12] What we do know may be proved wrong as future research is conducted. This is exciting; it means that there is a world of research possibilities. Pinker classifies two types of possibility: problems and mysteries.[12] In the face of a problem, we may not know its solution, but we have insight, increasing knowledge, and an idea of what we are looking for. In the face of a mystery, we can only stare in wonder and bewilderment, not knowing what an explanation would look like.

The fascination of organizational cognitive neuroscience is that it lies between finding solutions to problems and exploring mysteries. Research projects are designed to resolve problems, and research questions are addressed to fill gaps in an existing body of knowledge. Nevertheless, in organizational cognitive neuroscience, researchers conducting their research projects are also investigating the mystery of how the mind works, especially in organizational settings. Once we introduce the notion of compassion, the research agenda also has a noble cause.

REFERENCES

1. ELIOT, T.S. 1977. Four Quartets, Burnt Norton. *In* The Penguin Dictionary of Quotations. J.M. Cohen & M.J. Cohen, Eds.: 151. Book Club Associates. London.
2. FROST, P.J. 1999. Why compassion counts! Jnl. of Management Inquiry **8:** 127–133.
3. FROST, P.J. *et al.* 2006. Seeing organizations differently: three lenses on compassion. *In* The Sage Handbook of Organization Studies. S.R. Clegg, C. Hardy, T.B. Lawrence & W.R. Nord, Eds.: 843–866. Sage. London.
4. JOSSELSON, R. 1992. The Space Between Us: Exploring the Dimensions of Human Relationships. Jossey-Bass. San Francisco, CA.
5. MILLER, J.P. & I.P. STIVER. 1997. The Healing Connection. Beacon Press. Boston, MA.
6. FROST, P.J. 2003. Toxic Emotions at Work: How Compassionate Managers Handle Pain and Conflict. Harvard Business School Press. Boston, MA.
7. BRUNER, J.S. 1986. Actual Minds, Possible Worlds. Harvard University Press. Cambridge, MA.
8. WEICK, K.E. 1995. Sensemaking in Organizations. Sage Publications. Thousand Oaks, CA.
9. CAMERON, K.S. & A. CAZA. 2004. Contributions to the discipline of positive organizational scholarship. American Behavioural Scientist **47:** 731–739.
10. PORTER, M.E. 1980. Competitive Strategy. Free Press. New York, NY.
11. COLLINS, S. & A. LONG. Too tired to care? The psychological effects of working with trauma. Jnl. of Psychiatric & Mental Health Nursing **10:** 17–27.
12. PINKER, S. 1999. How the Mind Works. Penguin Books. London.